PN
1997.85   Bluestone
.B5   Novels into film

Date Due

FEB 2 1 1983			
11/15/94			
11/21/01			

NOVELS INTO FILM

NOVELS
into
FILM

GEORGE BLUESTONE

UNIVERSITY OF CALIFORNIA PRESS
Berkeley and Los Angeles 1966

University of California Press
Berkeley and Los Angeles, California

Cambridge University Press
London, England

© 1957, THE JOHNS HOPKINS PRESS, BALTIMORE 18, MARYLAND
THIRD PRINTING, 1966
(FIRST PAPER-BOUND EDITION, SECOND PRINTING)

LIBRARY OF CONGRESS CATALOG CARD NUMBER: 57-8449

PRINTED IN THE UNITED STATES OF AMERICA

To My Father

Preface

NEXT TO TELEVISION, THE FILM IS THE youngest of the arts. Certainly it is the youngest of the mature arts. Having at last discovered its classics, its historical cycles, its pivotal figures, and even its warring schools of critics, the film in recent years has become more and more insistent on its claim to serious recognition. Now that television has become the upstart, the film all at once seems mature and mellow, ready to accept respectability, adult consideration, and the right to look askance at the exuberance of youngsters. But because of the cinema's comparative youth, aesthetics has been tempted to treat it like a fledgling, measuring its capabilities by the standards of older, more traditional arts. The film's persistent claim to autonomy has too often been passed off as immature bawling. The temptation to judge by outmoded standards has been further strengthened by the film's surface borrowings from other disciplines. Because the film and the traditional arts, like intersecting circles, overlap at a number of points, the temptation, at first glance, seems understandable.

Like the drama, the film is a visual, verbal, and aural medium presented before a theater audience. Like the ballet, it relies heavily on movement and music. Like the novel, it usually presents a narrative depicting characters in a series of conflicts. Like painting, it is (except for the stereoscopic film) two dimensional, composed of light and shadow and sometimes color. But the ultimate definition of a thing lies in its unique qualities, and no sooner do we attend to the film's specific properties than differentiating characteristics begin to assert themselves.

This study attempts to gauge some of these characteristics in reference to *one* of the traditional arts; more specifically, to make this assessment by careful attention to a particular genre—the filmed novel—where both media apparently overlap. I have assumed, and attempted to demonstrate, that the two media are marked by such essentially different traits that they belong to separate artistic genera. Although novels and films of a certain kind do reveal a number of similarities—as in the case of novels which resemble shooting-scripts—one finds the differentia more startling. More important, one finds the differentia infinitely more problematic to the film-maker. These distinguishing traits follow primarily from the fact that the novel is a linguistic medium, the film essentially visual. (I have assumed, and attempted to demonstrate, that music and dialogue, while they reinforce the photographic image, are really subsidiary lines in the total film composition.) The governing conventions of each medium are further conditioned by different origins, different audiences, different modes of production, and different censorship requirements. The reputable novel, generally speaking, has been supported by a small, literate audience, has been produced by an individual writer, and has remained relatively free of rigid censorship. The film, on the other hand, has been supported by a mass audience, produced co-operatively under industrial conditions, and restricted by a self-imposed Production Code. These developments have reinforced rather than vitiated the autonomy of each medium.

We discover, therefore, in film versions of the novel an inevitable abandonment of "novelistic" elements. This abandonment is so severe that, in a strict sense, the new creation has little resemblance to the original. With the abandonment of language as its sole and primary element, the film necessarily leaves behind those characteristic contents of thought which only language can approximate: tropes, dreams, memories, conceptual consciousness. In their stead, the film supplies endless spatial variations, photographic images of physical reality, and the principles of montage and editing. All these differences derive from the contrast between the novel as a conceptual and discursive form, the film as a perceptual and presentational form. In these terms, the film-maker merely treats the novel as raw material and ultimately creates his own unique structure. That is why a comparative study which begins by finding resemblances between novel and film ends by loudly proclaiming their differences.

The first chapter, "The Limits of the Novel and the Limits of the Film," attempts a more or less comprehensive survey of relevant aesthetic principles but emphasizes the film on the grounds that the novel has been studied more substantially and more competently elsewhere. Though buttressed with illustrative examples, the approach is deliberately broad in order to give as clear a picture as possible of what the film-maker who adapts novels is up against. A certain density in the theoretical analysis is due to the paucity of film studies in American aesthetics. Except for isolated examples like Vachel Lindsay, John Howard Lawson, and Erwin Panofsky, who came to the film from other disciplines (the forthcoming book on film aesthetics by Siegfried Kracauer is eagerly awaited), no film critic or historian has attempted to enunciate the aesthetic principles of motion pictures. Lawson's study, for example, was appended to a revised edition of an earlier book on playwrighting. So far, no American writer has attempted a full theoretical analysis of our most influential cultural milieu. The result is that the classics on the theory of the cinema—Pudovkin, Eisenstein, Arnheim, Balázs—pay insufficient attention to American films which, ironically, have given the world some of its most startling examples of practical craftsmanship. That is why the process of doing a specialized study like the present one has often seemed like going through a wood where flashes of noonday sun appear only occasionally through tangled trees. The conclusions reached in the first chapter are therefore tentative and speculative rather than definitive or exhaustive.

My conclusions, however, do claim to raise the key questions which confront any filmist who attempts the adaptation of a novel to his own medium. This explains why, in an attempt to work out root-principles, a discussion of the Production Code is included.

Since the film-maker must attend both to formal and thematic requirements, to his medium and audience alike, I have tried to remain aware of the film as both an artistic and a social instrument. That the survey is deliberately broad and theoretical, however, may account for the change in tone from the first chapter to the more concrete analyses of the specimen films.

The choice of the specimen films was governed by almost equal parts of free will and necessity. Originally, I drew up a list of a dozen preferred films which seemed to present a variety of problems for investigation. For example, one was a successful film adapted from a mediocre novel; one a mediocre film based on a novel of excellent critical reputation; two were adaptations from the same novel. I wanted to study a wide variety of films based on novels which ranged from those closely resembling shooting-scripts to those bearing so little resemblance that one wondered how they could be adapted at all. I discovered very quickly, however, that in order to do the kind of detailed analysis I wanted, I would need both the shooting-script and a print of the film. It was largely the difficulty of ready access to research materials, the difficulty of locating shooting-scripts and proper conditions for seeing old films, that was responsible for cutting my original selection down to the present six. But because of the kindness of film archivists, the Library of Congress, and the studios themselves, the surviving films were viewed under optimum conditions and were therefore subjected to minute and exhaustive analysis. While the specimen films represent the period from 1935 to 1949, they are not intended to pose as indicative of the industry's general level of production during the same period. The films are arranged chronologically merely as a convenient method of organization.

The specimen studies are not examples of explication in the current sense of the word. What I have tried to do in each case is assess the key additions, deletions, and alterations revealed in the film and center on certain significant implications which seemed to follow from the remnants of, and deviations from, the novel. In short, instead of trying to lead the films, I let the films lead me. Since each film is allowed its own integrity, the novel is considered less a norm than a point of departure. The specimen studies, then, center on particular problems rather than follow a central line of argument. *The Informer* emerges as an example of how the film-maker attempts to externalize subjective states; *Wuthering Heights* as an example of changes which the film-maker necessarily adopts in order to make a nineteenth-century British novel comprehensible to a twentieth-century American audience; *Pride and Prejudice* as a film, modeled on a novel revealing certain resemblances to the shooting-script, that successfully exploits those resemblances for its own use, and that devises the spatial rhythms of the dance as analogues to dramatic relationships; *The Grapes of Wrath* as an instance of how, by a simple reversal of key sequences, the film alters the structure of the novel to fit its own popular conventions; *The Ox-Bow Incident* as an example of how the film alters an ending to accomplish the dual purpose of accommodating both its meaning and its structure to filmic terms; *Madame Bovary* as a film which falters because it fails to pick up an author's obvious use of spatial elements, fails to rethink the novel in plastic form. In each of these, discussions of peculiarly filmic devices (fade-in, fade-out, long shot, close-up) appear only when they seem to illustrate the central problem.

A final word on method. In order to correlate the film with the novel on which it was based, I adopted a modified version of the procedure originally suggested to me by Lester Asheim. Essentially, the method is a way of imposing the shooting-script on the book. By evolving an exact record of alterations, deletions and additions of characters, events, dialogue, I was able to reduce subjective impressions to a minimum. The method calls for viewing the film with a shooting-script at hand. During the viewing, notations of any final changes in the editing were entered on the script. After the script had become an accurate account of the movie's final print, it was then superimposed on the novel. Passages in the book which in no way appear on the screen were deleted; descriptive scenes which show up in the film were bracketed. Dialogue which was carried over into the film was underlined, added characters noted in the margin, and so on. Before each critical evaluation, I was able to hold before me an accurate and reasonably objective record of how the film differed from its model.

Here, as elsewhere, the research would have been impossible

without the co-operation of scholars and critics whose passion for the film as an art form continues to be strong and exploratory. For the judgments and the errors, however, I take full responsibility.

BALTIMORE   *George Bluestone*
NOVEMBER, 1956

Acknowledgments

LIKE FILM PRODUCTION ITSELF, FILM CRITI-
cism is a joint effort. The following pages will reveal, more than
any acknowledgment, my indebtedness to the scholars, professional
film-makers, and archivists whose generous assistance made this
study possible. On the theory that a film ought to be as closely
anatomized as a novel, or even a poem, the greater part of this
book is devoted to detailed analyses of particular motion picture
versions of the novel. In order to make such detailed comparisons,
I found it necessary to obtain, for each film, a shooting-script and
a screening, a combination more difficult to come by than I had
once imagined. Thus the six specimen films had to be screened in
five different cities—Baltimore, Washington, D. C., New York,
Rochester, and Los Angeles. This complicated procedure was considerably simplified through the kind services of Mr. George
Culver of the Film Archives at the Library of Congress; Mr.
James Card of the George Eastman House in Rochester, New
York; Mr. John W. Adams and Mr. Richard Griffith of the Mu-
seum of Modern Art Film Library; the Twentieth Century-Fox
distributors in Washington, D. C.; and the Metro-Goldwyn-Mayer
studios in Culver City, California. Dr. Lester Asheim, Dean of the
Graduate Library School, University of Chicago, apprised me of

techniques for gathering and handling research materials in a field where such techniques are still in their infancy.

I am also grateful to Dr. Siegfried Kracauer and Mr. Adams for reading and correcting early drafts of the first two chapters; to Mr. Walter Van Tilburg Clark for a sensitive appraisal of the chapter on *The Ox-Bow Incident;* and to Professor Harry Levin of Harvard University, Professor Kenneth MacGowan of the University of California at Los Angeles, Professor Alan Downer of Princeton University, and Professors Hillis Miller and N. Bryllion Fagin of The Johns Hopkins University for reading the entire manuscript. Their criticism and suggestions were invaluable during revisions of the book.

Several professional men in the movie industry itself, most of whom had worked on the specimen films, spared time from crowded schedules for correspondence and personal interviews, frequently providing valuable data which would not otherwise have been available: Messrs. Dore Schary, John Ford, Samuel Goldwyn, Nunnally Johnson, William Wyler, Dudley Nichols, William A. Wellman, and Julian Johnson. By watching Mr. Wyler on a studio set at work on a new film adaptation of a novel (Jessamyn West's *A Friendly Persuasion*), I learned more about directing than I would have from a dozen descriptive articles. Mr. Schary made several factual corrections in my chapter on *Pride and Prejudice*.

Parts of this study have appeared, in different form, in *The Sewanee Review*, *The Quarterly of Film, Radio, and TV*, and *The Carleton Drama Review;* I would like to thank the editors for permission to use them here.

I should also like to acknowledge my thanks to the faculty of the Aesthetics of Literature program at The Johns Hopkins University. Above all, I am indebted to Professor George Boas, without whose enduring sympathy, patient supervision, and critical insight this study would never have been written. Professor Leo Spitzer was kind enough to share with me his ideas on myths and the movies.

My wife, Natalie Harris Bluestone, was a source of constant support and encouragement through all stages of the work.

Contents

1 *The Limits of the Novel and the Limits of the Film*

I. THE TWO WAYS OF SEEING

SUMMING UP HIS MAJOR INTENTIONS
in 1913, D. W. Griffith is reported to have said, "The task
I'm trying to achieve is above all to make you see."[1] Whether by
accident or design, the statement coincides almost exactly with
an excerpt from Conrad's preface to *Nigger of the Narcissus* published sixteen years earlier: "My task which I am trying to achieve
is, by the power of the written word, to make you hear, to make
you feel—it is, before all, to make you *see*."[2] Aside from the
strong syntactical resemblance, the coincidence is remarkable in
suggesting the points at which film and novel both join and part
company. On the one hand, that phrase "to make you see" assumes
an affective relationship between creative artist and receptive audience. Novelist and director meet here in a common intention.
One may, on the other hand, see visually through the eye or imagi-
natively through the mind. And between the percept of the visual
image and the concept of the mental image lies the root difference
between the two media.

[1] Lewis Jacobs, *The Rise of the American Film* (New York, 1939), p. 119.
[2] Joseph Conrad, *A Conrad Argosy* (New York, 1942), p. 83.

Because novel and film are both organic—in the sense that aesthetic judgments are based on total ensembles which include both formal and thematic conventions—we may expect to find that differences in form and theme are inseparable from differences in media. Not only are Conrad and Griffith referring to different ways of seeing, but the "you's" they refer to are different. Structures, symbols, myths, values which might be comprehensible to Conrad's relatively small middle-class reading public would, conceivably, be incomprehensible to Griffith's mass public. Conversely, stimuli which move the heirs of Griffith's audience to tears, will outrage or amuse the progeny of Conrad's "you." The seeming concurrence of Griffith and Conrad splits apart under analysis, and the two arts turn in opposite directions. That, in brief, has been the history of the fitful relationship between novel and film: overtly compatible, secretly hostile.

On the face of it, a close relationship has existed from the beginning. The reciprocity is clear from almost any point of view: the number of films based on novels; the search for filmic equivalents of literature; the effect of adaptations on reading; box-office receipts for filmed novels; merit awards by and for the Hollywood community.

The moment the film went from the animation of stills to telling a story, it was inevitable that fiction would become the ore to be minted by story departments. Before Griffith's first year as a director was over, he had adapted, among others, Jack London's *Just Meat (For Love of Gold)*, Tolstoy's *Resurrection*, and Charles Reade's *The Cloister and the Hearth*. Sergei Eisenstein's essay, "Dickens, Griffith, and the Film Today,"[3] demonstrates how Griffith found in Dickens hints for almost every one of his major innovations. Particular passages are cited to illustrate the dissolve, the superimposed shot, the close-up, the pan, indicating that Griffith's interest in literary forms and his roots in Victorian idealism[4] provided at least part of the impulse for technical and moral content.

From such beginnings, the novel began a still unbroken tradi-

[3] Sergei Eisenstein, *Film Form*, trans. Jay Leyda (New York, 1949), pp. 195-255.
[4] Jacobs, pp. 98-99.

tion of appearing conspicuously on story conference tables. The precise record has never been adequately kept. Various counts range from 17 to almost 50 per cent of total studio production. A sampling from RKO, Paramount, and Universal motion picture output for 1934–35 reveals that about one-third of all full-length features were derived from novels (excluding short stories).[5] Lester Asheim's more comprehensive survey indicates that of 5,807 releases by major studios between 1935 and 1945, 976 or 17.2 per cent were derived from novels.[6] Hortense Powdermaker reports, on the basis of *Variety's* survey (June 4, 1947) that of 463 screenplays in production or awaiting release, slightly less than 40 per cent were adapted from novels.[7] And Thomas M. Pryor, in a recent issue of the *New York Times*, writes that the frequency of the original screenplay, reaching a new low in Hollywood, "represented only 51.8 per cent of the source material of the 305 pictures reviewed by the Production Code office in 1955." Appropriate modifications must be made in these calculations, since both Asheim and Powdermaker report that the percentage of novels adapted for high-budgeted pictures was much higher than for low-budgeted pictures.[8]

The industry's own appraisal of its work shows a strong and steady preference for films derived from novels, films which persistently rate among top quality productions. Filmed novels, for example, have made consistently strong bids for Academy Awards. In 1950, *Time* reported the results of *Daily Variety's* poll of 200 men and women who had been working in the industry for more than twenty-five years. *Birth of a Nation* was considered the best silent film; *Gone with the Wind* the best sound film and the best "all time film."[9] Originally, both were novels. The choice of *Gone*

[5] In Marguerite G. Ortman, *Fiction and the Screen* (Boston, 1935).

[6] In Lester Asheim, "From Book to Film" (Ph.D. dissertation, University of Chicago, 1949).

[7] In Hortense Powdermaker, *Hollywood: The Dream Factory* (Boston, 1950), p. 74.

[8] For example, Asheim reports that of the "Ten Best" films listed in the *Film Daily Yearbook* for 1935–45, fifty-two or 47% were derived from established novels.

[9] *Time*, LV (March 6, 1950), 92. From the point of view of thematic conventions, there may be further significance in the fact that both films

with the Wind was a happy meeting of commercial and artistic interests. For when, some five years later, *Time* reported *Variety's* listing of Hollywood's "all time money makers," Miss Mitchell's title stood ahead of all others with earnings of some $33.5 million. More important, of the ten most valuable film properties, five had been adapted from novels.[10] The high percentage of filmed novels which have been financially and artistically successful may be more comprehensible when we remember how frequently Pulitzer Prize winners, from *Alice Adams* to *All the King's Men*, have appeared in cinematic form.[11]

Just as one line of influence runs from New York publishing house to Hollywood studio, another line may be observed running the other way. Margaret Farrand Thorp reports that when *David Copperfield* appeared on local screens, the demand for the book was so great that the Cleveland Public Library ordered 132 new copies; that the film premier of *The Good Earth* boosted sales of that book to 3,000 per week; and that more copies of *Wuthering Heights* have been sold since the novel was screened than in all the previous ninety-two years of its existence. Jerry Wald confirms this pattern by pointing out, more precisely, that after the film's appearance, the Pocket Book edition of *Wuthering Heights* sold 700,000 copies; various editions of *Pride and Prejudice* reached a third of a million copies; and sales for *Lost Horizon* reached 1,-400,000.[12] The appearance, in 1956, of such films as *Moby Dick* and *War and Peace*, accompanied by special tie-in sales of the novels, has continued this pattern.

But when Jean Paul Sartre suggests that for many of these read-

---

deal with the Civil War and that both are sympathetic to the secessionists. To what extent has the Southern defeat haunted our national consciousness?

[10] *Time*, LXV (January 17, 1955), 74. The figures are quoted from *Variety's* forty-ninth anniversary issue. The filmed novels were: *Gone with the Wind, From Here to Eternity, Duel in the Sun, The Robe,* and *Quo Vadis.*

[11] Among other filmed Pulitzer Prize winners: *The Good Earth, Gone with the Wind, The Late George Apley, The Yearling, The Grapes of Wrath, A Bell for Adano, The Magnificent Ambersons, So Big, Arrowsmith, The Bridge of San Luis Rey, Alice Adams.*

[12] Jerry Wald, "Screen Adaptation," *Films in Review,* V (February, 1954), 66.

ers, the book appears "as a more or less faithful commentary" on the film,[13] he is striking off a typically cogent distinction. Quantitative analyses have very little to do with qualitative changes. They tell us nothing about the mutational process, let alone how to judge it. In the case of film versions of novels, such analyses are even less helpful. They merely establish the fact of reciprocity; they do not indicate its implications for aesthetics. They provide statistical, not critical data. Hence, from such information the precise nature of the mutation cannot be deduced.

Such statements as: "The film is true to the spirit of the book"; "It's incredible how they butchered the novel"; "It cuts out key passages, but it's still a good film"; "Thank God they changed the ending"—these and similar statements are predicated on certain assumptions which blur the mutational process. These standard expletives and judgments assume, among other things, a separable content which may be detached and reproduced, as the snapshot reproduces the kitten; that incidents and characters in fiction are interchangeable with incidents and characters in the film; that the novel is a norm and the film deviates at its peril; that deviations are permissible for vaguely defined reasons—exigencies of length or of visualization, perhaps—but that the extent of the deviation will vary directly with the "respect" one has for the original; that taking liberties does not necessarily impair the quality of the film, whatever one may think of the novel, but that such liberties are somehow a trick which must be concealed from the public.

What is common to all these assumptions is the lack of awareness that mutations are probable the moment one goes from a given set of fluid, but relatively homogeneous, conventions to another; that changes are *inevitable* the moment one abandons the linguistic for the visual medium. Finally, it is insufficiently recognized that the end products of novel and film represent different aesthetic genera, as different from each other as ballet is from architecture.

The film becomes a different *thing* in the same sense that a historical painting becomes a different thing from the historical event which it illustrates. It is as fruitless to say that film A is better or

---

[13] Jean-Paul Sartre, *What Is Literature?* trans. Bernard Frechtman (New York, 1949), p. 245.

worse than novel B as it is to pronounce Wright's Johnson's Wax Building better or worse than Tchaikowsky's *Swan Lake*. In the last analysis, each is autonomous, and each is characterized by unique and specific properties. What, then, are these properties?

II. A NOTE ON ORIGINS

At least part of our definition of the two media may be read at their respective points of origin. It is no accident that American writers, as Roger Manvell's bibliography shows,[14] have been pre-occupied with the industry's history and financial organization. For the American film began as a gadget and ended as a billion-dollar investment. Its primary appeals all along have been to our dual American love of innovation and splendor. Erwin Panofsky, in his perceptive essay on motion pictures, has been sensitive to the impact of these origins on the art of the film.[15] The origins of the film, according to Panofsky, suggest two fundamental implica-tions. First, that the "primordial basis of the enjoyment of moving pictures was not an objective interest in a specific subject matter, but the sheer delight in the fact that things *move*," no matter what things they are. I would amend Mr. Panofsky's statement to read, "sheer delight in the fact that *images* move." For it was a delight in an illusion resembling reality that first brought customers to the zoetrope, the nickelodeon, and the carnival sideshows. We take no special delight in the sight of a family eating, of a mother feeding her baby. But when precisely these images appeared as illusory images on a screen, they caused a sensation.

The second fact we are to understand, Panofsky goes on, is

that films . . . are originally a product of a genuine folk-art. At the very beginning of things we find the simple recording of movement, galloping horses, railroad trains, fire-engines, sport-ing events, street scenes. And these films were originally *pro-*

[14] Roger Manvell, *Film*, revised ed. (London, 1950), pp. 251–263.
[15] Erwin Panofsky, "Style and Medium in the Moving Pictures," *transi-tion*, No. 26 (1937), p. 121. A revised version appears in *Critique*, 1 (Janu-ary–February, 1947).

duced by people who did not claim to be artists, and were *enjoyed* by people who did not claim to be artists, and who would have been much offended had anybody called them art-lovers. They were taken by photographers who were anything but "directors," and were performed, when it had come to the making of narrative films, by people who were anything but actors.[16]

As if by instinct, even the earliest American films were already making use of their own peculiar properties. Before 1905, "Instead of emulating a theatrical performance already endowed with a certain amount of motion, the earliest films added movement to stationary works of art, so that technical invention could achieve a triumph of its own."[17]

The choice of subjects for these early animations were those three most appealing to the mass audience of the time: (1) melodramatic incidents, preferably of the sanguinary kind found in popular nineteenth-century historical paintings, or in plays, or in popular wax-works; (2) crudely comic incidents—the beginning of the pie-throwing genre; (3) scenes represented on mildly pornographic postcards. In point of fact, Panofsky concludes, the legitimate paths of evolution were opened up not by running away from the folk-art characteristics of the primitive film, but by developing it "within the limits of its own inherent possibilities." The three primordial species could develop ultimately into genuine film-tragedy, genuine film-comedy, and genuine film-romance, as soon as one realized that they could be transfigured "not by artificial injection of 'literary' values, but by exploiting the unique and specific possibilities of the new medium as such."

Because its history is longer and its materials more refined, the novel is more complex. In approaching the novel—a term we have used thus far with a confidence more apparent than real—we are faced internally with the fluidity of its boundaries and externally with its particular relationship to life. If the film is protean because it has assimilated photography, music, dialogue, the dance, the novel is protean because it has assimilated essays, letters, memoirs,

[16] *Ibid.*, p. 121.
[17] See also Jacobs, pp. 3–77.

histories, religious tracts, and manifestoes. There is no such thing as *the* novel.

A second difficulty arises because, as we shall also see in the film, aesthetic apprehension is constantly driven back to epistemology. Since the manipulation of visual stimuli in the film and verbal manipulation in the novel both presuppose a spectator, attention is constantly forced to move between subject and object. Where Rudolf Arnheim, the psychologist analyzing the film, begins from cognitive premises, Edwin Muir, the critic analyzing the novel, feels compelled to end with them. Early in his book, Arnheim says, "It is one of the author's fundamental principles that art is just as much and just as little a part of material life as anything else in the world; and that the only way to understand art is to start from the simplest forms of sensory-psychological impression and to regard visual and auditory art as sublimate forms of seeing and hearing."[18] Edwin Muir, toward the end of his study, *The Structure of the Novel*, finds that in trying to ascertain reasons for particular limitations in the novel he was driven "at least to the limitations of our vision of the world. We see things in terms of Time, Space, Causality . . . ."[19] We may expect, then, to cope with similar problems in a comparative study of the two media.

The novel's imprecise boundaries have made critics reluctant to classify it with absolute assurance, and have even doomed to failure those critics who have attempted strict definition. E. M. Forster recognizes the problem when he quotes Chevalley's definition of the novel, "*une fiction en prose d'une certain etendue*," and adds that he will consider as a novel any fictitious prose over 50,000 words.[20] Forster is aware that one must begin somewhere, and because the point at which one begins is a construct, the construct is necessarily naïve. Critical constructs distort the novel in much the same way that novels distort life, since in both cases one can hope to catch but a small fragment of the whole. Yet when Forster ends by doubting that "there is such a thing as a critical equip-

[18] Rudolf Arnheim, *Film*, trans. L. M. Sieveking and Ian F. D. Morrow (New York, 1933), p. 11.
[19] Edwin Muir, *The Structure of the Novel* (New York, 1929), p. 113.
[20] E. M. Forster, *Aspects of the Novel* (New York, 1927), p. 17.

ment," he is not discounting the value of his lectures. He is merely being clear about their limitations. True comprehensiveness comes only from reading the novel again and again, and sometimes not even then. When Forster satirizes the critic who classifies novels according to nine types of weather, and Henry James inveighs against the "clumsy separations" which "are made by critics and readers for their own convenience, and to help them out of some of their occasional queer predicaments,"[21] they are concerned not so much with the feebleness of criticism as with the presumptions of that particular kind of criticism which turns the reader away from the living fiction toward the empty construct. They are not despairing of any approach; they are merely discouraging the wrong one.

That much modern criticism comes close to despair is not only evident but understandable. Throughout *Forms of Modern Fiction*, for example, the collection of critical essays edited by William Van O'Connor, there runs a motif of anxiety, a recurring sense of collapse the moment formal criticism is brought to bear on the novel. "We cannot be both broad and critical,"[22] says Allen Tate, and adopts what he calls "the short view." By showing how Emma Bovary's mind, at a given moment, is rendered with perfect sensuousness, Tate offers a special angle from which to read the entire novel. Yet this is less a comment on the helplessness of criticism than on the limitations of the verbal process itself.

In a sense, this process of taking up a vantage point that is constantly aware of opposite tendencies has been typical of every major definition of the novel since its inception. Faced with new experiences, the novel has been forced to find new modes of rendering them. And criticism, faced with the *fait accompli*, has had to coin new terms. Thus criticism is perpetually a step behind the novel, as the novel is perpetually a step behind life. Each continually rejects its past. That is why the history of the novel reveals a constant warfare between opposite tendencies.

Harry Levin has reminded us of the conflicting tendencies even at the points of origin. The French *roman* suggests remote origins

[21] Henry James, *The Art of Fiction* (New York, 1949), p. 14.
[22] Allen Tate, "Techniques of Fiction," *Forms of Modern Fiction*, ed. William Van O'Connor (Minneapolis, 1948), p. 33.

in medieval romance. The Italian *novella*, the cognate of the English word, means "news" and suggests a new kind of anecdotal narrative claiming to be both recent and true. Thus the novel "touches heroic legend at one extreme and modern journalism at the other."[23] The eighteenth century finds Henry Fielding describing *Joseph Andrews*, "this species of writing, which I have affirmed to be hitherto unattempted in our language,"[24] as "a comic romance . . . a comic epic poem in prose." If the affectation of Samuel Richardson was to be made ridiculous, the comic element had to be introduced in order to correct, in Levin's compound phrase, "obsolete ideals and false ideologies."

Almost a century later, new social realities had made Fielding's familiar polarities obsolete. In his study of M. Beyle, which opened the third and concluding number of his *Revue Parisienne* (September 25, 1840), Balzac says, "I do not believe the portrayal of modern society to be possible by the severe method of the literature of the seventeenth and eighteenth centuries."[25] Distinguishing between the literature of imagery, exemplified by Victor Hugo, and the literature of ideas, exemplified by Stendhal, Balzac considers himself an exponent of literary eclecticism, combining the sensual luxuriance of the one and the ideational dryness of the other.

In America, with the appearance of *The House of the Seven Gables*, Hawthorne went on to place himself at one end of the novel's original polarity of *roman* and *novella*. Renouncing the "novel," which presumes "to aim at a very minute fidelity . . . to the probable and ordinary course of man's experience," Hawthorne defines his book as a "romance," which attempts to read the "truth of the human heart" and "has fairly a right to present that truth under circumstances, to a great extent, of the writer's own choosing or creation."

By the twentieth century, after the exhilarating discovery that consciousness, and the unconscious, possessed hitherto undis-

[23] Harry Levin, "The Novel," *Dictionary of World Literature*, ed. Joseph T. Shipley (New York, 1943), p. 405.

[24] Henry Fielding, *Joseph Andrews* (London, 1954), p. 23.

[25] Honoré de Balzac, "A Study of M. Beyle," *The Charterhouse of Parma*, trans. C. K. Scott Moncrieff (London, 1950), p. xii.

covered powers, new definitions began to force the setting up of new oppositions. Instead of distinguishing between two or more kinds of reality, epistemology questioned whether any fixed reality was possible at all. In *Don Quixote*, the mock hero continually confuses illusion and reality, but the reader is never in doubt about the distinction between armored knights and windmills. In Gide's *The Counterfeiters*, however, the reader is never certain where reality lies. Reality is too shifting, too elusive to be arrested with certainty. Like Edouard in *The Counterfeiters*, the novelist now begins by saying, "I should like to put everything into my novel,"[26] and ends by despairing of getting anything in. The inability to arrest a reality that is perpetually out of reach becomes a central theme. Not only does the novelist begin to doubt reality; he doubts his medium as well.

There is a sense, then, in which our twentieth-century novels have abandoned the drama of human thought and action for the drama of linguistic inadequacy. "It is almost as though language and subject had reversed roles. Where language was formerly used to comment on social and psychological conflicts, sociology and psychology now elucidate the traits of language itself." When Sartre concludes, "The literary object, though realized *through* language, is never given *in* language. On the contrary, it is by nature a silence and an opponent of the word . . ."[27] we realize that the great polarities have reached a new and striking conclusion. Language has become a character in the novel.

André Gide makes this point explicitly. In his journal, Edouard begins to catch sight of the "deep-lying" subject of his work-in-progress: "It is—it will no doubt be, the rivalry between the real world and the representation of it which we make ourselves . . . ." Language is no longer a secondary matter, "an external manifestation"; and technique, the manner in which one arranges his language, "not only . . . *contains* intellectual and moral implications, but . . . *discovers* them."[28] Finally, in A. A. Mendilow's study of

[26] André Gide, *The Counterfeiters*, trans. Dorothy Bussy (New York, 1949), p. 172.

[27] Sartre, p. 44.

[28] Mark Schorer, "Technique as Discovery," *Forms of Modern Fiction*, p. 16.

the novel, the limitations of language become a central preoccupation:

> Language cannot convey non-verbal experience; being successive and linear, it cannot express simultaneous experiences; being composed of separate and divisible units, it cannot reveal the unbroken flow of the process of living. Reality cannot be expressed or conveyed—only the illusion of it.[29]

But to recognize the disparity between language and that which language depicts is not to discover an impasse. The distinction between word and thing is, after all, not new. What does seem to be new is the intensification of polarity between the constructs of verbal expression and the elusiveness of nonverbal experience. In mystical writing, one could simply label nonverbal experience "ineffable" and leave it at that. But today even the attributes of the ineffable have changed. The emphasis has shifted from elucidating a fixed and unchanging reality to arresting a transient one. Where Fielding, Balzac, and Hawthorne could stake out their claims with a certain confidence—although "affectation," "modern society" and the "truth of the human heart" are each in turn a different kind of territory—the modern novelist is riddled with doubts. Not only does he doubt his ability to stake out claims; he also doubts the existence of what he is claiming. At the very least, he is tormented by its chameleon-like character. Reality is never the same from one moment to the next. Not only does it change according to its own laws, but the novelist himself makes it change. His very act of writing alters his subject matter. "To speak is to act"; says Sartre, "anything which one names is already no longer quite the same; it has lost its innocence."

The moment our attention with respect to nonverbal experience shifts from substance to process, from being to becoming, from stasis to flux, the discrete character of language no longer seems adequate. Where the recurrent trope depicting art as holding the mirror up to nature once suggested the possibility of a virtual image at least, the question now becomes whether any image is possible at all. Where words once seemed a rough vehicle for con-

---

[29] A. A. Mendilow, *Time and the Novel* (London, 1952), p. 81.

veying reality directly, they now seem to become weapons which puncture reality the moment they are applied. So that even creating the "illusion" which Mendilow speaks of becomes a torment.

If the tendency of the modern novel has been to escape the limitations of language, one must meditate on the extraordinary effects which have been revealed in the process. It seems as if Proust and Joyce, confronted by those limitations, had resolved to uncover every hidden resource which their medium allowed. Necessarily, the recognition that once you "enter the universe of significations, there is nothing you can do to get out of it,"[30] returns the novelist to a rather stoic acceptance of his medium. And this acceptance permits him to discover new possibilities, new permutations and combinations which he had not dreamed were there.

Active imagination on the one hand, and aesthetic apprehension on the other, take their place as types of ordinary cognition. The verbal constructs of language become inseparable from the non-verbal constructs of sense data. When Hugh Dalziel Duncan defines great literature as "the conscious exploration through the imagination of the *possibilities* of human action in society,"[31] he is rephrasing Harry Levin's observation that because the novel combines "the qualities of a human document and a work of art," it may be judged by what it says and how, by truth and beauty both. When Duncan argues that a theory which allows "action to go forward in terms of symbolic action" presumes "a theory of the imagination as part of action," he is deliberately blurring the distinction between sociology and aesthetics. If the imagination is viewed as a type of human behavior, then socio-psychological analysis becomes inseparable from aesthetic analysis. Each conditions and supports the other. We shall see to what extent the shaping power of the mass audience leaves its mark on the film, but we may note at this point the analogous way in which the reader's symbolic action leaves its imprint on the novel.

Already we can observe how contrasting origins and development have brought the media of film and novel to radically dif-

[30] Sartre, p. 24.
[31] Hugh Dalziel Duncan, *Language and Literature in Society* (Chicago, 1953), p. 3.

ferent points. Where the film has not yet begun to question its ability to render certain types of physical and even psychological reality, the novel is no longer so confident. In Mendilow's terms, the novel "first tries to reflect reality as faithfully as it can, and then, despairing of the attempt, tries to evoke the feeling of a new reality of its own."

III. CONTRASTS IN THE MEDIA

The Film: Raw Materials

Such differences as we have already noted in the two media become even more obvious when we examine, in more detail, the peculiar properties of each. The film is based on the optical principle known as persistence of vision. After exposure, the retina of the eye retains the image of a picture approximately 1/10 of a second longer than the duration of actual contact. The principle was applied in the old zoetrope, for example, where apertures were cut in a freewheeling disc. When the disc was revolved at a given speed, the light through the apertures would seem to be continuous. A series of separate images, run behind the apertures, would create the illusion of constant motion. The principle has remained the same from the flashcards of the nickelodeon to the splendor of the widescreen. In the movie theater we sit in darkness much of the time. Our eye fills in the gaps.

The silent film was made up of separate frames joined on rolls of celluloid at a standard rate of sixteen frames to the foot. In sound films, twenty-four frames or 1½ feet per second run before the lens of the standard projector. At this rate, the eye receives the illusion of normal movement. The average film runs about 80 minutes and measures about 7,200 feet in length, although historically films have varied from as little as 50 feet or less to as much as 48,000 feet or more. Full-length films are made up of 1,000- or 2,000-foot reels, so that in the latter case an average feature runs about four reels. The standard width of the film strip is 35 mm., and a substandard width of 16 mm. is popular for noncommercial use. Innovations in stereoscopic films have set off further experiments with 55 and 65 mm. film, which may very well render the conventional mechanics obsolete (see James L. Limbacher's survey, "Widescreen Chronology," *Films in Review* [October, 1955], p. 403 ff). Whatever the standards of the future, however, it is highly probable that the film's basic materials will remain more mechanically fixed than those of the more traditional arts.

Beyond these limitations, however, the camera is free to use almost endless visual variations. It is at this point that the camera, its reel of sensitized film sprocketed in place, announces itself as an artistic instrument. The camera can go anywhere, see anything, in the natural world. Placed in front of a church, it can effect a number of distortions without even moving. Beginning with a two-inch lens, the cameraman can shoot the church in its entirety and end with a forty-inch lens which reveals no more than a notice pinned to the door. The two-inch lens most nearly corresponds to the vision of human eyesight and may therefore be used as a norm. Lenses of less than two inches distort space by extending and exaggerating distances, as through the wrong end of a telescope; lenses of more than two inches distort space by reducing and compressing distances, as through the magnifying end. Gauzes can be used to soften the outlines of scenes; masks can be used to give the illusion of looking through a keyhole or a heart or a cathedral arch. Sometimes the lens is smeared to give blurred or watery effects. Even immobilized, the camera makes space pliable.

More significantly, however, the camera can move, and its mobility has enabled it to achieve unprecedented visual effects. At this point, the film declares its historical independence from the theater. Mobile, the camera can see over a hundred miles of prairie, or count the eyelashes on an actor's lids. It can whirl over ballrooms; ride on cranes up houses into windows; move on a truck alongside galloping horsemen; take nose dives on the fuselage of an airplane; pan up skyscrapers by pivoting vertically on its tripod; or, by pivoting horizontally, brood across a deserted battlefield.

Similarly, it can distort light to fit a desired mood—deepen shadows, highlight faces, amplify contrast, turn night into day or faintly defined clouds into sharp ones. John Howard Lawson emphasizes these capabilities by suggesting that "the light pattern is the key to the composition, which is never static. The composition is not merely a commentary on the action. There is a changing dynamic relationship between each person or object in the scene and the camera."[32] Thus, when the camera swings through the window to find the sleeping man in the first shot of *Body and Soul*, "the instrument itself is acting."

Like a precocious child, however, the camera can become offensive through sheer virtuosity. Basil Wright is correct when he says that "the good cameraman is as sparing as possible in the use of elaborate stunts."[33] The technique of the camera has, after all, been evolved by the demands of men making films for a specific end. Consequently, "the apparatus should be subservient to the idea."

The danger of the runaway camera never persists simply because the camera does not crank itself. Behind the lens is a creative brain directing its steady and often ruthless vision. And it is to the film-maker in relation to his instrument that we must look for the real center of the film's uniquely creative process.

On the face of it, to be sure, the camera approximates our ordinary perceptions. "It is the normal part of our behaviour," says Ernest Lindgren, "to look one moment at one thing, and the next moment at another, according to the direction in which our attention is attracted."[34] In order to alter our view, a mere movement of the eyes is sufficient. But sometimes we turn our head, or move it up or down. Sometimes the impulse for movement is transferred to our whole body, and, to get a particular angle of vision, we turn around or walk. Indeed, this selective and erratic manner of seeing, Lindgren argues, "is the keystone, not merely of the whole theory of film editing, but of the whole technique of filmic representation."

V. I. Pudovkin suggests the same thing in his axiom, "The lens of the camera replaces the eye of the observer."[35] But Basil

[32] John Howard Lawson, *Theory and Technique of Playwriting and Screenwriting* (New York, 1949), pp. 382–383.

[33] Basil Wright, "Handling the Camera," *Footnotes to the Film*, ed. Charles Davy and Lovat Dickson (London, 1937), p. 44.

[34] Ernest Lindgren, *The Art of the Film* (London, 1948), p. 53.

[35] V. I. Pudovkin, *Film Technique*, trans. Ivor Montagu (London, 1935), pp. xiii–xiv.

Wright, the British photographer, points out, as Pudovkin and Lindgren ultimately do, the essentially radical departure of eye from camera:

> First and foremost we must remember that the camera does not see things in the same way as the human eye. The brain behind your eye selects the points of emphasis in the scene before you. You can look at a crowd and see nothing but one umbrella, or you can look at an empty field and see millions of separate blades of grass. . . . Not so the camera. The lens soullessly records on a sensitised piece of celluloid simply the amount of light of differing values that passes through it. No amount of thinking on the part of the cameraman will achieve any other emphasis. Out of a wide landscape it will not pick out that certain tree. You, as a person, have got to interfere, to place the camera in such a way that the picture it records will somehow give the emphasis you require.[36]

With Pudovkin's observation that the marked difference between the natural event and its appearance on the screen is exactly "what makes the film an art," we are brought to the heart of the creative film process. Bound by its respect for physical reality, but unbound by the vision of any *one* spectator, the lens becomes an ideal, unrealistic eye; unbound by natural observation, the eye of the spectator becomes omniscient. It took several years for film-makers to understand that the film's angle of vision was non-naturalistic; that being non-naturalistic, yet bound by optical and mechanical laws, the film had found its formative power. In many early films, an immobilized camera, set at a given distance, recorded the action before it in sequences that corresponded roughly to theatrical acts. In spite of some amazing effects in Méliès, who used the technique, the results remained little more than animated postcards.

Then, in the history of film technique, there came two astral hours. In *Enoch Arden*, D. W. Griffith outraged his superiors by alternating a medium shot with a close-up instead of filming his scene continuously in the usual manner. Griffith, in mobilizing the camera, had discovered the principle of editing. Having found the

[36] Wright, pp. 38–39.

true nature of motion pictures, Griffith went on to discover, through the camera, a multitude of ways in which to render spatial movement through exciting visual rhythms. In a short time, the inter-cut, the parallel development, the extreme long shot, the fade-out, the fade-in, the dissolve, the flashback, all became common currency in editing techniques.

Once film technicians discovered that the strips of celluloid were their real raw material, and once directors interrupted the camera's naturalistic eye to join the film in ways contrary to nature, the mode of transition from one shot to the next became all important. Spatial transition, the core of editing, becomes, in Raymond Spottiswoode's phrase, "the grammar of the film." And the principle is as central today as it was in its infancy. Lindgren gives us the main design:

> The normal method of transition from shot to shot within a scene is by means of a cut which gives the effect of one shot being instantly replaced by the next. The normal method of transition from one scene to another is by means of the mix or dissolve which is always associated with a sense of the passage of time or of a break in time. A sequence is normally punctuated by a fade-in at the beginning and a fade-out at the end. The, fade may be quick or slow according to the emotional mood of the film at the moment it occurs and to the degree of emphasis which the director desires to give the pause at that particular point.[37]

Where Lindgren's statement has the matter-of-factness of assimilated tradition, Pudovkin's adumbration has the ring of a manifesto: "I claim that every object, taken from a given viewpoint and shown on the screen to spectators, is a dead object, even though it has moved before the camera. . . . Every object must, by editing, be brought upon the screen so that it shall have not photographic but cinematographic essence."[38] If by a "dead object" in this context we understand "dead" to mean lacking in significance with respect to a total structure, just as a phrase detached from a poem

[37] Lindgren, p. 67.
[38] Pudovkin, pp. xiv-xv.

is dead, then Pudovkin will not seem to be overstating his case. And if we remember that the analogy to poetry is figurative and not literal, then the domain of the film will remain autonomous. In his brilliantly pioneering work on film aesthetics, Vachel Lindsay grasped the difference firmly: "A list of words making a poem and a set of apparently equivalent pictures forming a photoplay may have entirely different outcomes. It may be like trying to see a perfume or listen to a taste." [39]

When, however, Pudovkin insists without reservation that the material of the film director consists not of real processes happening in real space and real time but merely of those pieces of celluloid on which those processes have been recorded—then aesthetic emphasis turns to distortion. So exhilarating was the discovery of the film's formative principles, that the rhythm of montage tended to obscure the photographic demands of the individual shot. It is becoming increasingly clear that in addition to its place in the sequence, the photograph must be granted its own integrity. In order for the shot to be integrated into a larger structure, the shot itself must be recognizable as a copy of physical reality. The sled in *Citizen Kane* must first be recognizable as a sled before it can be contrasted to the fantastic cluster of art works upon the lawn. If the cinematic eye can link diverse spatial images, the images themselves must be meticulously arranged. Like musical notes, each image must have the proper timbre before the entire sequence can be strong. Even though the photographic image is different in quality from the object it records, Panofsky's observation that what we work with in the film is *physical reality* seems highly relevant. For although it is true that all the objects and persons in the film can be arranged in all sorts of ways, "there is no running away from them."

Arnheim, in his discussion of film metaphor, suggests the same thing. Noting that the sound-film is so sensory a medium that things which belong together abstractly and not materially cannot be shown together, he goes on to say: "Just as a grinning death's-head does not in a film appear as a symbol but as an actual part of the human skeleton, so the connection between two objects shown

[39] Vachel Lindsay, *The Art of the Moving Picture* (New York, 1915), p. 272.

on a film simultaneously never seems metaphorical but always at once real and ontological."[40] Like Panofsky, Arnheim is suggesting that there is a photographic literalness in the film which is inescapable and which makes metaphor impossible except in a highly restricted sense. Even Thomas Mann, who seriously misjudges the film in other respects, supports the notion that almost any story will be accepted so long as it "is set in a frame of scenic and mimic detail which is true to life and reality . . . ."[41] Any discussion of editing, then, must remain at least peripherally aware of the shot's obligation to representational fidelity. The film's spatial freedom is always modified by realistic demands.

The Trope in Language

The film, then, making its appeal to the perceiving senses, is free to work with endless variations of physical reality. "Literature on the other hand," Mendilow points out, "is dependent entirely on a symbolic medium that stands between the perceiver and the symbolised percepta . . . ." Perhaps nothing better illustrates this root difference between language and photographed image than an appraisal of each medium's ability to render literary tropes.

Carrying Mendilow's statement a step further, we observe that word-symbols must be translated into images of things, feelings and concepts through the process of thought. Where the moving picture comes to us directly through perception, language must be filtered through the screen of conceptual apprehension. And the conceptual process, though allied to and often taking its point of departure from the percept, represents a different mode of experience, a different way of apprehending the universe.

The distinction is a crucial one, for it generates differences which run all the way down the line from the media's ability to handle tropes, affect beholders, render states of consciousness (including dreams, memories, feelings, and imagination), to their respective methods of handling conventions, time, and space.

The linguistic trope is the novel's special way of rendering the

[40] Arnheim, p. 265.
[41] Thomas Mann, "On the Film," *Past Masters and Other Papers*, trans. H. T. Lowe-Porter (New York, 1933), p. 263.

shock of resemblance. By juxtaposing similar qualities in violently dissimilar things, language gets its revenge on the apparent disorder of life. It binds together a world which seems atomized and therefore chaotic to the primitive mind. Modern theories of symbolic thinking demonstrate that we necessarily see resemblances in the most ordinary perceptions. Arnheim points out that an illusion, to be strong, does not have to be complete in every detail: "everyone knows that a clumsy childish scribble of a human face consisting of two dots, a comma, and a dash may be full of expression and depict anger, amusement, fear . . . ." A kind of basic tropism is involved in such a process: the mind sees resemblances in the disparate sources of scribbled drawing and angry face.

So similar are linguistic and cognitive processes in finding resemblances that critics like Cleanth Brooks build their analytical systems around the metaphor. The difference between the artist who coins metaphors and the ordinary mind which classifies objects derives largely from the fact that the artist casts his net much wider. Where the cognitive mind finds common traits in collies and boxers and calls them dogs, the maker of tropes finds common qualities in slings, arrows, and outrageous fortune. Literary tropes, however, are distinguished from cognitive classification, first, by their verbal origins and, second, by a kind of connotative luxuriance. Not only does the power of the trope inhere in its figurative character but in its ability to compound itself without damage to intended meanings. Virginia Woolf, contrasting the novel and film, is especially sensitive to the unique power of the figure of speech. The images of a poet, she tells us, are compact of a thousand suggestions, of which the visual is only the most obvious:

> Even the simplest image: "my love's like a red, red rose, that's newly sprung in June," presents us with impressions of moisture and warmth and the flow of crimson and the softness of petals inextricably mixed and strung upon the lift of a rhythm which is itself the voice of the passion and the hesitation of the love. All this, which is accessible to words, and to words alone, the cinema must avoid.[42]

[42] Virginia Woolf, "The Movies and Reality," *New Republic*, XLVII (August 4, 1926), 309.

We have already seen that a special kind of film trope is possible, but only when it is confined to cinematic terms: it must arise naturally from the setting (as Lilian Gish's knitting in *Way Down East*, or Marlon Brando's horse in *Viva Zapata*). If disparate objects are compared, the film metaphor must be predicated upon a clear suspension of realistic demands (as the invasion montage in the Marx Brothers' *Duck Soup*). Since the latter is rarely successful (the notable failure of the cradle linkage in *Intolerance*), the former technique must carry the burden of metaphor. James Agee, speaking of the metamorphic mobility of the silent-screen comedian, his ability to assume physical shapes suggesting objects or emotions, is able to say, "It was his business to be as funny as possible physically, without the help or hindrance of words. So he gave us a figure of speech, or rather a vision . . . ."[43] But if such figures work at all, they do so by becoming appropriated to the peculiar laws of the film, and not by simple conversion. The final and most central cinematic analogy to the metaphor may be found in the special case of editing (discussed below), where two disparate elements, as in the trope, are linked together to create a *tertium quid*.

That film tropes are enormously restricted compared to literary tropes is indicated by the character of the compacted imagery in almost any passage by Marcel Proust. Watching the aged Duc de Guermantes, Marcel marvels to find him showing his age so little, and understands why

> . . . as soon as he rose and tried to stand erect, he had tottered on trembling limbs (like those aged archbishops who have nothing solid on them except their metallic cross . . .) and had wavered as he made his way along the difficult summit of his eighty-three years, as if men were perched on giant stilts, sometimes taller than church spires, constantly growing and finally rendering their progress so difficult and perilous that they suddenly fall.[44]

---

[43] James Agee, "Comedy's Greatest Era," *Life*, XXVII (September 5, 1949), 70.

[44] Marcel Proust, "The Past Recaptured," *Remembrance of Things Past*, trans. Frederick A. Blossom, II (New York, 1932), 1123.

The images of metallic cross, men on stilts, in turn taller than church spires and still growing, depend for their effect precisely on the fact that they are not to be taken literally. The quality of precarious summits common to stilts and years is the resemblance which yokes these things together. In the process a new thing is created which resides neither in octogenarians nor in stilts. The moment such relationships lose their novelty and become habitual, they become cliches. So that besides conceptual appeal and figurative luxuriance the final property of the trope is its insistence on perpetual renewal. It is a way, then, of packed symbolic thinking which is peculiar to imaginative rather than to visual activity. Converted into a literal image, the metaphor would seem absurd. In such attempts, to adopt Virginia Woolf's formulation, "Eye and brain are torn asunder ruthlessly as they try vainly to work in couples." She is right in concluding that the results of conversion from linguistic to visual images are disastrous to both. The difference is too great to overcome.

Just as the cinema exhibits a stubborn antipathy to novels, the novel here emerges as a medium antithetical to film. Because language has laws of its own, and literary characters are inseparable from the language which forms them, the externalization of such characters often seems dissatisfying. The distinction between the character who comes to us through a screen of language and the character who comes to us in visual images may account, perhaps, for the persistent disclaimers of film commentators like Michael Orme[45] and Thomas Craven.[46] Protesting De Mille's butchering of *Four Frightened People* by E. Arnot Robinson, Orme reflects, "you cannot transpose any one character from page to screen and hope to present him entirely as the novelist created him or as the novelist's public knew him . . . . who can really recall hav-

---

[45] Michael Orme, "The Bookshelf and the Screen," *Illustrated London News*, CLXXXVI (March 10, 1934), 368.

[46] Craven's statement reads, "I doubt if the most astute and sympathetic reader ever visualizes a character; he responds to that part of a created figure which is also himself, but he does not actually see his hero. . . . For this reason all illustrations are disappointing." In "The Great American Art," *Dial*, LXXXI (December, 1926), 489–490.

ing seen a screen performance which really and truly portrayed his favourite character as he knew it?"

Editing: The Cinematic Trope

If the film is thus severely restricted in rendering linguistic tropes (despite dialogue which will be discussed presently), it has, through the process of editing, discovered a metaphoric quality all its own. We have already noted how the spatial liberation of the cinema was its unique achievement. But film editing, combining the integrity of the shot with the visual rhythm of the sequence, gives the director his characteristic signature.

"The first thing to be observed about the technique of editing," Lindgren observes, "is that it affords the film-maker a new field for his powers of selection." Since the complete action of any given scene is made up of a large number of moving components, the director must constantly choose which detail he will emphasize at a given moment. Selection, however, can go much farther than this. Through editing, the film-maker can eliminate meaningless intervals, concentrate on significant details, ordering his design in consonance with the central line of his narrative.

For example, Pudovkin poses the problem of presenting a man falling from a window five stories high. The director, in this case, would take one shot of a man falling from a window in such a way that the net (into which he safely falls) is not visible on the screen; then a shot of the same man falling from a slight height to the ground. Joined together, the shots would give the desired impression of continuous fall. It is precisely this technique that Griffith used in the Babylonian episode of *Intolerance*, which Pudovkin had seen and admired. The camera, it should be noted, has not followed nature. Instead, the director has selected two points in the process, leaving the intervening passage to be filled in by the mind of the spectator. This extraordinary power of suggestion is indeed unique in the dramatic arts. "It is not correct," Pudovkin warns us, "to call such a process a trick; it is a method of filmic representation exactly corresponding to the elimination of five years that divides a first from a second act upon the stage." The method corresponds roughly to the temporal gap between one panel and another in Renaissance frescoes depicting the lives of saints, except that in the film the action seems continuous.

In cinematic terms, then, the method of connecting the film strips becomes the basic formative function. For the two strips, joined together, become a *tertium quid*, a third thing which neither of the strips has been independently. This is the essence of that much abused concept of Eisenstein's which we have come to know as montage.

Given the transition, the relationship between shots as the center of the creative process, a high degree of discipline must be exercised in the editing. Long shots must dovetail with close shots. There must be a logical connection between the shots, a kind of visual momentum, or transference. We see a man about to cross a street. In a close-up, we see his face twist in horror. We cut immediately to a scene in front of him. A car is bearing down on a small child. We accept the instantaneous shift because, interested as we are in the cause of the horror, we are propelled visually to the next significant detail. Different points of view must thus be carefully blended to suggest a continuous action.

Building his design out of individual strips, always thinking plastically, the film-maker may use almost endless spatial combinations. He may, for example, use contrast ironically. When Alec Guinness, in *The Promoter*, achieves a social triumph by dancing with the Countess of Chell, the film cuts to a shot of greasy sausage frying in a skillet. It is the next day and the "card's" mother is preparing his meal in their dingy kitchen. Or the director may use what the Feldman brothers call parallel editing.[47] A wife, to make her husband jealous, is seen flirting with a willing lover. We cut to an office where the husband is seen making advances to his secretary. The director may use symbolism. In *Strike*, the shooting down of workers is punctuated by shots of the slaughter of a steer in a stockyard. In *The Blue Angel*, birds are used with consummate artistry as a kind of leitmotif. In the opening scene, Professor Unrat coos at a caged canary. Later, having devoted himself to Lola, a music-hall singer, he watches pigeons flying up against a clock whose bronze figures ominously mark the passage

[47] Joseph and Harry Feldman, *Dynamics of the Film* (New York, 1952), p. 86.

of time. And at the height of his degradation, the Professor crows like a cock. The possibility for plastic comments like these, as distinct from verbal renditions of the same effects, is unprecedented in the arts.

A new kind of relationship between animate and inanimate objects springs up, a relationship which becomes the key to plastic thinking. Pudovkin points out quite cogently that relationships between human beings are, for the most part, illumined by conversation, by words. No one carries on conversation with objects, and that is why an actor's relationship to objects is of special interest to the film technician.

Within the composition of the frame, the juxtaposition of man and object becomes crucial. "The performance of an actor linked with an object and built upon it will always be one of the most powerful methods of filmic construction."[48] We have only to think of Chaplin to see the principle in operation. The dancing rolls in *The Gold Rush*, the supple cane, the globe dance in *The Great Dictator*, the feeding machine in *Modern Times*, the flowers and drinks in *Monsieur Verdoux*, the flea skit in *Limelight*—these are only isolated examples of Chaplin's endless facility for inventing new relationships with objects. He leans on a doorman as on a lamppost, and the animate becomes inanimate. The spring of the watch in *The Pawnshop* comes alive, and the inanimate becomes animate. The confusion dynamizes the relationship, and the distinction between man and object is obliterated. Man and object become interchangeable, and the inanimate joins the animate as an actor. Certainly this accounts for a good part of Chaplin's filmic genius.

Not only has the film discovered new ways to render meanings by finding relationships between animate and inanimate objects, but the human physiognomy itself has been rediscovered. So pervasive has been the power of the close-up to convey emotion that in "*Der Sichtbare Mensch*" Béla Balázs places the film on

---

[48] Pudovkin, p. 115. A telling account of a familiar phenomenon appears in Lindsay, p. 15: " . . . there came to our town not long ago a film of a fight between Federals and Confederates, with the loss of many lives, all for the recapture of a steam-engine that took on more personality in the end than private or general on either side, alive or dead."

a par with the invention of the printing press. The method of conveying meaning by facial expression, a method which according to Balázs fell into desuetude with the advent of printing, has been revived by the "microphysiognomy" of the screen image. The face becomes another kind of object in space, a terrain on which may be enacted dramas broad as battles, and sometimes more intense. Physiognomy preëmpts the domain of nonverbal experience: "The gestures of visual man are not intended to convey concepts which can be expressed in words, but such inner experiences, such nonrational emotions which would still remain unexpressed when everything that can be told has been told."[49]

Just as words are not merely images expressing our thoughts and feelings, but in many cases their *a priori* limiting forms, the subtleties of the mobile face not only render hitherto unrecorded experiences but also create the conditions for new experiences to come into being. If, then, "the film increases the possibilities for expression, it will also widen the spirit it can express." If Balázs goes too far in calling for an "encyclopedia of comparative gesturology," he at least draws attention to the unprecedented possibilities of the human face. These possibilities have given rise to a wholly different kind of acting. The microdrama of the human countenance permits the reading of the greatest conflicts in the merest flicker of an eye. Understatement becomes the key to film characterization. The subtleties of Mme. Falconetti's face in Dreyer's *The Passion of Joan of Arc*, or of Giulietta Massina's in Fellini's *La Strada* would have been incomprehensible to anyone in the dramatic arts before 1900.

In a real sense, then, Pudovkin is right when he says, "In the discovered, deeply imbedded detail there lies an element of perception, the creative element that gives the event shown its final worth." By selecting and combining, by comparing and contrasting, by linking disparate spatial entities, photographed images of "the deeply imbedded detail" allow the film-maker, through editing, to achieve a uniquely cinematic equivalent of the literary trope.

[49] Béla Balázs, *Theory of the Film*, trans. Edith Bone (New York, 1953), p. 40.

Sound in Editing

If the emphasis so far has been on spatial movement, I do not mean to overlook the function of sound in editing. I mean only to emphasize that sound is subsidiary to the moving image, that dialogue, music, aural effects take their place as separate lines in the ensemble which editing creates. Just as the first narrative films erred by imitating the fixed frame of the stage, the first sound films erred by imitating theatrical dialogue. Sound films, like the early silents, aroused curiosity as a toy and, in the process, were almost talked to death. Intelligent critics were quick to attack this fault, and some even argued against the sound track itself. An art, they said, thrives on the limitations of its materials and every gain in realism (like painting plaster of Paris figures in lifelike colors) must be accompanied by an aesthetic loss. But the aesthetic loss was temporary and the film learned the proper use of its new dimension. "One can imagine," writes Panofsky, "that, when the cave-men of Altamira began to paint their buffaloes in natural colors instead of merely incising the contours, the more conservative cave-men foretold the end of palaeolithic art. But palaeolithic art went on, and so will the movies."

A case in point is René Clair's initial resistance to sound. So repelled was he by the early dissonance that Clair for a time seriously considered abandoning the film for a career in fiction. Even after he resigned himself to the inevitablity of the soundtrack, as Georges Sadoul tells us, Clair satirized the medium. In *Sous les Toits de Paris*, "The glass-panel door that slams to before certain of the characters are about to speak is in this respect something of a symbol." Not until the recent *Les Belles de Nuit* does Clair seem to accept symbolically this entrenched nemesis of the silent film. Clair's poor composer reacts to a rash of discordant noise, aural representatives of a disordered world, by retreating into a world of dreams. In his dream-world, the sounds—a bugle blast, the tenor-manager of an opera house accepting the young hero's opus, a seductive temptress singing her affections against exotic settings —fall more gently on the ear. But gradually the dreams become frantic and distasteful, the sounds more harsh than any in the hero's waking hours. And when he awakes, highly relieved to escape the madness of his dream-world, he symbolically accepts the harsh acoustic world from which he had fled. With the discovery that sound could thus be integrated into the total film structure, Clair seems to have become reconciled to the aural dimension of motion pictures.

Yet in one sense the conservatives who objected to sound were right. Every filmic innovation from sound to 3-D and the wide-screen processes has been accompanied by a throwback to false theatrical conventions. But these throwbacks have been brought on less by the innovation than by a misunderstanding of its proper role in the film medium.

With sound, as with the subsequent innovation of color and stereoscopic film, came a new dimension and new possibilities for selection. But the proper role of sound became apparent only when the film, as in the work of René Clair, once again asserted its fundamental editing principles. Although Pudovkin's early notes are speculative rather than definitive, there is from the beginning, supplementing the *parallel* use of sound in dialogue and music, the guiding principle of counterpoint, a logical extension of the technique of editing. Pudovkin visualizes "a film in which sounds and human speech are wedded to the visual images on the screen in the same way in which two or more melodies can be combined by an orchestra . . . . " To urge the contrapuntal use of sound and image was to point up hidden resources that the filmist might easily overlook. But Pudovkin goes too far when he suggests that one must never show on the screen a man and reproduce his words exactly synchronized with the movement of his lips. To forego the right of synchronization is to forego another valuable and essentially contrapuntal device, namely the contrast between a line of dialogue and the speaker's face.

The classic statement on the aesthetic use of sound came as an articulate statement from the Russians after the Americans had presented the first commercially practical example. *The Jazz Singer* opened in October, 1927. In August of the following year, a statement by Eisenstein, Pudovkin, and Alexandrov appeared in a Leningrad magazine, arguing essentially for a strict use of "non-synchronization." The statement ignores, of course, the realistic tug of synchronized speech, just as an emphasis on editing tends to overlook the photographic demands of the individual shot. If, however, we exempt dialogue from the onus of strict non-synchronization (Eisenstein violated his own credo by synchronizing speech and image in *Alexander Nevsky*, his first sound film), the statement can and has stood as a guide to most serious filmists. In *Alexander Nevsky*, the camera tracks along bleak wastes of ice. But the Prokofieff score, suggesting quiet, ominous preparations, adumbrates the coming Battle of the Ice. In *High Noon*, the theme of the ballad, introduced during the credit titles, is carried over into the marriage ceremony, suggesting the coming desertion, the lonely conflict. Thus sound is used to reinforce, comment on, anticipate the film's visual images.

That the final word on sound has not yet been pronounced is indicated when we contrast the aural work of various film directors. Discussing his scenario for *An American Tragedy* (which Paramount paid him for but never produced, substituting the melodramatic version directed by Josef von Sternberg in 1931), Eisenstein says flatly, "The true material of the sound film is, of course, the monologue." But such a recent tour de force as *The Thief*, which abandons dialogue entirely, seems to restate the case for movement, music, and nonverbal sound effects as the emblems of subjective moods. Between these extremes, is the combination which Laurence Olivier uses in the sound track of *Hamlet*. Sometimes Hamlet's voice is rendered in interior monologue; sometimes, when his emotions burst out naturally, in spoken soliloquy. At times, the words are synchronized with the speaker's lips; at other times they merely accompany the face of the listener. Suffice it to say that dialogue, interior monologue, sound effects, music are ultimately determined by and therefore subservient to the demands of the visual image.

Like color, like stereoscopic film, the talkies opened up new cinematic possibilities. But each innovation has conformed in the end to pictorial requirements. Sometimes the innovation has been consciously suppressed. In *Modern Times*, Chaplin kept his mechanized tramp from talking when talking did not suit his purposes. After filming *Henry V* in technicolor, Olivier did *Hamlet* in black and white.

What the dimension of sound implies for the film's ability

to render experiential time we shall see in our discussion of time and space in the two media.

IV. THE AUDIENCES AND THE MYTHS

The Novel

Differences in the raw materials of novel and film cannot fully explain differences in content. For each medium presupposes a special, though often heterogeneous and overlapping, audience whose demands condition and shape artistic content. Because the shaping power of reader and movie-goer has, perhaps, been too often neglected in considerations of the filmed novel, it requires special emphasis here.

When Sartre, speaking of literature, points out that, by a reversal which is "characteristic of the imaginary object, it is not [Raskolnikov's] behavior which excites my indignation or esteem, but my indignation and esteem which give consistency and objectivity to his behavior,"[50] he is pushing to its limits the spectator's claim to an active role in the aesthetic response. But if the history of aesthetics proves anything, it is that a given set of myths, symbols, conventions is unable to satisfy all spectators at all times in all places. On the other hand, according to Sartre, one "cannot write without a public and without a myth—without a *certain* public which historical circumstances have made, without a *certain* myth of literature which depends to a very great extent upon the demand of this public." It follows, then, that in a society like ours, "where we are conscious of separation in time (through our historical sense) as well as in space, literature is assigned the task of creating and sustaining communal symbolic characters who must become part of the experience of every individual who is to take part in this society."[51] If we take seriously Tobler's classic definition of philology as "that branch of the humanities which strives to understand the manifestations of the intellectual life of a nation, period or person as far as this life manifests itself in lan-

[50] Sartre, pp. 50–51.
[51] Duncan, p. 5.

guage," it follows that linguistic analysis distorts literature insofar as it neglects symbolic levels which, only by entering the public domain, as it were, become comprehensible to particular audiences.

The precise contours of such approved myths in literature need not concern us here beyond our noting what any number of literary historians have already pointed out, that the rise of the novel "coincides with the educational diffusion of literacy, the technological perfection of printing, and the economic ascendancy of the middle classes."[52] The coincidence has led to the recurrence, in the Western novel, of root-problems derived from the conflicts and adjustments between Protestant ethics grounded in Judaeo-Christian religion, and the rise of a middle-class society founded on an industrial organization of production. Whether one uses the technique of a Kenneth Burke in searching out the associational clusters of images in literary expression; of a Perry Miller in explicating the history of ideas in a relatively homogeneous culture like New England; of an F. O. Matthiessen in bringing the resources of history, language, and psychology to bear on the texts of given novels—one finds recurring again and again, under the aegis of conflicts between good and evil, the great oppositions between the individual and society, sin and morality, mind and heart, flesh and spirit. One needs only to trace recurrent attitudes to the novel's typological characters—the usurer, the virgin, the frontiersman, the egoist, the artist, the criminal, the entrepreneur, the landed aristocrat, the transgressor and law-enforcer—to find common patterns of approval and disapproval. In spite of inevitable "ambiguities, differences, every kind of divisiveness"[53] in our linguistic appeals to one another, the novel has retained a complex but common body of themes, settings and attitudes which are characteristic of middle-class refraction. If, in Mendilow's phrase, even the most independent writer "is grappled to the soul of his times with hoops of steel," it is reasonable to expect that the novelist will use notations which are comprehensible to his readers and, today especially, will pit himself against some startling new

[52] Levin, p. 405.
[53] Duncan, p. 140 ff.

experiences which are entering the public domain. One of his most important discoveries, for example, is that status as well as sexual repression can cause anxiety.

This mutual extension of the boundaries between social and imaginative action lends increasing support to the value of approaching literature as an "institution." David Daiches' assumption that the most significant modern fiction "represents an attempted adjustment between literature and a certain state of transition in civilization and culture generally"[54] supports Levin's definition of realism as "a continuous effort, from one generation to the next, to adjust the techniques of literature to the changing conditions of life." In the institutional approach, the critic assumes a necessary difference between art and life and considers literary convention the gentlemen's agreement between them.[55] He assumes that even though literature, "instead of reflecting life, refracts it," literature is, at the same time, always "an intrinsic part of life." He assumes that in the steady adjustment of literature to life literary conventions change with experience and that judgments are therefore falsified if we apply current standards to old works, if, for example, we judge the heroic couplet by the credo of the Imagist Manifesto, or *Le Cid* by Strindberg's psychology. Since there is that in literature which is at once perpetually dying and perpetually coming into being, the institutional approach assumes that literature, like other institutions, the church, or the law,

> . . . cherishes a unique phase of human experience and controls a special body of precedents and devices; it tends to incorporate a self-perpetuating discipline, while responding to the main currents of each succeeding period; it is continually accessible to all the impulses of life at large, but it must translate them into its own terms and adopt them to its peculiar forms. Once we have grasped this fact, we begin to see how art may belong to so-

[54] David Daiches, *The Novel and the Modern World* (Chicago, 1939), p. 2.

[55] Harry Levin, "Literature as an Institution," *Criticism: The Foundations of Modern Literary Judgment*, ed. Mark Schorer, Josephine Miles, and Gordon McKenzie (New York, 1948), p. 550. "Convention," says Levin, "may be described as a necessary difference between art and life."

ciety and yet be autonomous within its own limits, and are no longer puzzled by the polarity of social and formal criticism.[56]

The Film

How the institutional approach, appropriating the influences of both audience and medium, may be applied to comparative film criticism is indicated by the manner in which the director must attend to the requirements of the mode of industrial production (the profit motive dividing bourgeois artist from mass audience), unofficial and official censorship (the Production Code), modern folk myths (the perpetuation of symbolic heroes—the actor, the tramp, the cowboy, the gangster, the Disney stable of fable—and the popularization of melodrama, slapstick, spectacle). Each contributes to a complex but common body of conventions which, as in the novel, are perpetually being broken.

The product of a commercial society, the Hollywood commodity must make a profit; to make a profit, it must please consumers. Where a novel can sell 20,000 volumes and make a substantial profit, the film must reach millions. This explains, perhaps, why writers accustomed to working in isolation are continually unnerved by the co-operative demands of film production. More than anyone else, novelists with screen-writing experience have been responsible for scathing indictments of the film industry.[57] The playwrights have been both less frequent and less severe in their attacks.[58] And the directors, being too busy making films,

[56] *Ibid.*, p. 552.

[57] Novels about Hollywood which are sardonic and critical in tone include Budd Schulberg, *What Makes Sammy Run* and *The Disenchanted;* F. Scott Fitzgerald, *The Last Tycoon;* Jay Richard Kennedy, *Prince Bart;* Nathaniel West, *Day of the Locust;* Robert Carson, *The Magic Lantern;* Horace McCoy, *I Should Have Stayed Home;* James Cain, *Serenade;* Aldous Huxley, *After Many a Summer Dies the Swan;* Peter Viertel, *White Hunter, Black Heart;* Norman Mailer, *The Deer Park.* Manfred A. Wuerslin (University of Wisconsin) is at work on a dissertation considering "The Image of Hollywood in Modern American Literature, 1920–1950."

[58] *The Big Knife* by Clifford Odets is a rare and angry theatrical indictment of Hollywood. In Robert Aldrich's film adaptation of the play, a conscious effort is made to dissociate the villain-producer, Stanley Hoff, from the industry as a whole.

have complained little or not at all. Discontent, it seems, has been directly proportional to one's lack of training in joint production. This accounts, too, both for the antipathy of individualistic scholars to film research and for the neglect of scenario-writing as an independent art form. If it is true, as Margaret Kennedy points out, that screen writing "is no more a work of literature than is the recipe for a pudding,"[59] both the resistance and the unhappiness of screen writers are more understandable. But the contradictions generated by the exigencies of the market and the tendencies of the medium make the problem more complicated than this.

On the one hand, we find the elaborate apparatus of the studios, the orchestral nature of the production crew, the necessity of catering to the tastes of a mass audience, the profit motive, the official and unofficial censorship imposed by state and industry. On the other hand, the filmic thinking of the individual craftsman, the rightness of the screen for the freewheeling, plastic imagination, the resistance of film to any kind of rigid code, the rich and complex subject matter offered by the film's heterogeneous audience, the adaptability of that audience to thematic and formal innovation. On the one hand, acceptance of the most implausible heroics; on the other, insistence on absolute fidelity to realistic detail. The ordinary comforts of reliable conventions are all but impossible when the conventions themselves conflict. This tug of contradiction, this pull of opposite tendencies, has both strengthened and weakened the film from its inception. Just a step behind the artist, and sometimes overtaking him, has been the shaping power of censor and audience. In the film, more than in any of the other arts, the signature of social forces is evident in the final work.

Directly and indirectly, the structure of the film has been conditioned by a carefully supervised content. This control is not surprising since big business has always treated the film as a commodity. As early as 1915-16, French Pathé, then the world leader in the newsreel field, formed an alliance with DuPont, which had risen to industrial eminence in 1915 through war munitions contracts with England.[60]

[59] Margaret Kennedy, *The Mechanized Muse* (London, 1952), p. 13.
[60] Lawson, p. 327.

In 1915, American Tobacco tried to effect a merger between Paramount and the leading independents, but the agreement fell through because Adolph Zukor of Paramount wanted to keep monopolistic control of the field. Then the Kuhn, Loeb investors, Jeremiah Milbank, of Chase National Bank, and others became actively interested in the new industry. With various modifications, this pattern of close alliances between investment banking and corporate production has persisted to the present day.[61]

Along with the rise of Hollywood as a business community, trading in the commodity of art, came the rise of self-appointed moral censors. Individual states set up their own censorship codes, reflecting the preferences of particular regions. When *Volpone* was shown in Boston, a note had to be appended on the screen to the effect that, of course, Mosca was duly apprehended and received the punishment he deserved. Thus, moral control has continually altered filmic content. Religious, social, and cultural defenders of public morality continue to buffet Hollywood's conscience with a mélange of ethical arguments. Most powerful of these has been the Catholic Legion of Decency, whose A, B, and C ratings are significant emblems for every Hollywood producer.

Pressured in one way or another during the twenties, before the Legion of Decency ever came into being, Hollywood, in 1934, almost in self-defense, adopted a revised version of the much-publicized Production Code.[62] With minor revisions, the Code has been, or has attempted to be, standard operating procedure in Hollywood ever since. The censor, in his explicit restrictions against verbal and visual sin, makes no bones about tampering with the film-maker's subject matter. But the Code, on the other hand, says nothing about artistic techniques. And the conflict between artistic freedom and thematic control has had the practical

[61] For more detailed analyses of film financing and its effect on film production, see May D. Huettig, *Economic Control of the Motion Picture Industry* (Philadelphia, 1944); Ernest Borneman, "Rebellion in Hollywood," *Harper's Magazine*, cxciii (October, 1946), 337–343; "Movies: End of an Era?" *Fortune*, xxxix (April, 1949), 99–102, 135–150; Helen B. Shaffer, "Changing Fortunes of the Movie Business," *Editorial Research Reports*, ii (September, 1953).

[62] See Ruth Inglis, *Freedom of the Movies* (Chicago, 1947).

effect of taxing the ingenuity of directors, writers and camera-
men who try to evade the Code's specific strictures. Hortense Powdermaker has noted the Code's basic absence of logic.[63] Since
"moral concepts are not distinguished from physical facts," the
Code "simply does not belong to this world." While the prohibitions fit very well with the general studio atmosphere of meticu-
lous attention to small details and very little emphasis on meaning,
"no one connected with motion picture production believes in the
system of morality it embodies." Everyone knows that houses have
toilets, love gets physically consummated, childbirth is a biological
function, and marriages frequently end in divorce. But this information may never be explicitly conveyed on the screen.

The artificiality of the Code, which fails to distinguish between
obscenity and honesty, is bound to submit to the corrosion of time
and practice. If the film, as George Bernard Shaw once said, is
"reeking with morality but does not touch virtue,"[64] then virtue
will find other means of asserting itself. It is true that the absence
of censorship is no guarantee against bad taste and pornographic
sensationalism, as any number of pre-Code films will graphically
attest, but a liberal censorship at least creates favorable conditions
for good taste and honesty. Inevitably, the exigencies of commercial interests which find sex saleable and of artistic integrity which
deplores restriction combine to work modifications. That is why
recent challenges to the Code have come from extremes in film
mediocrity and excellence. Within the industry, the challenge has
come both from Howard Hughes' release of *The French Line* and
United Artists' release of Otto Preminger's *The Moon is Blue* and
The Man With the Golden Arm, all three without the Breen
Office seal of approval. Conversely, and less obtrusively, a kind
of modification has come from pictures which have received the
seal but which contain scenes that might once have been elided
by the Hollywood censors. For example, there are scenes depicting a house of prostitution in *The Egyptian*, unusual violence in
On the Waterfront, a married couple lying together in a double

---

[63] Hortense Powdermaker, *Hollywood: The Dream Factory* (Boston,
1950), p. 77 ff.
[64] George Bernard Shaw, "The Drama, the Theater, and the Films,"
Harper's Magazine, CXLIX (September, 1924), 426.

bed in *Anna*, and adulterers who are not mortally punished in *Tea and Sympathy*.[65] Each in its own way has modified the sanctity of the Code. The challenge from outside the industry has come in an action by Dr. Hugo Flick, the New York State censor head, permitting the retention of a scene showing the birth of a buffalo in Walt Disney's *The Vanishing Prairie;* in Supreme Court decisions refusing to uphold local censorship suits against Hollywood's *M*, France's *La Ronde*, and Italy's *The Miracle;* in Maryland, Kansas, and Ohio state courts which have reversed censorial prohibitions against *The Moon is Blue*.

In spite of these inroads, Hollywood still begs off from the charge of censorship by pointing to its audience. Every innovation is greeted with the cry, "The box-office won't stand it," even after innovations again and again prove the cry wrong. The prospect is less dismaying when we remember that the Hollywood producer is governed less by the laws of aesthetics than by the laws of the marketplace. It is significant, for example, that *The Jazz Singer*, after the rejection of sound by most major studios, was released by Warner Brothers as a means of averting bankruptcy; and that wide-screen and stereoscopic innovations were adopted only after television had become an economic competitor of some magnitude.

Faced with the charge of mediocrity, Hollywood pleads the heterogeneous nature of its customers, pointing to differences in taste between region and region, city and farm, men and women, adults and children, educated and illiterate, race and race, religion and religion. And although there is always a Shaw to argue that "levelling, though excellent in incomes, is disastrous in morals,"[66] the industry almost always quietly returns the responsibility to its vague and tyrannous audience. The fact that a few courageous independents like Stanley Kramer and Robert Aldrich have been able to produce quality films that also sell is merely the exception that proves the rule.

Margaret Farrand Thorpe reminds us that the Lynds' *Middle-*

[65] Charles Samuels, "The Great Censorship Rebellion," *True*, xxxv (February, 1955), 39–40, 65–68.
[66] George Bernard Shaw, "The Cinema as a Moral Leveller," *New Statesman: Special Supplement on the Modern Theater*, iii (June 27, 1914), 2.

town sets the responsibility for the level of the average movie squarely in the lap of the average citizen's wife: "What the adult female chiefly asks of the movie is the opportunity to escape by reverie from an existence which she finds insufficiently interesting."[67] That is why, according to Mrs. Thorp, there is social and psychological significance in the fact that 70 per cent of Gary Cooper's fan mail comes from women who write that their husbands do not appreciate them.

When no less a novelist than Elizabeth Bowen can lend support to this analysis by writing, "To get back to my star: I enjoy sitting opposite him or her, the delights of intimacy without the onus, high points of possession without the strain,"[68] the analysis uncovers a real demand which the film-maker must fulfill. It helps explain, perhaps, the shaping conventions of both glamor and the star system. Since Mrs. Thorp and Miss Bowen are both women, we should not be surprised to find some of their impressionistic insights being supported by any number of audience research projects. The studies in Leo Handel's *Hollywood Looks at its Audience* reveal that women's preferences do in fact differ from men's. These studies, if they are accurate, bear out Mrs. Thorp's observation that the whole glamor system depends on the identity of star and role: "To the majority of spectators the stars are not so much actors as *alter egos,* or at least close personal friends, and to see them behaving out of character is to see one's universe rock, to feel one's personality dim, a sensation not unlike going mad." Miss Bowen adds, glamor "is a sort of sensuous gloss: I know it to be synthetic, but it affects me strongly."

In brief, the Hollywood film is faced with the search for a formula that cannot be found; with satisfying needs that cannot be satisfied. The tension has created demands, both real and illusory, either originated by, or imposed upon, the heterogeneous audience, and the demands have built up over the years a loose but well-defined series of conventions which add an unofficial code to the written one. The stipulations of Code and censor

[67] Margaret Farrand Thorp, *America at the Movies* (New Haven, 1939), p. 5.

[68] Elizabeth Bowen, "Why I Go to the Movies," *Footnotes to the Film,* p. 213.

may prohibit the acknowledgement of biological realities, but no one forces the evasion of social realities. The official Code may disallow religious satire; but the unofficial code disallows pro-labor sentiment. The existence of an unwritten code suggests that the industry is interested in imposing ideas as well as in reflecting them. Working together, the two codes have been responsible for creating a set of myths which, even in the reputable Hollywood product, is rarely questioned. Ben Hecht, who has learned the tyranny of formula by growing rich on it, bitterly attacks the industry's "organized lying":

Two generations of Americans have been informed nightly that a woman who betrayed her husband (or a husband a wife) could never find happiness; that sex was no fun without a mother-in-law and a rubber plant around; that women who fornicated just for pleasure ended up as harlots or washerwomen; that any man who was sexually active in his youth later lost the one girl he truly loved; that a man who indulged in sharp practices to get ahead in the world ended in poverty and even with his own children turning on him; that any man who broke the laws, man's or God's, must always die . . . or go to jail, or become a monk, or restore the money he stole before wandering off into the desert; that anyone who didn't believe in God (and said so out loud) was set right by seeing either an angel or witnessing some feat of levitation by one of the characters; that an honest heart must always recover from a train wreck or a score of bullets and win the girl it loved; that the most potent and brilliant of villains are powerless before little children, parish priests or young virgins . . . that injustice could cause a heap of trouble but it must always slink out of town in Reel Nine; that there were no problems of labor, politics, domestic life or sexual abnormality but can be solved by a simple Christian phrase or a fine American motto.[69]

While most of these moral judgments are, of course, based on the Ten Commandments, the behavior depicted does not square with the facts of life.

[69] Ben Hecht, *A Child of the Century* (New York, 1954), p. 469.

Lest the uniqueness of the film's virtues be extended to its vices, one ought to remember that similar conventions have existed in most of our mass-arts. When Merle Curti discovers, for example, that the nineteenth-century dime novel, as promoted by the Beadle brothers, George Lippard, and others, consistently found the remedy to social evils not "in a social attack on the problem but rather in single-handed effort,"[70] he is merely noting the precedent for the film's finding personal solutions to universal problems.[71] Every persistent convention which Curti finds in the older genre has its Hollywood counterpart: the triumph of virtue over vice; the happy ending; the emphasis on adventure, suspense, melodrama; the exaltation of common virtues against aristocratic snobbishness; the homage to God and country and rugged individualism; the norms of Anglo-Saxon Christianity. In short, a kind of folk appropriation of Protestant ethics in which self-reliance, perseverance, pluck, and individual prowess are the keys to, but not the warranties of, personal luck, and in which fortuitous grace is bestowed by a fate over which the individual, finally, has no control. Every major American novelist, from Herman Melville to William Faulkner, has had to fly in the face of such popular myths. And now, in muted or modified form, the film has hardened these conventions into a governing tradition.

If recognizing this continuity has the advantage of placing the film in the perspective of traditional mass arts in our culture, it does not necessarily mitigate the force of those precedents described by Curti. The unconscious or conscious adherence to convention has an enduring influence on film content. No small measure of the screen writer's rancor comes from the knowledge that while the nineteenth-century reader, if he had the price, could choose Melville and Hawthorne as well as dime novels, the twentieth-century fan can only rarely choose Chaplin and Griffith. Movies are simply too expensive to permit the kind of variety which the novel allows.

Even Chaplin violates conventional totems at his peril. For the Chaplins and Griffiths and Capras, insofar as they have survived

[70] Merle Curti, "Dime Novels and the American Tradition," *Probing Our Past* (New York, 1955), p. 175.
[71] See Lester Asheim, "Mass Appeals" in "From Book to Film," p. 138 ff.

at all, have done so within the domain of traditional sanctions. Hardly any subject matter submitted to the film has been able to avoid the twin conventions of theme and medium. Lester Asheim, in his sample of twenty-four film adaptations, found that seventeen increased the love emphasis; that sixty-three per cent of all the films in the sample had a romantic happy ending, but forty per cent (one-fourth the entire sample) required an alteration of the story to accomplish it; and that in no case was a "negative" ending retained.

If filmic deviations from the novel can be quantitatively measured in this fashion, there is another stratum of underlying assumption which is more elusive. Political and social attitudes, though less precise, are operative nonetheless. Supplementing the taboos which rankle Ben Hecht, these assumptions appear whenever Hollywood even verges on controversial issues. The use of fake newsreels to defeat Upton Sinclair in his gubernatorial campaign in 1934 was only a more obvious outcropping of a generally scrupulous defense of business mores. Rose Terlin's observation that typical labor films like *Black Fury* and *Riff-Raff* assume there is "no cause for the strike save personal animosities or someone's personal ambition,"[72] remains, with rare exceptions like the modern story in *Intolerance* and *The Grapes of Wrath*, an accurate description of movie protocol, even down to recent efforts like *On the Waterfront*.

Upon the medium, then, lies the shaping power of businessman and audience. On the one hand, commercial production; on the other, mass consumption; and a Code that mediates between them. The resulting tensions are enormous. And yet, to the invisible hand which hovers above the filmist, guiding him, pressuring him, wheedling him, there is a counter-irritant. For the Code succeeds in inducing a kind of inverted world which ultimately works against itself. Movie dreams feed and quicken ordinary desire. Desire, unable to achieve the dream, turns to discontent, and greater discontent intensifies the need for dreams. So the film helps to build a circular process of increasing tension. Constantly enticing,

[72] Rose Terlin, *You and I and the Movies* (The Woman's Press, 1936), p. 28. See, too, Upton Sinclair, "The Movies and Political Propaganda," *The Movies on Trial*, ed. William J. Perlman (New York, 1936), p. 189.

the dream-world strengthens the very rebelliousness which its makers try to quell. There is still no way out of the circle. For after the plush and glamor, there must still come too many bleak houses, friendless streets, dull jobs.

What we find distasteful, then, is nothing but the worst aspects of Victorianism in modern dress. It is the hypocrisy rather than the sentiment which repels us. What is pernicious is not that the audience accepts, and even believes, the movie myths, but that the industry tries to institutionalize those beliefs to the exclusion of others. The restrictions are unmistakable; penalties await the transgressor. Chaplin's *Monsieur Verdoux* and the union-sponsored *Salt of the Earth,* two recent challenges to Hollywood conventions, had to be made with great difficulty outside the industry, and even then both ran afoul of distribution outlets. For the film has greater consequences than Victorian novels. Not only does it influence fashions and mores, but it threatens to replace reality with illusion outside the movie theater. What might happen was indicated when the Gary Cooper Fan Club of San Antonio made a serious and determined effort to nominate their hero vice-president of the United States. Their platform was his perfect adaptation for the office: "he doesn't talk much, said they; he knows what it's all about; and he gets things done. They could cite any number of instances, on the prairies or in the Himalayas."[73] When old ladies use umbrellas to swat actors who play movie villains, and youngsters back away from the real Boris Karloff, then what Jung calls the "participation mystique" becomes a kind of national psychosis.

It is against this kind of unreality that the counter-irritant works surreptitiously. For in spite of the cant, Hollywood films have been imbued with an extraordinary amount of earthy energy. Siegfried Kracauer, and Wolfenstein and Leites have convincingly demonstrated that the psychological history of a nation can be read in its motion pictures.[74] If this is true, then the particular case of the Hollywood product reveals certain redeeming traits.

[73] Thorp, p. 93.
[74] See Siegfried Kracauer, *From Caligari to Hitler* (Princeton, 1947), and Martha Wolfenstein and Nathan Leites, *Movies: A Psychological Study* (Glencoe, Ill., 1950).

For it seems as if the pioneer virtues—courage, energy, hard work, the refusal to be disheartened by difficulties—having reached their last outpost on the Pacific frontier, had become absorbed by the film. And we may assume, with Mrs. Thorp, that "these are qualities that America still cherishes and she insists on finding them in her ideal men and women."

So pugnacious is this counter-irritant that the movies, together with radio, television, and the comic strip, are building up a whole new American folklore. It is the creatures of these media, Mrs. Thorp points out, "that our children want to hear stories about, to keep models of on their desks, to have printed on their sweaters, to take to bed with them." The only real characters for whom they have anything like the same kind of affection are the heroes of the Western serials who share a good many of the cartoon characters' traits, namely personality, energy, the ability to win against odds. Pogo and L'il Abner share these traits with Chaplin and the Marx brothers, and certainly we tend to take them all more or less seriously.

If Hollywood has excelled in slapstick, gangster films, romance, adventure and musical comedy, it is because all of them manifest a broad and nervous kind of energy. For it is here that moral qualities and the qualities of the medium combine to turn out some gold with the dross. The best of Griffith, Von Stroheim, Chaplin, Ford, Capra, Huston, no mean achievement for a new art, have been less a tribute to the liberality of censors than, borrowing Alistair Cooke's phrase, to the film's "innate and impenitent democracy." After all is said and done, the serious filmist has shown remarkable cunning in slipping reality through an all but impenetrable door. Whenever the parlor has grown stuffy with stale decorum or strait-laced convention there has always been a Charlie to come crashing through the floor.

The complexity of society's shaping power, then, is enormous. That is why, as Mrs. Thorp points out, "the movies seem to be quite as capable of proceeding on two levels as Elizabethan tragedy: poetry and psychology for the gentlemen's gallery, action and blood for the pit. . . . In the picture on two levels may lie the whole solution of movies for the millions." In any event, the prospect is exciting. For out of the constant warfare between the spirit of the prude and the boldness of the pioneer, between the ethics of the buccaneer and the niceties of the boudoir, has come a usable artistic tradition.

What can the film-maker who essays adapting novels to the screen make of this tradition? Mrs. Thorp's suggestion that the film proceed on two levels assumes optimum conditions, of course, but the film adapter must work with what he has. Leda Bauer and Nelson Algren[75] may write amusing accounts of what happens when the movies tackle novels and novelists respectively. But the film adapter, beyond understanding the limits and possibilities of his medium, must make a serious adjustment to a set of different and often conflicting conventions, conventions which have historically distinguished literature from the cinema and made of each a separate institution.

V. OF TIME AND SPACE

A clearer understanding of the reciprocity between spectator and art object, of the shaping power of audience and thematic convention, enables us to return more confidently to an appraisal of the media's fundamental ability to handle time and space. Any comparative analysis of novel and film reverts, finally, to the way in which consciousness absorbs the signs of both language and photographed image.

It is difficult enough to delineate the separate bodies of conventional myth which distinguish novel from cinema. But a further difficulty arises when we realize that convention's adjustment to the changing facts of life has necessarily accelerated because change itself has accelerated. Attempting to explain the time obsession of the twentieth-century novel, Mendilow reminds us of Whitehead's observation that

> . . . in the past the time-span of important change was considerably longer than that of a single human life. Thus mankind was trained to adapt itself to fixed conditions.

[75] See Leda V. Bauer, "The Movies Tackle Literature," *American Mercury*, XIV (July, 1928), 288–294, and Nelson Algren, "Hollywood Djinn," *The Nation* (July 25, 1953), pp. 68–70.

Today this time-span is shorter than that of human life, and accordingly our training must prepare individuals to face a novelty of conditions.[76]

If language has become a protagonist in the novel, there is a sense in which time has become its foil. Like the novel and the film, language and time begin in apparent harmony and end in hostility.

The Modes of Consciousness

It is a commonplace by now that the novel has tended to retreat more and more from external action to internal thought, from plot to character, from social to psychological realities. Although these conflicting tendencies were already present in the polarity of Fielding and Sterne, it was only recently that the tradition of *Tristram Shandy* superseded the tradition of *Tom Jones*. It is this reduction of the novel to experiences which can be verified in the immediate consciousness of the novelist that Mendilow has called modern "inwardness" and E. M. Forster the "hidden life." Forster suggests the difference when he says that "The hidden life is, by definition, hidden. The hidden life that appears in external signs is hidden no longer, has entered the realm of action. And it is the function of the novelist to reveal the hidden life at its source." But if the hidden life has become the domain of the novel, it has introduced unusual problems.

In a recent review of Leon Edel's *The Psychological Novel: 1900-1950*, Howard Mumford Jones sums up the central problems which have plagued the modern novelist: the verbal limitations of nonverbal experience; the dilemma of autobiographical fiction in which the novelist must at once evoke a unique consciousness and yet communicate it to others; the difficulty of catching the flux of time in static language. The summary is acutely concise in picking out the nerve centers of an increasingly subjective novel where "after images fished out of the stream of past time . . . sub-

[76] Alfred North Whitehead, *Adventures in Ideas* (London, 1934), p. 94; quoted in Mendilow, p. 9.

stitute a kind of smoldering dialectic for the clean impact of drama."[77]

Béla Balázs has shown us how seriously we tend to underestimate the power of the human face to convey subjective emotions and to suggest thoughts. But the film, being a presentational medium (except for its use of dialogue), cannot have direct access to the power of discursive forms. Where the novel discourses, the film must picture. From this we ought not to conclude like J. P. Mayer that "our eye is weaker than our mind" because it does not "*hold* sight impressions as our imagination does."[78] For sense impressions, like word symbols, may be appropriated into the common fund of memory. Perceptual knowledge is not necessarily different in strength; it *is* necessarily different in kind.

The rendition of mental states—memory, dream, imagination—cannot be as adequately represented by film as by language. If the film has difficulty presenting streams of consciousness, it has even more difficulty presenting states of mind which are defined precisely by the absence in them of the visible world. Conceptual imaging, by definition, has no existence in space. However, once I cognize the signs of a sentence through the conceptual screen, my consciousness is indistinguishable from nonverbal thought. Assuming here a difference between *kinds* of images—between images of things, feelings, concepts, words—we may observe that conceptual images evoked by verbal stimuli can scarcely be distinguished in the end from those evoked by nonverbal stimuli. The stimuli, whether they be the signs of language or the sense data of the physical world, lose their spatial characteristics and become components of the total ensemble which is consciousness.

On the other hand, the film image, being externalized in space, cannot be similarly converted through the conceptual screen. We have already seen how alien to the screen is the compacted luxuriance of the trope. For the same reasons, dreams and memories, which exist nowhere but in the individual consciousness, cannot be adequately represented in spatial terms. Or rather, the film, having only arrangements of space to work with, cannot

[77] *Saturday Review*, xxxviii (April 25, 1955), 19.
[78] J. P. Mayer, *Sociology of Film* (London, 1946), p. 278.

render thought, for the moment thought is externalized it is no longer thought. The film, by arranging external signs for our visual perception, or by presenting us with dialogue, can lead us to *infer* thought. But it cannot show us thought directly. It can show us characters thinking, feeling, and speaking, but it cannot show us their thoughts and feelings. A film is not thought; it is perceived.[79]

That is why pictorial representations of dreams or memory on the screen are almost always disappointing. The dreams and memories of *Holiday for Henrietta* and *Rashomon* are spatial referents to dreams and memories, not precise renditions. To show a memory or dream, one must balloon a separate image into the frame (Gypo remembering good times with Frankie in *The Informer*); or superimpose an image (Gypo daydreaming about an ocean voyage with Katie); or clear the frame entirely for the visual equivalent (in *Wuthering Heights*, Ellen's face dissolving to the house as it was years ago). Such spatial devices are always to some degree dissatisfying. Acting upon us perceptually, they cannot render the conceptual feel of dreams and memories. The realistic tug of the film is too strong. If, in an effort to bridge the gap between spatial representation and nonspatial experience, we accept such devices at all, we accept them as cinematic conventions, not as renditions of conceptual consciousness.

Given the contrasting abilities of film and novel to render conceptual consciousness, we may explore further the media's handling of time.

Chronological Time

The novel has three tenses; the film has only one. From this follows almost everything else one can say about time in both media. By now, we are familiar with Bergson's distinction between two kinds of time: chronological time measured in more or less discrete units (as in clocks and metronomes); and psychological time, which distends or compresses in consciousness,

[79] See Maurice Merleau-Ponty, "Le Cinéma et la Nouvelle Psychologie," *Les Temps Modernes*, No. 26 (November, 1947), pp. 930–943.

and presents itself in continuous flux. What are the comparative abilities of novel and film to render these types of time?

To begin with, Mendilow describes language as "a medium consisting of consecutive units constituting a forward-moving linear form of expression that is subject to the three characteristics of time—transience, sequence, and irreversibility." But we must remember that Mendilow is here referring to chronological time only. And chronological time in the novel exists on three primary levels: the chronological duration of the reading; the chronological duration of the narrator's time; and the chronological span of the narrative events. That the three chronologies may harmonize in the fictive world is due entirely to the willingness of the reader to suspend disbelief and accept the authority of convention. As long as the novelist is not troubled by the bargain into which he enters with his reader, the three levels do not come into any serious conflict.

But Laurence Sterne saw a long time ago the essential paradox of the convention. If the novelist chooses to chronicle a series of events up to the present moment, he discovers that by the time he commits a single event to paper, the present moment has already slipped away. And if the novelist discovers that it takes a chronological year to record a single fictional day, as Sterne did, how is one ever to overcome the durational lag between art and life? If the present moment is being constantly renewed, how can prose, which is fixed, ever hope to catch it? Whenever a novelist chooses for his province a sequence of events which cannot be completed until the present moment, the three levels come into open conflict. In Sterne and Gide, that conflict becomes more central than conflicts between the characters.

The film is spared at least part of this conflict because one of the levels is omitted. Since the camera is always the narrator, we need concern ourselves only with the chronological duration of the viewing and the time-span of the narrative events. Even when a narrator appears in the film, the basic orientation does not change. When Francis begins to tell the story of Dr. Caligari, the camera shows his face; then the camera shifts to the scene of the story and there takes over the telling. What has happened is not so much that Francis has turned over the role of narrator to the omniscient camera as that the omniscient camera has included Francis as part of the narrative from the beginning.

The ranges of chronological time for reader and viewer are rather fluid, yet more or less fixed by convention. Where a novel can be read in anywhere from two to fifty hours, a film generally runs for one or two. *Intolerance* runs over two hours; the uncut version of *Les Enfants du Paradis* over three; and *Gone with the Wind* and *War and Peace* slightly less than four. Since the fictional events depicted in both novel and film may range anywhere from the fleeting duration of a dream (*Scarlet Street* and *Finnegans Wake*) to long but finite stretches of human history (*Intolerance* and *Orlando*), the sense of passing time is infinitely more crucial than the time required for reading or viewing.

We may note, of course, that a fifty-hour novel has the advantage of being able to achieve a certain density, that "solidity of specification" which James admired, simply because the reader has lived with it longer. Further, because its mode of beholding allows stops and starts, thumbing back, skipping, flipping ahead, and so lets the reader set his own pace, a novel can afford diffuseness where the film must economize. Where the mode of beholding in the novel allows the reader to control his rate, the film viewer is bound by the relentless rate of a projector which he cannot control. The results, as may be expected, are felt in the contrast between the loose, more variegated conventions of the novel and the tight, compact conventions of the film.

Sometimes, to be sure, the conventions governing quantity do affect the end product. The silent version of *Anna Karenina* with Garbo (called *Love*) and the subsequent sound versions (the first with Garbo and Fredric March; the second with Vivien Leigh and Ralph Richardson) dropped the entire story of Levin and Kitty. And Philip Dunne, the veteran screen writer, tells us that the boy in the film *How Green Was My Valley* never grew up, thus leaving out half the novel; that the *Count of Monte Cristo* contained no more than 5 per cent of its original; that *The Robe* and *The Egyptian* used less than a third of theirs.[80] While such quantitative deletions do alter the originals, it is, in the last analysis,

[80] Wald, p. 65.

the qualitative rather than the quantitative differences that militate against film adaptations of the novel.

If, as Mendilow says, "Fictional time is an ineluctable element in the novel," and fictional time treats of both kinds of time, then we discover that the moment we shift from chronological to psychological time, certain special problems arise.

Psychological Time: Variability in Rate

We speak of psychological time here in at least two roughly defined ways. The first suggests that the human mind is capable of accelerating and collapsing the "feel" of time to the point where each individual may be said to possess his own "time-system." The second suggests, beyond this variability in *rate*, the kind of flux which, being fluid and interpenetrable, and lacking in sharp boundaries, can scarcely be measured at all.

As long as the kind of time we are talking about in any sense implies discrete units in a series, language seems roughly adequate to the task. For example, the observation that chronological time crowded with activity, the sense of time passing quickly, seems "long" in retrospect, whereas chronological time taken up with dull and undifferentiated activity (the sense of time passing slowly) seems "short" in retrospect still has built into it a concept of measurement. It assumes the clock as a standard of measurement, for this kind of psychological time seems "long" or "short" in terms of certain normative expectancies. It assumes a normative "feel" for chronological time which may be distended or compressed by the stress of the moment, or by memory.

Here language is still appropriate to its task. Mendilow points out, for example, that in *Tom Jones* each book draws on a progressively greater length of the reader's clock time to cover a progressively shorter period of fictional time. So that where Book Three covers five years, Book Nine and Ten cover twelve hours each. The implication is that both for Tom and the reader, the events of the five weeks which occupy the last two thirds of the novel will seem "longer" than the events of the twenty years which occupy the first third.

Compression and distension of time has its exact equivalent in the film's use of speed-up and slow-motion. We have already noted how Pudovkin found the creative element of film in "the discovered, deeply imbedded detail." But that the deeply imbedded detail is in constant motion has further implications for filmic structure. Like the principles of editing, the principles of movement seem to collect around centers of gravity dictated by the film's persistent and almost willful self-assertion. "A sure folk instinct was shown," writes Panofsky, "when the photoplay immediately became known as the movies." Lawson extends this insight by making movement the pivotal element in film structure: "The conflict of individuals or groups projected on the screen has one characteristic that is not found in other story structures. *The conflict is in constant motion.*"

From this there develops a new kind of artistic reality, what Pudovkin calls filmic time and filmic space; what Panofsky calls the Dynamization of Space, and the Spatialization of Time. The theatrical producer, says Pudovkin,

> . . . works with real actuality which though he may always remould, yet forces him to remain bound by the laws of real space and real time. The film director, on the other hand, has as his material the finished recorded celluloid. . . . The elements of reality are fixed on those pieces; by combining them in his selected sequence according to his desire, the director builds up his own "filmic" time and "filmic" space.[81]

The director, then, creates a new reality, and the most characteristic and important aspect of this process is that laws of space and time which are ordinarily invariable or inescapable become "tractable and obedient." Hollywood's silent comedians made use of this freedom in their own unique way. James Agee has noted how Mack Sennett, realizing "the tremendous drumlike power of mere motion to exhilarate,"[82] gave inanimate objects a mischievous life of their own, *"broke every law of nature* the tricked camera could serve him for and made the screen dance like a

[81] Pudovkin, p. 53. See, too, A. Nicholas Vardac, *Stage to Screen* (Cambridge, Mass., 1949) for the influence of nineteenth-century theater on early American cinema.
[82] Agee, p. 74.

witches' Sabbath" (italics mine). And other comedians, energized by the liberation of untrammeled movement, "zipped and caromed about the pristine world of the screen." No previous narrative art has been able to achieve such graphic effects.

Not only is space liberated, but *because* it is liberated, time is, too. In thirty seconds, we see shoot, stem, bud, and blossom grow gracefully one from the other, a process that takes weeks in ordinary time. Just as space can be molded, time can be arrested and quickened. Anyone who has seen the remarkable slow-motion sequence in *Zéro de Conduite* can attest to the dramatic power of distended time. By interfering and only by interfering with natural time was Jean Vigo able to render the dream-like essence of the pillow fight.

Similarly, it is easy to find innumerable examples of accelerated motion in Hollywood where the emphasis has always been, for example, on the murderous pace of the comic chase. Chaplin outraces the Keystone cops. W. C. Fields dodges in and out of traffic at eighty miles an hour. Time is distorted in the opposite direction, but the principle remains the same. Spatial mobility makes time more flexible. A man is trying to find a job without success. The film may suggest the dreary routine of job-hunting by intercutting shots of the man's feet walking along asphalt streets with close-ups of other men shaking their heads, saying no. Four or five such alternate shots, taking a few seconds of running time, can suggest a process taking months, or even years. Thus the film is able, in an instant, to suggest the sense of monotonous events that seem "short" in retrospect, even though the duration of those events is "long" by clock time.

As for the kind of rhythmic progression one finds in music, the film has an exact parallel in the thoroughly discussed theory of montage. Not only does each shot take its meaning both from preceding shots and future expectations, but the use of sound (music, dialogue) provides a complex system of counterpoint.

Psychological Time: The Time-Flux

As soon as we enter the realm of time-in-flux, however, we not only broach all but insoluble problems for the novel but we also find a sharp divergence between prose and cinema. The transient, sequential, and irreversible character of language is no longer adequate for this type of time experience. For in the flux, past and present lose their identity as discrete sections of time. The present becomes "specious" because on second glance it is seen as fused with the past, obliterating the line between them.

Discussing its essential modernity, Mendilow lends support to the idea that the whole of experience is implicit in every moment of the present by drawing from Sturt's *Psychology of Time*. For Sturt tries to work out the sense in which we are caught by a perpetual present permeated by the past:

> One of the reasons for the feeling of pastness is that we are familiar with the things or events that we recognize as past. But it remains true that this feeling of familiarity is a *present* experience, and therefore logically should not arouse a concept of the past. On the other hand, a present impression (or memory) of something which is past is different from a present impression of something which is present but familiar from the past.[83]

How this seeming contradiction operates in practice may be seen when we attempt to determine precisely which of two past events is prior, and in what manner the distinction between the memory of a past thing and the impression of a present thing is to be made. At first glance, we seem perfectly able to deduce which of two remembered events is prior. For example, on the way to the store this morning, I met a group of children going to school. I also mailed my letter just as the postman came by. I know that ordinarily the children go to school at nine o'clock and the postman comes by at eleven. Therefore, I deduce that I went to the store *before* I mailed my letter. Although I have not been able to give the act of my going to the store an exact location in the past, I have been able to establish its priority.

On second thought, however, it seems as if (apart from the deductions one makes by deliberate attention to relationships) the memory of a past event comes to me with its pastness already intended. The image I have of my friend *includes* the information that this is the way he looked the year before he died. Similarly, if

[83] Quoted in Mendilow, p. 98.

I have a mental image of myself on a train to Kabul, then summon up an image of myself eating chestnuts, I know that the first is an image of a past thing and the second an image of a present thing because the image of myself on the train includes the information that the event took place last year. At the same time, I know that I am eating chestnuts right now. Here the perceptual witnessing of my present action checks and defines my mental images, confirming both the priority of the train ride and the presentness of the eating.

But suppose I bring my attention to bear on an object which is present now and which was also present yesterday at the same time, in the same place, in the same light. If, for example, I look at the lamp in my room, which fulfills all these requirements, then close my eyes and behold the mental image, how am I to know if that image refers to the lamp which was there yesterday or to the lamp which is there today? In this instance, which is tantamount to fusing a thing's past with its present, my present image, for all practical purposes, no longer respects the distinction between past and present. It offers me no way of knowing the exact location of its temporal existence.

This obliteration between past and present is precisely the problem which faces the novelist who wishes to catch the flux in language. If he is faced with the presentness of consciousness on the one hand, and the obliteration of the discrete character of past and present on the other, how is he to express these phenomena in a language which relies on tenses?

Whether we look at William James' "stream of consciousness," Ford Madox Ford's "chronological looping," or Bergson's "*durée*," we find the theorists pondering the same problem: language, consisting as it does of bounded, discrete units cannot satisfactorily represent the unbounded and continuous. We have a sign to cover the concept of a thing's "becoming"; and one to cover the concept of a thing's "having become." But "becoming" is a *present* participle, "become" a *past* participle, and our language has thus far offered no way of showing the continuity between them.

So elusive has been the *durée* that the novelist has submitted to the steady temptation of trying to escape time entirely. But here, too, the failure has served to dramatize the medium's limitations.

Speaking of Gertrude Stein's attempt to emancipate fiction from the tyranny of time, E. M. Forster notes the impasse: "She fails, because as soon as fiction is completely delivered from time it cannot express anything at all."

To be sure, there seem to be intuitive moments of illumination in Proust and Wolfe during which a forgotten incident floats up from oblivion in its pristine form and seems thereby to become free of time. Proust's involuntary memory fuses the experience of his mother's madeleine cake with the former experience of Aunt Léonie's, and the intervening time seems, for the moment, obliterated. But it is the precise point of Proust's agonizing effort that— despite our ability, through involuntary memory, to experience simultaneously events "with countless intervening days between" —there is always a sense in which these events remain "widely separated from one another in Time." The recognition of this conflict helps us understand why every formulation which attempts to define a "timeless" quality in a novel seems unsatisfactory, why Mendilow's attempt to find an "ideal time" in Kafka seems to say little more than that Kafka was not plagued by the problem. In the end, the phrase "timeless moment" poses an insuperable contradiction in terms.

We can see the problem exemplified concretely in a passage from Thomas Wolfe's *The Hills Beyond*. The passage describes Eugene Gant's visit to the house in St. Louis where his family had lived thirty years before. Eugene can remember the sights, shapes, sounds, and smells of thirty years ago, but something is missing— a sense of absence, the absence of his brother Grover, of his family away at the fair:

> And he felt that if he could sit there on the stairs once more, in solitude and absence in the afternoon, he would be able to get it back again. Then would he be able to remember all that he had seen and been—that brief sum of himself, the universe of his four years, with all the light of Time upon it—that universe which was so short to measure, and yet so far, so endless, to remember. Then would he be able to see his own small face again, pooled in the dark mirror of the hall, and discover there in his quiet three years' self the lone integrity of "I," knowing: "Here

is the House, and here House listening; here is Absence, Absence in the afternoon; and here in this House, this Absence, is my core, my kernel—here am I!"[84]

The passage shows the characteristic, almost obsessive longing of the modern novel to escape the passage of time by memory; the recognition that the jump, the obliteration, cannot be made; the appropriation of non-space as a reality in the novel—not the feeling of absence alone, but the absence of absence.

We arrive here at the novel's farthest and most logical remove from the film. For it is hard to see how any satisfactory film equivalents can be found for such a paragraph. We can show Eugene waiting in the house, then superimpose an image of the boy as he might have looked thirty years before, catch him watching a door as if waiting for Grover to return. But as in all cinematic attempts to render thought, such projection would inevitably fail. How are we to capture that combination of past absence and present longing, if both are conditions contrary to spatial fact?

The film-maker, in his own and perhaps more acute way, also faces the problem of how to render the flux of time. "Pictures have no tenses," says Balázs. Unfolding in a perpetual present, like visual perception itself, they cannot express either a past or a future. One may argue that the use of dialogue and music provides a door through which a sense of past and future may enter. Dialogue, after all, is language, and language does have referential tenses. A character whose face appears before us may *talk* about his past and thereby permeate his presence with a kind of pastness. Similarly, as we saw in our discussion of sound in editing, music may be used to counterpoint a present image (as in *High Noon* and *Alexander Nevsky*) and suggest a future event. In this way, apparently, a succession of present images may be suffused with a quality of past or future.

At best, however, sound is a secondary advantage which does not seriously threaten the primacy of the spatial image. When Ellen, the housekeeper, her withered face illumined by the fire,

[84] Thomas Wolfe, *The Hills Beyond* (New York, 1941), pp. 37-38. In *Thomas Wolfe: The Weather of His Youth* (Baton Rouge, 1955), pp. 28-53, Louis D. Rubin, Jr. analyzes in some detail Wolfe's handling of time.

begins telling her story to Lockwood in *Wuthering Heights*, we do sense a certain tension between story-teller and story. But in the film we can never fully shake our attention loose from the teller. The image of her face has priority over the sound of her voice. When Terry Malone tells Edie about his childhood in *On the Waterfront*, the present image of his face so floods our consciousness that his words have the thinnest substance only. The scars around his eyes tell us more about his past than any halting explanation. This phenomenon is essentially what Panofsky calls the "principle of coexpressibility," according to which a moving picture—even when it has learned to talk—remains a picture that moves, and does not convert itself into a piece of writing that is enacted. That is why Shakesperian films which fail to adapt the fixed space of the stage to cinematic space so often seem static and talky.

In the novel, the line of dialogue stands naked and alone; in the film, the spoken word is attached to its spatial image. If we try to convert Marlon Brando's words into our own thought, we leave for a moment the visual drama of his face, much as we turn away from a book. The difference is that, whereas in the book we miss nothing, in the film Brando's face has continued to act, and the moment we miss may be crucial. In a film, according to Panofsky, "that which we hear remains, for good or worse, inextricably fused with that which we see." In that fusion, our seeing (and therefore our sense of the present) remains primary.

If, however, dialogue and music are inadequate to the task of capturing the flux, the spatial image itself reveals two characteristics which at least permit the film to make a tentative approach. The first is the quality of familiarity which attaches itself to the perceptual image of a thing after our first acquaintance. When I first see Gelsomina in *La Strada*, I see her as a stranger, as a girl with a certain physical disposition, but without a name or a known history. However, once I identify her as a character with a particular relationship to other characters, I am able to include information about her past in the familiar figure which now appears before me. I do not have to renew my acquaintance at every moment. Familiarity, then, becomes a means of referring to the past, and this past reference fuses into the ensemble which is the present

Gelsomina. The spatial image of Gelsomina which I see toward the end of the film includes, in its total structure, the knowledge that she has talked to the Fool and returned to Zampano. In a referential sense, the pastness is built in.

That the film is in constant motion suggests the second qualification of film for approximating the time-flux. At first glance, the film seems bound by discrete sections, much as the novel is bound by discrete words. At the film's outer limit stands the frame; and within the frame appear the distinct outlines of projected objects, each one cut as by a razor's edge. But the effect of running off the frames is startlingly different from the effect of running off the sentence. For whether the words in a novel come to me as nonverbal images or as verbal meanings, I can still detect the discrete units of subject and predicate. If I say, "The top spins on the table," my mind assembles first the top, then the spinning, then the table. (Unless, of course, I am capable of absorbing the sentence all at once, in which case the process may be extended to a paragraph composed of discrete sentences.) But on the screen, I simply perceive a shot of a top spinning on a table, in which subject and predicate appear to me as *fused*. Not only is the top indistinguishable from its spinning, but at every moment the motion of the top seems to contain the history of its past motion. It is true that the top-image stimulated in my mind by the sentence resembles the top-image stimulated by the film in the sense that both contain the illusion of continuous motion. Yet this resemblance does not appear in the *process* of cognition. It appears only after the fact, as it were, only after the component words have been assembled. Although the mental and filmic images do meet in rendering the top's continuity of motion, it is in the mode of apprehending them that we find the qualitative difference.

In the cinema, for better or worse, we are bound by the forward looping of the celluloid through the projector. In that relentless unfolding, each frame is blurred in a total progression. Keeping in mind Sturt's analysis of the presentness of our conceptions, a presentness permeated by a past and therefore hardly ruled by tense at all, we note that the motion in the film's *present* is unique. Montage depends for its effects on instantaneous successions of different spatial entities which are constantly exploding against each other. But a succession of such variables would quickly become incomprehensible without a constant to stabilize them. In the film, that constant is motion. No matter how diverse the moving spaces which explode against each other, movement itself pours over from shot to shot, binding as it blurs them, reinforcing the relentless unrolling of the celluloid.

Lindgren advances Abercrombie's contention that completeness in art has no counterpart in real life, since natural events are never complete: "In nature nothing at any assignable point begins and nothing at any assignable point comes to an end: all is perfect continuity." But Abercrombie overlooks both our ability to perceive spatial discreteness in natural events and the film's ability to achieve "perfect continuity." So powerful is this continuity, regardless of the *direction* of the motion, that at times we tend to forget the boundaries of both frame and projected object. We attend to the motion only. In those moments when motion alone floods our attention and spatial attributes seem forgotten, we suddenly come as close as the film is able to fulfilling one essential requirement of the time-flux—the boundaries are no longer perceptible. The transience of the shot falls away before the sweeping permanence of its motion. Past and present seem fused, and we have accomplished before us a kind of spatial analogue for the flux of time.

If the film is incapable of maintaining the illusion for very long, if its spatial attributes, being primary, presently assert themselves, if the film's spatial appeal to the eye overwhelms its temporal appeal to the mind, it is still true that the film, above all other non-verbal arts, comes closest to rendering the time-flux. The combination of familiarity, the film's linear progression, and what Panofsky calls the "Dynamization of Space" permits us to intuit the *durée* insofar as it can, in spatial art, be intuited at all.

The film, then, cannot render the attributes of thought (metaphor, dream, memory); but it can find adequate equivalents for the kind of psychological time which is characterized by variations in rate (distension, compression; speed-up, *ralenti*); and it approaches, but ultimately fails, like the novel, to render what Bergson means by the time-flux. The failure of both media ultimately reverts to root differences between the structures of art and consciousness.

Our analysis, however, permits a usable distinction between the two media. Both novel and film are time arts, but whereas the formative principle in the novel is time, the formative principle in the film is space. Where the novel takes its space for granted and forms its narrative in a complex of time values, the film takes its time for granted and forms its narrative in arrangements of space. Both film and novel create the illusion of psychologically distorted time and space, but neither destroys time or space. The novel renders the illusion of space by going from point to point in time; the film renders time by going from point to point in space. The novel tends to abide by, yet explore, the possibilities of psychological law; the film tends to abide by, yet explore, the possibilities of physical law.

Where the twentieth-century novel has achieved the shock of novelty by explosions of words, the twentieth-century film has achieved a comparable shock by explosions of visual images. And it is a phenomenon which invites detailed investigation that the rise of the film, which preëmpted the picturing of bodies in nature, coincides almost exactly with the rise of the modern novel which preëmpted the rendition of human consciousness.

Finally, to discover distinct formative principles in our two media is not to forget that time and space are, for artistic purposes, ultimately inseparable. To say that an element is contingent is not to say that it is irrelevant. Clearly, spatial effects in the film would be impossible without concepts of time, just as temporal effects in the novel would be impossible without concepts of space. We are merely trying to state the case for a system of priority and emphasis. And our central claim—namely that time is prior in the novel, and space prior in the film—is supported rather than challenged by our reservations.

VI. CONCLUSION

What Griffith meant by "seeing," then, differs in quality from what Conrad meant. And effecting mutations from one kind of seeing to another is necessary not only because the materials differ but also because the origins, conventions, and audiences differ as well.

What happens, therefore, when the filmist undertakes the adaptation of a novel, given the inevitable mutation, is that he does not convert the novel at all. What he adapts is a kind of paraphrase of the novel—the novel viewed as raw material. He looks not to the organic novel, whose language is inseparable from its theme, but to characters and incidents which have somehow detached themselves from language and, like the heroes of folk legends, have achieved a mythic life of their own. Because this is possible, we often find that the film adapter has not even read the book, that he has depended instead on a paraphrase by his secretary or his screen writer. That is why there is no necessary correspondence between the excellence of a novel and the quality of the film in which the novel is recorded.

Under these circumstances, we should not be surprised to find a long list of discontented novelists whose works have been adapted to motion pictures. The novelist seems perpetually baffled at the exigencies of the new medium. In film criticism, it has always been easy to recognize how a poor film "destroys" a superior novel. What has not been sufficiently recognized is that such destruction is inevitable. In the fullest sense of the word, the filmist becomes not a translator for an established author, but a new author in his own right.

Balázs has, perhaps, formulated the relationship most clearly. Recognizing the legitimacy of converting the subject, story, and plot of a novel into cinematic form, Balázs grants the possibility of achieving successful results in each. Success is possible because, while "the subject, or story, of both works is identical, their content is nevertheless different. It is this different *content* that is adequately expressed in the changed form resulting from the adaptation." It follows that the raw material of reality can be fashioned in many different forms, but a *content* which determines the form is no longer such raw material. If I see a woman at a train station, her face sad, a little desperate, watching the approach of a hissing engine, and I begin to think of her as a character in a story, she has already, according to Balázs, become "semi-fashioned" artistic content. If I begin to think of how to render her thoughts in words, I have begun to evolve a character in a novel. But if, returning to my impression of that woman at the station, I begin to imagine Garbo in the role of Anna Karenina, I have again transformed her into a new artistic content.[85]

In these terms, says Balázs, the fully conscious film-maker who sets out to adapt a novel

> . . . may use the existing work of art merely as raw material, regard it from the specific angle of his own art form as if it were raw reality, and pay no attention to the form once already given to the material. The playwright, Shakespeare, reading a story by Bandello, saw in it not the artistic form of a masterpiece of story-telling but merely the naked event narrated in it.

Viewed in these terms, the complex relations between novel and film emerge in clearer outline. Like two intersecting lines, novel and film meet at a point, then diverge. At the intersection, the book and shooting-script are almost indistinguishable. But where the lines diverge, they not only resist conversion; they also lose all resemblance to each other. At the farthest remove, novel and film, like all exemplary art, have, within the conventions that make them comprehensible to a given audience, made maximum use of their materials. At this remove, what is peculiarly filmic and what is peculiarly novelistic cannot be converted without destroying an integral part of each. That is why Proust and Joyce would seem as absurd on film as Chaplin would in print. And that is why the great innovators of the twentieth century, in film and novel both, have had so little to do with each other, have gone their ways alone, always keeping a firm but respectful distance.

As we go on to trace the mutations from book to film in six specimen adaptations, our task will be greatly simplified if we remain aware of these crucial differences between the media. An

[85] For an excellent analysis of contrasting ways in which a literary story, a filmed story, and human consciousness order reality, see Albert Laffay, "Le Récit, le Monde, et le Cinéma," *Les Temps Modernes*, No. 20 (May, 1947), pp. 1361–1375; No. 21 (June, 1947), pp. 1579–1600. See, too, Siegfried Kracauer, "The Found Story and the Episode," *Film Culture*, II, No. 1 (1956), 1–5.

art whose limits depend on a moving image, mass audience, and industrial production is bound to differ from an art whose limits depend on language, a limited audience and individual creation. In short, the filmed novel, in spite of certain resemblances, will inevitably become a different artistic entity from the novel on which it is based.

2   The Informer

The Informer, BY LIAM O'FLAHERTY AP-
peared in 1925 to a reception of mixed reviews. O'Flaherty was
recognized as a "subjective naturalist,"[1] a peripheral voice in the
Irish Renaissance who possessed a passionate, even compelling
style, and as a kind of psychological realist who understood the
violent tendencies beneath the calm exterior of human behavior.
If his work was uneven, or inconclusive, or poorly plotted, it was,
nevertheless, deeply felt. Earlier that year, a kind of allegorical
composite of O'Flaherty's main themes—the Irish peasant, his
struggles, his explosive passions, his rebellious nationalism—had
appeared in his novel, *Black Souls*. The main character, Fergus
O'Connor, a wanderer who alights in the quiet peasant community
of Rooruck on the shores of Inverara, and sets off a violent erup-
tion because of his passion for the wife of a native villager, looks
ahead to the explosive style of *The Informer*.

Around 1930, John Ford, who had already been directing Hollywood films for sixteen years, became interested in the story, and
began, without success at first, to get his studio to approve it. In
1935, encouraged by the success of *The Lost Patrol*, a low-

[1] See John M. Manley and Edith Rickert, *Contemporary British Literature*,
3rd edition (New York, 1935), p. 45.

budgeted production the year before, Ford and his writer, Dudley Nichols, all but sneaked the film into production on their own. Known as a "sleeper" in trade jargon, *The Informer* is said to have cost $243,000, a small sum by present-day standards. The picture was shot in three weeks and "Ford declared it was the easiest he ever made."[2] The executives had reason to be astounded when Victor McLaglen's acting (in the role of Gypo Nolan), John Ford's direction, and Dudley Nichols' script all won Academy Awards, and the New York film critics judged *The Informer* the best film of 1935. For certainly *The Informer* defied most of Hollywood's conventions. It had no happy ending. The hero, though physically powerful, did not repel whole armies of Indians or Arabs with a single carbine. The hero's woman was unmistakably a prostitute. The hero's romantic dreams remained unfulfilled. The setting and circumstances of the drama were, as we shall see, more controversial than Ford had imagined. Why, then, did it make such a lasting impression on critics and audiences alike?

The bare story, as portrayed in the film, is simple enough. On "a certain night in strife-born Dublin—1922" during the height of the Sinn Fein rebellion against the British, Gypo Nolan, a brutish hulk of a man, betrays his friend Frankie McPhillip for twenty pounds by revealing his whereabouts to enemy soldiers. As a result, Frankie is shot down while trying to escape from his own home. In order to protect himself, Gypo accuses another man, the tailor Rat Mulligan, then tries to drown his sin in a long night of drink and revelry. Taken before a rebel court of inquiry, which is supervised by Commandant Dan Gallagher, head of the revolutionary organization, he finally breaks down and confesses. Mulligan has an airtight alibi; and Mary McPhillip, the dead man's sister, proves Gypo's testimony false. Awaiting execution, Gypo manages to escape and hide away in the room of the street-walker for whom he had wanted the money in the first place. While he sleeps, Katie Madden, the girl, goes to Commandant Gallagher to plead for Gypo's life and unwittingly gives him away. Gypo, pursued by the revolutionaries, is mortally wounded by pistol fire. Finally he drags himself into a church where the dead man's

[2] Lewis Jacobs, *The Rise of the American Film* (New York, 1939), p. 480.

mother kneels at her morning prayers. Gypo confesses and begs forgiveness, which Mrs. McPhillip grants. Exultant in the mother's mercy, Gypo collapses into death.

In outline, these events roughly follow the movement of the book. The film's major characters are generally derived from the novel, and whole selections of dialogue remain more or less intact. For example, when O'Flaherty's Katie first finds Gypo in a pub, after he has received the reward money, she asks him if he has robbed a church. When he sees that the notion is repugnant to her, he says, "It wasn't a church. It was a sailor off an American ship," and he warns her that he will get into trouble if she says anything about it.[3]

"Who? Me?" Katie laughs aloud, "What d'ye take me for? An informer or what?" At the sound of the word, Gypo bounds up, as if struck, and cries, "What are ye talkin' about informin' for?"

These lines, with slight pruning, appear intact in the film. And the novel's closing scene reads almost exactly like the film scenario.

But to trace the literal carry-over from book to film is to say very little about the artistic mutation. It tells us nothing of how a linguistic medium is changed to a visual medium. It sheds little light on how the director arranges his scenes, or composes his shots, or uses his lighting, or edits his sound-track, or prunes his dialogue, or what governs the director's deletions, additions, and alterations. Yet in tracing the history of any adaptation, a consideration of deletion, addition, and alteration presses itself upon one very quickly. For almost invariably these are more striking, if not numerically greater, than the carry-over. The very confrontation of a different medium imposes a different mode of thinking. Dudley Nichols, the screen writer who worked with Ford on the film, even goes so far as to suggest that deviations from the original had become his central problem: "I am prompted," he writes, "to explain the method by which I *translated* Mr. O'Flaherty's novel into the language of the film; some new method had to be found by which to make the psychological action photo-

[3] Liam O'Flaherty, *The Informer* (Harrisburg, Pa., 1945), p. 30. Originally published by Harcourt, Brace, New York, in 1925. The text is from the 1945 edition.

graphic"[4] (italics mine). It is almost as if the film-maker must destroy the old medium in order to catch its essence in the new.

Daniel Taradash, who did the adaptation of *From Here to Eternity*, makes a similar statement about this duality of retention and deletion. He writes: "The matter of responsibility in adapting a fine novel is, I guess, mostly a matter of respect for the material. . . . You have to be bold in breaking away from the book when it becomes necessary. But there are certain key scenes and definite aspects of character, which have to be retained."[5]

If we can fix upon those elements in the film version that are carried over from their source, and those which depart from it, we ought, in the process, to illuminate the essential limits and possibilities of film and novel both.

Lester Asheim, in his content analysis of twenty-four film adaptations of novels, breaks down his deviations into the general areas of dialogue, character, action, setting, and narrative summary. For the purposes of *The Informer*, these distinctions are not quite so clear. As one reviewer pointed out, " . . . rarely has an American picture achieved such a consistent unity of emotional tone" because "outer and inner world are interfused."[6] We may, then, examine character and action together, because alterations in the first so closely influence alterations in the second. In an urban setting charged with political tension, and especially under Ford's direction, where setting and space severely highlight Gypo's inner moods, the elements are inextricable.

The inextricable relationship is not accidental. Nichols himself says, "I transferred the action of the drama from its original, rather special setting to a larger and more dramatic conflict which had national connotations."[7] John Howard Lawson seems to agree that this mutation is an improvement: "Nichols recognized the importance of establishing a social framework that was not defined in

[4] Dudley Nichols, *Twenty Best Film Plays*, ed. with John Gassner (New York, 1943), p. xxxvi.

[5] Jerry Wald, "Screen Adaptation," *Films in Review*, v (February, 1954) 64.

[6] William Troy, "Judas in Dublin," *The Nation*, CXL (May 22, 1935), 610.

[7] Nichols, p. xxxvii.

O'Flaherty's novel."[8] And earlier, "*The Informer* reflected the changing temper of the American people in 1935, the impact of social forces breaking through the barriers that monopoly had erected around the industry."[9] In the transference we ought to expect, then, that the particular circumstances of the Irish Revolution, will be generalized for American consumption. What we may perhaps be unprepared for (granting that Lawson and Nichols have evaluated the process correctly) is the way in which such mutations parallel changes in the characters and reinterpret O'Flaherty's original intention.

Let us look first at some of the characters who are dropped completely. Frankie McPhillip's father, in the novel, is a chairman of the bricklayers' trade-union, "a thoroughly respectable, conservative Socialist" who is "utterly fanatical in his hatred of the status of the working man." He prides himself on having put Frankie into a good job as an insurance agent and resents his failure to live up to his respectable position. When Gypo appears at the wake and Mrs. McPhillip identifies him as a friend, Mr. McPhillip bursts out:

> What kind of friend d'ye call that waster that never did a day's work in his life? That ex-policeman! . . . It's the likes o' him that's brought Frankie to his death an' destruction. Them an' their revolutions. It's in Russia they should be where they could act the cannibal as much as they like, instead of leadin' good Irishmen astray. Why don't they get out of here and go back to England where they came from.

In the film, for all practical purposes, Frankie has no father, and the absence is never questioned, let alone explained.

Gypo's girl in the book, Katie Fox (who becomes Katie Madden in the film), has a rival named Connemara Maggie, who works at Aunt Betty's, a high-class brothel. It is Connemara Maggie rather than Katie who favors Gypo toward the end of his nocturnal revelry. Katie is furious not only because Gypo abandons

[8] John Howard Lawson, *Theory and Technique of Playwrighting and Screenwriting* (New York, 1949), p. 437.

[9] *Ibid.*, p. 350.

her when he finds himself solvent but also because Katie is associated with Biddy Burke's, a much seedier, lower-class brothel.

Katie, too, has a roommate, named Louisa Cummins, an old bed-ridden hypochondriac with whom Gypo must contend when he takes refuge from his pursuers. Her presence does little but add grotesqueness to the room, which, as we shall see, is alien to the mood which the film tries to evoke. On Louisa Cummins' bedpost hangs a statue of Saint Joseph,

> . . . suspended from a thick nail by a rough, knotted cord. The cord was hung around the statue's neck, in a noose. That statue was not suspended there out of crude respect, as might be supposed. It was hung there as a blasphemous protest against the incompetence of the saint. Four years before she had made a Novena to Saint Joseph, requesting a cure for muscular rheumatism, and because her request was not granted she hung up the statue by the neck.

Neither Connemara Maggie nor Louisa Cummins appears in the movie.

One more deletion among these peripheral characters ought to shed additional light on the nature of the film's omissions. One of the figures whom Gypo encounters in the course of his drunken binge is a character named Crank Shanahan. Shanahan shows up drunk at the fish-and-chips shop where Gypo is treating his friends to food. Described as a crank who is in the habit of attending every political meeting in the city, Crank Shanahan takes up his usual occupation of "agitating and preaching in a loud shrill voice his own peculiar philosophy of social life. That philosophy was revolt against every existing institution, habit or belief. He was called an anarchist, but he was not an anarchist. He was just a fanatic who was dissatisfied with life." Shanahan takes part in the general tumult which passes for political discussion, but his reputation as a neurotic who is given "to fearfully morbid thoughts," to locking himself up at night and putting cotton-wool in his ears "lest he might hear a sound," precludes anyone's taking him seriously. With a single roar from Gypo, he and everyone else fall silent. The voice of strength makes political discussion seem querulous and weak. Thus the deleted characters, who are capable of slipping into the anonymity of a crowd, are grotesque, vehement about political convictions (usually absurd ones), or given to pointing up class distinctions. All these, apparently, were irrelevant to the film-makers' intention.

The addition of characters in the film, on the other hand, is much more sparse. Aside from a few Black and Tan officers who appear in a scene that was written into the film, there are only two major additions—a blind man who functions more as a symbol than a character, and a little crony named Terry whom Gypo picks up early in his night of carousing. Terry is a sharp-tongued and totally opportunistic little Irishman who tags along with Gypo, inflating his ego and pacifying him, but only as long as Gypo has money in his pocket. He becomes a kind of nimble mind governing the actions of Gypo's strong but more slow-witted body. Terry's motive is unmistakable. At one point, when he thinks Gypo has run out of cash, he tauntingly deserts him. But when Gypo pulls out another roll of bills, Terry quickly ingratiates himself again. Gypo has gone in search of Katie Madden, but through a kind of glib repartee which Gypo cannot match, Terry leads him to Aunt Betty's—"the finest shebeen in town"—continually flattering the big man by calling him "King Gypo," or bragging to the brothel's middle-class patrons that his friend is "rich as Craysus." When the emissaries come to take Gypo to the court of inquiry, Terry is stuck with the last round of drinks. Aunt Betty calls the bouncer, for whom Terry is clearly no match without Gypo. Now he is helpless. But his wit does not fail him. These are the last words we hear him say: "I have a queer feeling there's going to be a strange face in heaven in the morning." Like the porter's soliloquy in Macbeth, Terry's comic words have a deeper meaning. For it is Gypo's face, not his, which will be seen in heaven by morning. In the novel Gypo goes to his fate alone. In the film, he has a kind of clever fool to goad him there.

If additions and deletions are striking, alterations in the surviving characters are perhaps more significant. For in almost every carry-over we find a marked change. In the case of Dan Gallagher, the change is nothing less than startling. As portrayed by Preston Foster in the film, Gallagher is a clean-cut, pipe-smoking, trench-coated revolutionary leader who inspires respect and confidence. Rational in his decisions, Gallagher is fair-minded in Gypo's case without failing to be decisive. He constantly reiterates the motif that the informer must be found because the entire organization is in danger. "One traitor can destroy an army," he tells his confederates after his first meeting with Gypo. And when Dan tells Katie, who comes to plead for Gypo's life, that the organization gave Gypo the benefit of every doubt, that he, Dan, is powerless to grant her request because "I didn't pass sentence on him. The court did . . . . " He has no other choice because Gypo has endangered "the lives of hundreds of other men who are fighting for what they believe in," and we have no reason to doubt his sincerity. If anything, the neatness of the characterization tends to make Dan Gallagher dull.

In his relations to Mary McPhillip, Frankie's sister, Dan is wholly honorable. They profess love for each other on several occasions, and, though it is never overtly stated, the implication is that only the conditions of war prevent their being married.

The novel's Dan Gallagher bears little correspondence to Preston Foster's portrayal. O'Flaherty presents him as a complex public figure. His position is indicated by three contrasting reports which have appeared in three diverse sources. The leading organ of "the English aristocracy" prints a story which reads in part:

> This flower of Irish manhood grew on an obscure dunghill, in the daily practice of all these virtues, which are indigenous to the Irish soil, if one is to believe the flowery utterances of the politicians on St. Patrick's Day. His father was a small peasant farmer in Kilkenny. Having assisted very probably in the gentle assassination of a few of his landlord's agents in the past, he reverently decided to devote the activities of his promising son to the service of God. He succeeded in making himself famous in the ecclesiastical seminary in which he was being prepared for the priesthood, by smashing the skull of one of the Roman priests during a dispute on the playground.

An extract from an article in the leading organ of the American Revolutionary Organization reads in part:

When the glorious history of the struggle for proletarian liberation in Ireland comes to be written, the name of Comrade Dan Gallagher will stampede from cover to cover in one uninterrupted blaze of glory. . . . No other living man has given nobler service to the world revolution than this sturdy fighter, who rules the workers of Dublin with greater power than is wielded by the Irish bourgeoisie, who are still nominally in the saddle.

And finally, a secret report sent back to the "International Executive of the Revolutionary Organization," which had sent an agent over from the Continent for a three month tour of Ireland, reads in part:

For the moment it would be a tactical blunder to expel Comrade Gallagher from the International. At the same time there can be no doubt that the Irish section has deviated entirely from the principles of revolutionary Communism as laid down in the laws of the International. Comrade Gallagher rules the national Organization pure and simply as a dictator.

Ironically, the film's Dan Gallagher corresponds to the portrait suggested by the American Revolutionary Organization, while the novel's Dan corresponds to a cross between the character in the English journal and the report to the Continental International. In the novel, he is clearly ruthless, sadistic, loveless, terrified at losing power, a kind of incarnation of the naked intelligence.

A contrast between corresponding scenes in the film and book will sufficiently dramatize the alteration. In both media, Dan asks Mary to testify at the court of inquiry. In the film, after establishing the loophole in Gypo's alibi, Dan gently asks Mary to appear as a witness. "I will if you need me," she says. She expresses fear for Dan's safety and longs deeply for an end to the fugitive life. Now that Frankie is dead, she couldn't bear having something happen to Dan, too. The dialogue is conventional, almost stilted, and the scene begins and ends with a show of affection.

The novel's Dan likewise expresses fear, but the fear is only for himself. Before visiting Mary, he vows to stamp out the informer because "The least little rift . . . Then it's all up with *me*." Shortly after, at the McPhillip house, he asks Mary to come with him to the court of inquiry. Instead of complying, she is terrified and Gallagher has to persuade her. Mary is less moved by his plea than by his physical magnetism. "She wanted to rush away and to shout, but the fascination of his voice was upon her." They enter into a discussion of their relationship, and Gallagher persists in asking her to "join him." Finally, she asks hesitantly, "Do you mean . . . to . . . to . . . marry you?" This is part of his answer:

> Oh rot . . . These ridiculous conventions. Not only have I no respect for them, but they don't enter my consciousness. . . . Marriage . . . is truly a capitalist word meaning an arrangement for the protection of property so that legitimate sons could inherit it. So I don't have to argue with it in my own mind in order to rid myself of a belief in it. . . . I am a hundred years before my time.

"Tell me, Dan," Mary asks, "do you believe in anything?" In the kind of near-ranting we have already observed in two deleted characters, Mr. McPhillip and Crank Shanahan, Gallagher goes on:

> No . . . I believe in nothing fundamentally. And I don't feel pity. Nothing fundamental that has consciousness capable of being understood by a human being exists, so I don't believe in anything, since an intelligent person can only believe in something that is fundamental. . . .

Small wonder that occasionally Dan will pull himself up short and say, "But wait a minute. I haven't worked out that fully yet."

If Gallagher's capacity for theorizing is inconclusive and ambiguous, his sadism and cruelty are not. At the court of inquiry, the novel's Gallagher reveals none of Gallagher's patient reasonableness in the film. He indulges in sheer mental torture to break Gypo down and relishes the big man's agony. He becomes "demented, drunk with the fury of hatred." Even when the ordinarily hardened revolutionaries are reviled by Gypo's humiliation, by "the sight of a human soul stripped naked of the covering of civilization," Gallagher still revels in the spectacle. The combination of Gallagher's barely audible voice, gone suddenly "soft and sweet like a girl's," and Gypo's trying to kiss Gallagher's boots in a final plea for mercy is so grotesque as to be virtually impossible to render in cinematic terms. Later, when Gypo escapes, Gallagher vows, in the throes of his own terror, to catch the informer at all costs. "That hulking swine can do his best," he tells Mary, "I will drain his blood before dawn." Where the Dan of the film sends his confederates to get Gypo, and mercifully draws the shade to shield Katie from the sight, the Dan of the novel is eagerly in at the kill. He fires the mortal shot and stands there, in front of Gypo "smiling dreamily now, with distant, melancholy eyes."

Let it be said, in Mary's defense, that even though her fictional characterization is more complicated than the placid colleen we see on the screen, O'Flaherty's Mary is at once more recognizable and more intense. When we first see her in the novel, she is truly grieved over Frankie's death, but we are told that ever since "she got a position two years before as clerk in the offices of Gogarty and Hogan," she had hated Frankie's revolutionary activities. Once a sympathizer without organizational affiliation, she has allowed her white-collar job to turn her against the "whole theory of revolution." She has also turned religious and has gotten the notion that she would like to convert Dan Gallagher. Drawn to him by his cold but magnetic power, she turns against him at the end when it is clear he is beyond redemption. After the court of inquiry, she asks, exactly like the Mary of the film, "Why can't we have peace? Why must we be killing one another?" And when Dan sets out in his final pursuit of Gypo, Mary assails him bitterly. "Murderer, murderer," she cries after him "until they stuffed her mouth."

Like Dan and Mary, Gypo's girl Katie undergoes a metamorphosis from the book to the film. In the film, she is still a prostitute but has good reason to be one. Gypo doesn't support her, and when he disposes of a dandy who is trying to pick her up, she gets angry and tells him to keep his fine principles because she "can't afford them." She is willing to offer him companionship even when he has no money, and agrees to hide him when he escapes from Gallagher's men. She has scruples about informing, and when Gypo tells her what he has done, she replies sadly, "You don't know what you've done to me. . . . I'd lay down my life for you, ye poor blind old boy." While Gypo sleeps, she goes to Gallagher to plead for Gypo's life and tries to take part of his guilt upon herself. She is sorry for the words spoken to him in anger, "Shamin' him for his poverty and blamin' him for mine and puttin' the idea into his head." Only unwittingly does she reveal where Gypo is hiding.

O'Flaherty's conception of Katie is quite different. The novel's Katie has been expelled from the Revolutionary Organization on a charge of public prostitution. But her fall is not forced by poverty; it is gratuitous. She is known even among her colleagues as "a drug fiend, a slattern, an irresponsible creature." She is physically less attractive, more degenerate than John Ford's Katie. Though she also loves Gypo "in her own amazing way," she neither motivates his informing nor shares his guilt. Moreover, she does not try to intercede for him with the revolutionaries. On the contrary, for reasons which are not entirely clear in the book, she decides, while Gypo sleeps, to turn him over to Gallagher. When we last hear of her, before she wilfully betrays Gypo, she has been intercepted running down a road, "mad with dope."

Finally, Frankie McPhillip himself, the betrayed man, undergoes a marked change from book to film. In the hands of John Ford, he is a fugitive from the Black and Tans, who want him for murder. Although we never learn whom he has murdered, or under what circumstances, it does not seem to matter. We are left to infer that Frankie killed his victim in the line of patriotic duty, that the Tans are after him for political reasons. Clean-cut and likable, he has slipped into the city with the fog to see his family. When he talks to Gypo to ask if the Tans have set a guard around his house, he reminds the big man of the old days when they used to pull off "jobs" together. A great pair they were, with Gypo's muscles and Frankie's brain. Before he leaves, Frankie signals encouragingly and says, "Up the rebels." When Gypo informs, we feel that Frankie has been utterly and unjustly betrayed.

O'Flaherty's Frankie is not quite so engaging. We learn that he has murdered "the secretary of the local branch of the Farmers' Union during the farm labourers' strike at M——." Later we learn that the farm secretary was killed not during a political skirmish but during a drunken binge. Carousing with Gypo and two women, Frankie runs across his victim quite by accident and shoots him without provocation. He and Gypo bolt without making any attempt to cover their tracks and come into Dublin with a flimsy tale which endangers the entire organization. Moreover, Frankie has come into the city at this point not only to see his mother before he dies but also to communicate with the executive committee as well. Frankie is afraid he's dying of consumption, and has come to ask for money. The phrase "Up the rebels" never appears. O'Flaherty's characterization does not by any means justify Gypo's betrayal. But because the novel's Frankie is much less worth saving, Gypo's act seems less monstrous.

What do these deletions, additions, and alterations amount to? In general, they endow the film characters with a nobility, honesty, and reasonableness which the originals do not possess. The grossest physical characteristics are played down. The contrasts between Gypo's brutishness and the placid goodness of Mary and Mrs. Mc-Phillip, on the one hand, and the verbal dexterity of Frankie and Terry on the other, are sharply delineated. In the case of Dan Gallagher, the quantitative change is so great that a qualitative change results. Like the harsh naturalistic details, the political issues are toned down or relegated to the background. At least part of Ford's change is understandable for nonaesthetic reasons. Aside from the general problem of translating an Irish tale for American audiences, we know that Liam O'Flaherty was deeply concerned with the intricacies of Irish nationalism, whereas John Ford was more centrally concerned with constructing a film story. In 1941, an interviewer for the *Christian Science Monitor* raised the question of whether Ford, after *The Informer* and *The Grapes of Wrath*, had committed himself to doing movies with social significance. Pointing out that he had done a great variety of films, including westerns, comedies, and films with tragic endings, Ford answered, " . . . when I make a picture, I try to find people I like in situations that I think are dramatic,"[10] and Ford, as always, seemed content to leave it at that. Add Ford's primary interest in dramatic stories to the exigencies of the Production Code and the necessity of working for an American audience, and the shifted emphasis becomes more comprehensible.

[10] Frank Daugherty, "John Ford Wants It Real," *Christian Science Monitor* (June 21, 1941), p. 5.

At any rate, Ford should not have been surprised that his careful pruning of grotesqueries and politics would still not satisfy local interests. An enlightening exchange on the content of *The Informer*, which appeared in the pages of *Commonweal*, in 1936, serves to shed light on the impossibility of ever dissociating entirely a controversial setting from its dramatic story. In the issue of March 6, Rev. E. Oliver Boyle writes a communication to the magazine, protesting the recent award by the New York film critics to *The Informer* as the best production of the year.[11] Father Boyle argues that the film distorts facts: (1) In 1922—after Dail Eireann, in the wake of such Black and Tan barbarism as the destruction of the city of Cork in December, 1920, had officially declared the republic—the word "informer" had become a term of opprobrium and horror to all good Irishmen, but O'Flaherty and Ford lead us to believe that informing was not an uncommon occurrence. (2) The sign "10 pounds to America," which leads Gypo to inform is misleading; Father Boyle argues that even if an Irishman had twenty pounds, he would have found it impossible either to get a passport or to buy passage for the money. (3) At a time when every grammar-school child was singing "The Soldier's Song," it was unthinkable that a patriotic Irishman would *want* to go to America. (4) Father Boyle disapproves of the way the Gaelic chant is mumbled at Frankie McPhillip's wake. (5) The scene in the brothel and the characterization of Katie Madden is degrading to Irish womanhood.

In the issue of April 3, an answer to Father Boyle appears by Rev. Edward S. Schwegler.[12] Father Schwegler states quite strongly that he doubts whether the film can be criticized either on "historical" or "decency" grounds. He is amazed at the class-C rating which was conferred on the film by the Legion of Decency, and he argues that, on the contrary, it is the precise point of the picture that Gypo's betrayal *was* exceptional, that we are shown quite clearly, after all, the tragic effect of such perfidy. He demonstrates that with the twenty pounds commonly offered for information leading to the whereabouts of Irish Republican Army leaders, one *could* get a passport *and* afford a ticket. He says that

[11] Rev. E. Oliver Boyle, *Commonweal*, XXIII (March 6, 1936), 525.
[12] Rev. Edward S. Schwegler, *Commonweal*, XXIII (April 3, 1936), 637–638.

the Gaelic chant *is* sometimes mumbled at wakes and that an old Irish lady had remarked to him on how realistic had seemed to her this sequence in the film. And what, Father Schwegler wants to know, has the mumbling of the Gaelic chant got to do with the decency of a film anyway? Furthermore, the only suggestion of prostitution in the film occurs when the dandy tries to pick up Katie, but Gypo gallantly cuts it short by tossing him into the street. Besides, the character of Katie is not at all typical of Celtic womanhood, which, according to Father Boyle, had been severely maligned. Much more typical of Irish womanhood is Frankie's sister, Mary. Surely one could scarcely find a sweeter and more wholesome colleen. Finally, it is not quite accurate, says Father Schwegler, to say that the Legion of Decency had condemned the film. Catholics were clearly split on the issue, and the Legion of Decency's decision had merely represented Catholic opinion in Chicago. The International Federation of Catholic Alumnae, on the other hand, had recommended the film highly as adult enter- tainment. The proof of the pudding is that now, according to Father Schwegler, the International Federation is doing the re- viewing for the Legion of Decency, while the Chicago faction is out in the cold. We may concur in Father Schwegler's observa- tion that the weakness in the position of the Chicago school, and of Father Boyle himself, results inevitably from the dual fallacy of overlooking the positive aspects of a film, and of generalizing from particulars which falsify the whole.

If Ford and Nichols intended to avoid such controversy by widening the specific Dublin setting, they were not wholly suc- cessful. And if they intended to tone down the horror, it is hard to account for the impression of William Troy, who reviewed the film for *The Nation*. The film, Mr. Troy contends, gives an even more terrifying impression than the novel of the events of 1922.[13] The changes, apparently, were not going to protect the film or the studio either from controversy or from sheer misunderstanding. If the mutations we have already noted are to be justified, they must be justified on other grounds.

Perhaps a more direct and closer examination of the central figure, Gypo Nolan, will help uncover some of these grounds. The

[13] Troy, p. 610.

first thing we notice is that in the novel much of the special flavor of Gypo's character, the manner of his involvement with others, is achieved through peculiarly linguistic devices. More particularly, O'Flaherty relies heavily on internal monologue, metaphor, and especially on recurrent animal imagery. The idea of informing on Frankie appears to Gypo as an "uncouth ogre that was prowling around in his brain." At another point, "His jaws set like the teeth of a bear trap that has been sprung fruitlessly." There is repeated reference to his tufted eyebrows, "twitching ominously like snouts." Without his hat, Gypo's head appears "naked, hummocked . . . like a badly shorn sheep." At the fish-and-chips shop, he towers above the crowd "like some primeval monster." Later, the street "with its dirt and its squalor, was a savage sauce to whet his appetite for the riotous feast . . . ." When a woman in the brothel resists him and calls him a "pig," his face contorts, his head going from right to left "like a ram that is going to charge an enemy." In his terror at the court of inquiry, he lets go a "muffled scream like a dumb animal in mortal agony," and when he tries to escape with five men hanging on to him, he appears "like Laocoön entwined with snakes." At other points in the narrative, Gypo or his compatriots are likened to insects, heifers, snails, vipers, oxen, swine, bulls, and cats. The savage, primeval, and demonic run like motifs through O'Flaherty's prose.

Aside from bestial analogies, similes frequently appear to reinforce a physical action: "He raised Mulholland's body from the ground . . . like a book which he wanted to read"; he hits a man who goes down "like a bag of nails dropped on an iron deck"; Gypo walks away, his trousers "brushing with the sound of hay being cut with a scythe."

Internal monologue and literary figures of speech are all but impossible to translate to celluloid. The film, which must render its meanings in moving images, resists both these devices. And yet the texture of the narrative prose, which is so largely supported by both monologue and metaphor, must be rendered in cinematic equivalents. Ford and Nichols have solved this problem by devising an elaborate set of symbols which function on both literal and analogical levels. These symbols are in turn supported by a careful arrangement of visual and aural renditions of Gypo's subjective conflicts.

Some of these symbols, like the all-pervasive fog, relieved only occasionally by the flare of light from a doorway or the bloom of a fireplace in a room, are direct carry-overs from the novel. In the book, Gypo's hat is used explicitly as a symbol of security. At one point, he loses it, and hence becomes irrational: "terror again invaded his mind. If they discovered the hat they might be able to discover the identity of that ponderous fellow who had gone into the police-station . . . ." But the moment he retrieves the hat, his confidence returns. In the film, the cap is also used as a symbolic prop. When Gypo is cocky and sure of himself, the cap sits on his head at a jaunty angle. When he is nervous and unsure, as in the Tan headquarters, or at the court of inquiry, he twists it nervously in his hand, or uses it to wipe the perspiration from his face. Toward the end, from the time of his imprisonment to his death, Gypo goes bareheaded.

Similarly, in both book and film, the twenty pounds is used literally for cash transactions, and analogically as a symbol of Gypo's undoing. He spends the money in two ways—either as an act of desperate self-gratification, to forget his deed, or as an act of impulsive generosity, to share what he has. In both versions, he treats his fair-weather friends to food and drink, gives a despised woman in the brothel enough money to get her home, and delivers the rest to Katie. But in the film, the meaning of the money is reinforced. An epigraph is added at the beginning: "Then the Judas repented himself—and cast down the thirty pieces of silver —and departed," which makes explicit the implied theme of the novel, and helps round out the religious framework. But in the long run, whether Gypo spends the money selfishly or generously, the reward is cursed. Bartley Mulholland, Gallagher's cat-eyed man, trails Gypo relentlessly, adding up the pounds which Gypo spends, each pound becoming another tally in Gypo's final accounting.

A series of visual symbols which do not appear in the novel, however, are boldly added to the film, and it is here, more than anywhere else, perhaps, that we find the greatest evidence of the

Ford-Nichols signature. Working from mere clues in O'Flaherty's narrative, Ford and Nichols construct a series of full-blown cinematic details which become suffused with subjective ideas. For example, O'Flaherty shows the betrayal growing in Gypo exclusively through interior monologue. As Gypo talks to Frankie at the Dunboy House, a "monstrous idea" prowls into his head "like an uncouth beast straying from a wilderness into a civilized place where little children are alone." Later, the "ghoulish thing" comes back like a specter into his mind until finally, "There were two facts in his brain. First, the fact of his meeting with McPhillip. Second, the fact of his having no money for the night."

Dudley Nichols tells us precisely how this growing awareness appears in the film: "A poster offering a reward for information concerning Gypo's friend became the symbol of the evil idea of betrayal, and it blows along the street, following Gypo; it will not leave him alone. It catches on his leg and he kicks it off. But still it follows him and he sees it like a phantom in the air when he unexpectedly comes upon his fugitive friend." [14] Still later, during Gypo's first interview with Dan, a copy of the poster burns slowly in the fireplace, the flames distorting and consuming Frankie's features. No such poster appears in the novel, but its adoption enables the film-makers to render O'Flaherty's meaning in purely visual terms.

Again, when Gypo leaves Tan headquarters in the novel, with the money still fresh in his pocket, he hears a menacing footstep. It turns out to be only a ragged old woman. She mutters something unintelligible. "Then she bared her ragged teeth. Was it an omen?" The woman does not appear again. In the film, the old woman becomes a blind man, who is not dropped but appears at intervals throughout the film. When Gypo encounters him outside Tan headquarters, he grips the blind man's throat in sudden guilt. The blind man, Nichols tells us,

> . . . is a symbol of the brute conscience, and Gypo releases him when he discovers the man cannot see. But as Gypo goes on to drown his conscience in drink, the tapping of the blind man's stick follows him; we hear it without seeing the blind man as

[14] Nichols, p. xxxvi.

Gypo hears his guilt pursuing him in his own soul. Later, when he comes face to face with his conscience, for a terrifying moment he tries to buy it off—by giving the blind man a couple of pounds, a lordly sum.[15]

Nichols might have added that the blind man appears for the last time at the court of inquiry where his sheer presence is even more electrifying than his brief testimony as a witness.

Even more striking is what Ford and Nichols do to O'Flaherty's Chapter II. In its entirety, the chapter reads:

At thirty-five minutes past seven Francis Joseph McPhillip shot himself dead while trying to escape from No. 44 Titt Street, his father's house. The house had been surrounded by Detective-Sergeant McCartney and ten men. Hanging by his left hand from the sill of the back-bedroom window on the second floor, McPhillip put two bullets into McCartney's left shoulder. While he was trying to fire again, his left hand slipped and lost its hold. The pistol muzzle struck the edge of the sill. The bullet shot upwards and entered McPhillip's brain through the right temple.

When they picked him out of the orange box in the back garden where he fell, he was quite dead.

In the film, we see, as at the end of the novel's Chapter I, Gypo making his nervous claim for the reward money. But we cut instantly to a shot of the soldiers loading onto lorries. We hear the motors revving up. Back in the office, Gypo sits in the foreground, his head bare and bowed, the major and his officer at the window in the background, watching the preparations outside. Gypo looks up at a clock, whose ticking we hear quite clearly. The flashing light of the pendulum, underscoring the headlights of the lorries, casts an hypnotic gleam in Gypo's eyes. The clock reads five minutes past six. In Lewis Jacobs' phrase, "we have a prescience of relentless evil."[16] The ticking continues into the next scene, where we see Frankie entering his house to surprise his mother and sister.

[15] *Ibid.*, p. xxxvii. Arthur Mizener acknowledges the structural effectiveness of this and other symbolic devices in "The Elizabethan Art of Our Movies," *Kenyon Review*, IV (Spring, 1942), p. 189 ff.
[16] Jacobs, p. 482.

There, another clock, reading sixteen minutes after six, "welds the transition structurally." The soldiers surprise Frankie at his meal. In the confusion, he climbs out on the windowsill, but the Tans rush in to block the alleyway. Frankie fires, hitting one of the men, but another soldier shoots him mortally with a sub-machine gun. The violent noise stops as suddenly as it began. We see only Frankie's hand now, slipping slowly from the window, hear only the sound of his nails dragging across the sill. Stunned with horror, Frankie's mother sinks to the floor.

Back at headquarters, Gypo is still sitting in the same position. The ringing of a phone breaks the silence, sharply replacing the ticking of the clock. A sentry answers and informs the major that Frankie McPhillip was killed trying to escape. In cold silence, the major throws some bills upon the table, and an officer contemptuously pushes the money toward Gypo with his cane. "Show him out the back way," the officer says.

The last important innovation is that very model of a ship, representing the dream of passage to America, which so disturbed Father Boyle. At the moment that Gypo is seized in the novel with the impulse to report Frankie, he is not looking at a ship model (with a sign above it reading "10 pounds to America: Information Within"). He is looking into the window of a saddler's shop, but all he sees are a pair of spurs. Later, he daydreams not about himself and Katie sailing to America in formal wedding attire, but of his lost romantic youth: " . . . a mad longing seized him for the protection of the environment of his youth, the country-side of a Tipperary village, the little farm, the big red-faced kind-hearted mother, who hoped he would become a priest." To American audiences the injected dreams of marriage and ocean voyage are likely to seem more familiar than the longing for a Tipperary village, but the film has the added advantage of giving the symbol greater continuity. Gypo passes the window once with Katie; then again with Terry; and he ends with the superimposed fantasy. These appearances are joined, both visually and dramatically, in a way which the bright spurs and boyhood reminiscences of the novel never achieve. (Both Father Boyle and Father Schwegler, incidentally, seem unaware that the ship image never appears in the book, or that Liam O'Flaherty had little to do with the film adaptation.)

Curiously, it is at precisely these points of deviation from the novel that the film seems to have won its greatest critical support. William Troy considered Frankie's death scene one of the finest in cinema literature. And even Otis Ferguson, the reviewer for *The New Republic,* who raised one of the very few dissenting voices against the film, admitted the power of the early sequences, where most of these innovations appear.[17]

As suggested earlier, the symbols which conform to the film's realistic demands are reinforced by still other cinematic devices. A carefully worked out musical score is used to parallel rather than counterpoint the action. Some of the musical accents arise from the scene itself. In the first sequence, for example, Gypo stops to listen to a street tenor sing the romantic ballad, "Rose of Tralee."

> The pale moon was rising above the green mountain,
> The sun was declining beneath the blue sea
> When I strayed with my love to the pure crystal fountain . . .

As he sings, a patrol of Tan soldiers come by and frisk him for weapons, then toss him a coin. Although the tenor sings on without interruption, the oppressed atmosphere of the city has been strikingly suggested. Moreover, Gypo has been vaguely moved by the song, and a moment later he is looking at the ship model in the tourist window, dreaming.

The street singer appears again outside Frankie's house where the wake is being held. Once more, his ballad is appropriate to the occasion:

> The minstrel boy to the war has gone,
> In the ranks of death you'll find him.

With Terry, Gypo goes carousing through the streets singing "Wearing the Green," which is picked up at later intervals by the sound track. At Aunt Betty's, to bolster another kind of mood,

---

[17] Otis Ferguson, "The Informer," *The New Republic,* LXXXIII (May 29, 1935), 76.

Gypo calls for a rendition of "All Those Endearing Young Charms."

The sound-track score is carefully cued to emphasize the emotional tones of particular scenes. The themes of "the blind man and the minstrel boy," "the money," "the informer," and " 'Wearing the Green' " are woven together in a loose kind of medley which sounds at appropriate tempos. For example, at the court of inquiry, while Dan is adding up the money that Gypo has spent, the music builds to a crescendo and quickly breaks at the moment when Gypo, trapped by the evidence, drops all pretences and breaks down.

More revealing than the musical accompaniment, however, is the way in which Ford finds visual and aural substitutes for Gypo's interior monologues. When Gypo, for example, first sees the poster we see, superimposed upon the screen, an image of Gypo and Frankie in a bar singing a soldier's song. When Gypo is met by the real Frankie at the Dunboy House, we see a different image superimposed. This time it is the poster which Gypo had seen a little while before. We know that his temptation has begun. Again, during Gypo's last escape toward Katie's room, the superimposed poster appears once more, like a misty dream, this time dark and glowering, full of accusation. At the brothel, the despised woman, to whom Gypo later gives the money, dissolves for a moment, and Gypo thinks he is seeing Katie. Finally, after the betrayal, Gypo sits in a pub trying to formulate a plan. He seems to hear Frankie's mocking voice, "Ah, Gypo, I'm your brain. You're lost . . . You're lost . . . ."

Considering all these devices, it is surprising to find the *Christian Science Monitor* reporter explaining that Ford "rarely uses trick shots, but frames every take carefully from the straight-on angle." What Ford has really done here is neither to employ the trick shot nor the straight-on angle—it is hardly a question of that—but to use every resource of the camera to render the tortured consciousness of Gypo Nolan.

After a careful tracing out of the mutations which take place in John Ford's film, we are left with one remaining problem. How, in searching out these visual equivalents, does Ford evoke the kind of pity and terror for Gypo which the novel apparently failed to do? As we indicated earlier, the novel met with nothing like the unanimity of approval accorded the film. *The New Statesman,* appreciating the book as a study in the "psychology of revolution," seemed uneasy because "the terrors of fact mow and gibber through these pages."[18] The *Saturday Review of Literature* said, "One contemplates Gypo with a purely objective emotion, as one might look upon a figure by Rodin, equally brutish, equally strong, equally impotent."[19] *The New Republic* was even more severe. It complained that a "harsh, unrhythmic play of words occasionally rises to a flash of power, but more often becomes monotonous. The Dublin underworld is here—backstreets, brothels, and bestiality—but nothing of significance emerges from background or theme."[20] *The Spectator,* on the assumption that "It is good sometimes that the Beelzebub in humanity should be made manifest," was one of the few which broke through the hard bindings of a modifying clause to say something positive: "Gypo, though a brute, cunning and malevolent as any hungry tiger, is truly a man and dies like a man, strong in his soul."[21]

At first glance one would think that John Ford's Gypo would be even harder to center on sympathetically. The softening of supporting characters—the diminution of their harshness—ought to make his sin less venial, for the offense is greater. In the novel, Gypo is less sharply distinguished from the other characters. They all seem more or less covered with the gray mire of sin. In O'Flaherty's world, Gypo has much less to sin against, as we have already noted in the case of Frankie McPhillip. In Ford's world, Frankie is more innocent, Gallagher more benevolent, Katie more noble, and each is hurt as well as offended by Gypo's act. But in a curious way, this sharper differentiation throws Gypo's character into the kind of dramatic relief which is hard to find in the book. Because his sin in the film appears to be greater, his suffering and redemption take on more tragic overtones. In the book, Katie's jealousy and Dan's hatred are unequivocal. But in the film, Gypo succeeds in dividing his characters against themselves. He induces

[18] *New Statesman,* xxv (October 10, 1925), 727.
[19] *Saturday Review of Literature,* ii (October 17, 1925), 227.
[20] *The New Republic,* xlv (December 9, 1925), 93.
[21] *The Spectator,* cxxxv (October 3, 1925), 560.

emotional conflict in Katie and Dan and even in Mrs. McPhillip. Their affection for Gypo begins to war against their sense of justice, and the affection derives from the added dimension of goodness in themselves. Of the four major supporting roles, only Mary, and Katie for no more than an instant, exhibit this conflict in O'Flaherty's original. Having little or no affection for Gypo to begin with, the novel's characters respond more simply than they do in the film. Since the beast imagery is so insistent in O'Flaherty, we can feel little more than horror at Gypo's final degradation. In the film, the depths and the heights are both more clearly defined and more clearly contrasted. If O'Flaherty has the worst of the terror, then Ford has the best of the pity.

Again, looking at clues in the novel, we can see how Ford visually builds up our sympathy for Gypo. In the novel, Gypo is put upon by intelligent men. What frightens him most about the Revolutionary Organization is its likeness to an all-pervasive mind. Gypo suffers the loss of Frankie's intelligence, and the severe, almost malignant oppression of Dan's. In the film, Terry is introduced to enforce the continuity between them. "King Gypo," he keeps calling him, and we remember, dramatically, how unlike a king he is.

In the novel, Gypo undergoes a kind of psychological division of identity. At moments, he actually forgets that it was he who had gone into the police station. When he runs into Bartley Mulholland at the fish-and-chips place, he asks, "Hear anythin' about what I was tellin' ye? I mean about the fellah that informed on Frankie McPhillip?" Moments of that forgetfulness are carried over into the film. Outside the pub, a man sees Gypo and asks, "Usen't he be pals with Frankie McPhillip who was shot by the Black and Tans tonight?" With Terry's help, Gypo forces the man to say, "May the Lord have mercy on his soul," as if he were genuinely, if drunkenly, concerned about treating a friend's name with respect. He really *has* forgotten. At the court of inquiry, he sees Rat Mulligan and, forgetting the circumstances of the meeting, greets the sick man with friendly concern. He consistently meets Bartley's coldness with warmth and openness. And when he blurts out at the wake, "I'm sorry for yer trouble Mrs. McPhillip," we feel that his grief is genuine. By the time he breaks down and tells Dan, "I didn't know what I was doing, I didn't know what I was doing," we are prepared to believe him. It is as if he were trying to suppress a monstrous part of himself. That he recognizes it as monstrous endows his repentance with a kind of tragic awareness.

In the film, Gypo carries even farther the acts of instinctive generosity which occur in the book. Not only does he share his money with friends and cronies and the girl in the brothel, but he presses money on the blind man, remains faithful to Katie throughout, and submits to the betrayal as much for her sake as for the price of a meal and a bed.

Finally, we are made to feel grudging admiration for his strength. Forced to drop the bestial tropes of O'Flaherty's prose, Ford substitutes a series of visual movements which amply demonstrate Gypo Nolan's enormous strength. In every instance, there is a sense in which the exhibition is either innocent or partially justified. First we see him picking up the dandy who tries to accost Katie, and tossing him into the street. The man outside the pub whom Gypo challenges for staring at him strikes Gypo first before Gypo lays him out. The policeman who ends up in the street beside this man, "sweet and peaceful as the babes in the woods," as Terry says, also initiates the assault on Gypo. Later, Gypo picks up Katie as if she were weightless, and at Aunt Betty's and the fish-and-chips shop, he is continually hoisting women upon his shoulder with hardly any effort at all. The little man who challenges him at the shebeen is brushed off like a fly. Gypo's exhibitions of strength, then, are never cruel, or at least there is nothing in them to compare with the sadism of O'Flaherty's Dan Gallagher. Yet we have been prepared for his breaking out of the cell where he sits awaiting death. During his escape, he turns a guard's jaw into "jelly," but this time he is fighting for his life. Even after he has been shot several times, he summons enough strength to reach the church. His sheer vitality reinforces all the other carefully constructed traits which are used to enlist our sympathy. At the end, Gypo is more a victim than a victimizer.

Granted, then, the medial, formal, and thematic changes which are dictated almost as much by a shift in audience, taboos, and conventions as by the artistic sensibility of the film-makers, shall we say that the film is a violation of the original? I think not. What the film loses in savagery, brutality, violence, pessimism and terror, it gains in consistency of tone, sharper delineation of character, tighter integration of theme, and greater enlistment of pity. Margaret Kennedy makes a relevant observation on the general problem in *The Mechanized Muse*. "In a great work of art," she writes, "the medium is so wedded to the subject that it becomes impossible to think of them apart. To take the *writing* out of a great novel is to run the risk of emptying out the baby with the bath . . . if any story has been perfectly told in one medium, what motive can there be for retelling it in another?"[22] That is why, she continues, "Most screen writers prefer to work on an ill-written, second-rate book, towards which they have no conscience, but which has some situation or character which has caught the imagination."

In the particular instance of *The Informer*, though Ford retains the kind of respect toward his original which Daniel Taradash calls for, the cumulative changes are so great that the result is a new species. A quantitative concern with additions, deletions, and alterations ends up as a qualitative problem. There is a sense, as we have seen, in which a careful film adaptation goes to the original not as a finished work (though this tends to be less true of the classics), but as a kind of raw material, much as the novelist approached *his* experiences. Like D. W. Griffith, such a director scarcely needs the writer at his side. Dudley Nichols tells us that Griffith, like Shakespeare, "took his stories where he found them —*Broken Blossoms* from Thomas Burke, *The Birth of a Nation* from a second-rate historical novelist. . . . Collaborating in a sense with such writers, he was able by his own genius to create masterpieces, just as Shakespeare found the seed for *Hamlet* in Saxo Grammaticus . . . ."[23]

That is why, if one is asked, "How do you like the Greek 'Electra?' " one must reply, "By whom? Sophocles or Euripides?" And, if one is asked, "How do you like *The Informer?*" one must reply, "By whom? O'Flaherty or Ford?"

[22] Margaret Kennedy, *The Mechanized Muse* (London, 1942), p. 29.
[23] Nichols, p. xxii.

3   *Wuthering Heights*

lems of screening novels, once made a distinction which must be familiar to all experienced script writers. "Some novels," said Mr. Goldwyn, "read like scenarios. Look at *Rebecca*. *Rebecca* reads like a scenario. But not *Wuthering Heights*. *Wuthering Heights* we had to cut. And Ben Hecht and Charles MacArthur did a brilliant job."[1]

Since Mr. Goldwyn, Hollywood's most successful independent producer, keeps close and fatherly watch over all his films, we may assume that he knows whereof he speaks. *Wuthering Heights* was a strong contender for the Academy Award in 1939, the same year which produced *Gone with the Wind*. A prestige item among the credits attributed to Samuel Goldwyn and its director, William Wyler, the film represents an association which goes back to *Dead End* and *The Westerner*, and looks ahead to *The Best Years of Our Lives*. All these films were somewhat bold, somewhat offbeat productions, each financially successful, and each, in its own way, a challenge to standard Hollywood conventions. Even if the film's salutary effect on sales of the novel were not enough, the challenge of scripting *Wuthering Heights* would inspire us to examine Mr. Goldwyn's results.

[1] In conversation with the author.

Hecht and MacArthur, the screen writers, began their job with a surgical and remarkably simple operation. They cut the book in half.

Within the framing device of Lockwood's and Ellen Dean's narration, the novel's Catherine Earnshaw dies at the novel's midway point. The film retains the flashback scheme, including an epilogue in which Heathcliff's body is found dead along the snowbound moors, but the story proper concludes with Cathy's death and with Heathcliff's plaintive cry for Cathy's spirit to haunt *him* the rest of his natural life. This major deletion includes, of course, a substantial number of scenes from the novel, primarily those devoted to the suffering and redemption of the third generation. In the novel, Catherine Earnshaw, Heathcliff, and Edgar Linton transmit the curse of evil to their children, and the young Catherine, Hareton Earnshaw, and Linton Heathcliff must expiate that evil through suffering. From this central deletion in the film follows almost every other deviation from Emily Brontë's text. Concurrent omissions, additions, and alterations combine, as we shall see, to shift the meaning and emphasis of the novel and, at the same time, to sharpen the contours of its plot.

We lose, for example, the total working out of Heathcliff's revenge. Where in the film Heathcliff acquires Wuthering Heights by paying Hindley's gambling debts, in the novel he also acquires Thrushcross Grange. It is true that at one point in the film Lockwood says that he is Heathcliff's new tenant at the "Grange," but the film never explains that the Grange and the Linton house are one and the same. Certainly we have no rendition of that devastating process outlined by C. P. Sanger in which Heathcliff manipulates events so that both the Earnshaw and Linton property devolve upon him.[2] We lose, then, the full extent of Heathcliff's vengeance, the twenty-year fulfillment of his curse, the undeviating success of his conquests. Finally we lose, too, the crucial scene in which that indomitable will cracks, when, about to do violence to young Cathy, Heathcliff's "fingers relaxed, he shifted his grasp from her head, to her arm, and gazed intently into her face." What he sees there at that moment is the spirit of Catherine Earnshaw, those eyes haunting him beyond the grave (he had seen those

[2] C. P. Sanger, *The Structure of Wuthering Heights* (London, 1926).

eyes before in young Hareton's face). And we lose, in this fashion, a number of subsidiary details—for example, Heathcliff's telling Ellen Dean that he harmed no one who was not already doomed by his own infirmity; Cathy's willful self-destruction in a manner that will parallel Heathcliff's death later on; and, since detailed genealogy becomes superfluous once the third generation is dropped, such characters as Frances Earnshaw, who has no other function in the novel but to bear Hareton. Such deletions are more or less serious, but they reflect the minor adjustments which become necessary all the way down the line.

One kind of deletion which does not follow from severe cutting, however, is the explicitly temporal reference which knits the book together. Sanger has shown that a precise chronological table can be derived from Emily Brontë's narrative hints, which, though often concealed, are consistently carried through the novel. No such precise chart can be drawn up on the basis of what we see and hear on the screen. In the novel, Heathcliff returns six months after his departure from Wuthering Heights. In the film, the interval might be one year, or three—we are never told precisely. In a similar fashion, we witness the children's growing up; the death of Mr. Earnshaw; Cathy's marriage to Edgar; Isabella's visit to Heathcliff; Cathy's death—but never do we discover how much calendar time has elapsed from one sequence to the next. The curious thing is that this lack of precision does not seem to matter. Since the film is primarily a succession of spatial images, we seem to need only the barest indication of time's passing. Only in films like *High Noon*, where the clock becomes a virtual protagonist in the drama, does the exact chronological moment need to be known.

Generally speaking, if the film's spatial coördinates are clear enough, the audience has sufficient information to locate itself in the filmic world. As long as we can identify the seasons, the general age limits of the actors, the varying levels of maturity—childhood, adolescence, old age—the chronology will seem more or less adequate. Spatial changes, by implication, embody temporal changes. The actor's face and clothing become the rough calendar of events.

Thus, in *Wuthering Heights* the major narrative deletions result from cutting out half the novel; the temporal deletions from the properties of the film medium itself.

We find a seeming paradox, however, when we attend to the film's additions. In spite of the fact that half the book is dropped at a stroke, roughly thirty new scenes, by Lester Asheim's count, appear in the screen version. This contrasts sharply with seven new scenes in *The Grapes of Wrath* and twelve in *Pride and Prejudice*, both of which more closely approximate the narrative events of their originals.

Of a total of fifty scenes, why was it necessary to add thirty? Part of the answer is found in the fact that the screen writers developed several whole scenes from the most casual hints in Emily Brontë's narrative. Consider, for example, the passage in which we learn that Cathy and Edgar have been married:

> Edgar Linton, as multitudes have been before and will be after him, was infatuated by Cathy; and he believed himself the happiest man alive on the day he led her to Gimmerton chapel, three years subsequent to his father's death.

In the film, these events are fully dramatized. We are shown a scene in which Cathy is convalescing at the Lintons' following the illness contracted during her frenzied search for Heathcliff in the storm. The scene closes with Edgar's proposal of marriage. The next scene reveals a church exterior. Here Emily Brontë's single narrative sentence appears in fully visual terms. A beadle throws open the doors, scattering children, clearing the way for Edgar and Cathy, who emerge a moment later to a chorus of good wishes. Cathy is smiling and happy as Edgar leads her to a waiting carriage. As she approaches the carriage, however, she seems suddenly troubled, even frightened. "A cold wind went across my heart just then," she tells Edgar. "A feeling of doom. . . . You touched me and it was gone."

Cathy allows herself to be seated in the carriage. When Edgar goes to comfort her, she cries out, "Oh, Edgar, I love you! I do," and remains clinging to him at the fade-out, her heart not quite convinced of what her words have professed. That cold wind serves as a premonition of disaster to come, dramatizes the contending emotions which shall possess Cathy until her death, and looks ahead to the recurrence of her passion for Heathcliff which triggers her illness and decline. Although the fact that Cathy virtually wills her own death does not appear in the film, the wedding scene does serve to indicate how the film-makers use undramatic narrative summary, sometimes even a single line, to visualize dramatic events.

Another kind of addition occurs frequently in the film as a corollary to the omission of half the novel. Since the third generation does not appear, appropriate adjustments must be made to retain cohesion in the plot. The frame of the Ellen Dean-Lockwood colloquy, as we have seen, is carried over from book to film. But in keeping with the film-makers' general strategy, young Cathy, Hareton and Zillah (Emily Brontë's housekeeper who replaces Ellen Dean at Wuthering Heights) are dropped from the opening sequence. Isabella and Ellen Dean take their place. Joseph, the Bible-quoting handyman, and Heathcliff remain. The story which Ellen Dean subsequently tells Lockwood—in one night, however, instead of over a period of several weeks—loosely follows the narrative line of the novel's first half. But two of the hostile, somber faces which greet Lockwood at his first introduction to Wuthering Heights have necessarily been replaced.

Still another kind of addition occurs by virtue of exaggeration, what Asheim calls a sort of justified sensationalism. Asheim calls attention to three of these: the episode in which Heathcliff cuts his hands; the scene in which Cathy becomes ill after Heathcliff's departure; and the general use made of Penistone Crag.[3] In the film, Cathy is getting dressed for a ball in anticipation of Edgar's arrival. Heathcliff, wearing stable garments, appears to complain, to protest her becoming "a vain, cheap, wordly fool." In retaliation, Cathy berates him for being dirty, following the novel's view of clothes and cleanliness as status symbols. The insult infuriates Heathcliff; his hands leap out to strike her. "That's all I've become to you—a pair of dirty hands. . . . Well, have them then." A moment later, utterly dismayed by what he has done, Heathcliff climbs into the stable loft and drives his hands through the glass panes, one by one. Emily Brontë employs this opposition of dirt and

[3] Lester Asheim, "From Book to Film" (Ph.D. dissertation, University of Chicago, 1949), p. 32, p. 101.

fine clothes also as symbols of disfavor and respectability, and, as we shall see, she has more than her share of violence. But this particular scene appears nowhere in the novel. And yet it functions effectively as a cinematic equivalent to Heathcliff's anger, torture, and self-hatred.

In a similar fashion, the book's Cathy becomes ill, following Heathcliff's departure, by staying up all night at Wuthering Heights and working herself into a delirium. By extension, the film's Cathy runs out into the teeth of the storm, from which Edgar brings her in drenched and unconscious. Here, again, the storm scene is a more effective cinematic rendition of Cathy's troubled emotions than the original. E. M. Forster holds the theory that the emotions of Cathy and Heathcliff function differently from other emotions in fiction: "Instead of inhabiting the characters, they surround them like thunder clouds, and generate the explosions that fill the novel."[4] By adding the storm scene, the film-makers seem to be in the position of taking Forster literally.

Finally, the various glens and tarns, which Cathy and Heathcliff frequent in their wild jaunts across the countryside, are all compressed into a single location in the film, the "Castle" at Penistone Crag. Here the lovers meet, in their affinity for the desolate beauty of the moors, to spin their dreams and feel the wind and gather up the heather. This compression has the advantage not only of budget economy, but of story economy as well. It suggests the rugged, wild character of the Yorkshire terrain without extensive location shots, and it provides a unified physical symbol for the fierce passions of the novel. These additions, then, serve as cinematic figures of speech, meeting the film's special requirements (i.e., they arise naturally from the spatial setting). While these tropes have no immediate precedent in the book, they do manage to convey book ideas.

There is another kind of addition, however, which, since it neither elaborates narrative clues nor renders emotional states in filmic metaphors, is different from those I have mentioned, and has the effect of altering Emily Brontë's intentions. Through a number of carefully blended images and fragments of dialogue, the film attributes motives to Cathy which do not exist in the novel.

[4] E. M. Forster, *Aspects of the Novel* (New York, 1927), p. 209.

In an early scene, for example, while Cathy and Heathcliff are still children, we see them engaging in a kind of elaborate romantic game. After Heathcliff wins a horse race out on the heath, he claims his prize. "You've got to do as I say," he says. "You've got to water my horse and brush it down."

Cathy protests, "Oh, that's not fair. It's too real."

Two scenes later, they are back at Penistone Crag, the "Castle," and Cathy is trying to cheer Heathcliff because Hindley has just thrashed him. She wants to pretend that Heathcliff is a prince in disguise, a hero of high birth, that his father was the "Emperor of China," and his mother "an Indian queen." When Heathcliff does not respond, Cathy gives in and offers the prize she had, at first, refused. In play, she declares herself his slave. But Heathcliff will not take the prize now. "No, Cathy. You're my queen. Whatever happens out there—here you'll always be my queen."

Later, when the children have been superseded by Merle Oberon and Laurence Olivier as the more mature Cathy and Heathcliff, they are again seen together at the Castle. Hindley Earnshaw, now master of Wuthering Heights, has been mistreating Heathcliff, and Cathy is commiserating. She urges him to run away. "You could come back to me rich and take me away," she says. "Why aren't you my prince like we said long ago . . . ?" A moment later, they are running off to catch a glimpse of an elegant party at the Linton estate. That, Cathy says, is what she wants: "Dancing and singing and a pretty world! And I'm going to have it!" After Cathy has been carried into the house, following a sudden attack by one of the Linton dogs, Judge Linton orders Heathcliff out of his house. When Heathcliff calls a curse on the assembled company and leaves in a fury, Cathy calls out, "I'll be waiting . . . ."

As in the novel, Heathcliff's first attempt to leave is abortive. His passion for Cathy will not permit him to go through with it. In a subsequent scene at the castle, we see the lovers again, this time at the height of the passionate mood which we have come to associate with their moorland retreat. For the moment, they lose all thought of the obstacles between them. Cathy abjures Heathcliff to "Make the world stop right here—make everything stop and stand still—" and sends him to gather armfuls of heather. Doing as he is bid, Heathcliff calls back to her, "Cathy, you're still my queen." For an instant, they have retrieved a deathless moment from a childhood that is quickly vanishing and a future that is painfully uncertain. But the moment is achieved at the expense of facing the demands of that "other world." It is a fragile moment, and Cathy is aware of it. "Don't talk," she tells Heathcliff. "All this might disappear."

Indeed, the moment does not last. In the very next scene, Ellen is helping Cathy adjust an effulgent and highly becoming dress which she is donning for a party. When Heathcliff interrupts to protest her reverting to the lures of Linton society, Cathy quickly resorts to her former goading. This time it is no longer suggestive and hopeful. It has become cruel, taunting: "Thief or servant were all you were born to be—or beggar beside the road . . . ."

I have reviewed these events at length in order to point out both the strong mythopoeic tendencies and the troubling social ambitions which motivate Cathy. The consistency of the pattern bears emphasis, for one discovers with surprise that the pattern has little precedent in the novel. The twin motivations are almost wholly the work of the screen writers. Emily Brontë provides none of Cathy's elaborate romanticizing, and little of her goading Heathcliff to improve his status. In the novel, the activities of Cathy and Heathcliff are directed more toward sheer mischief than toward the shrewish promptings mouthed by Cathy in the film, more toward the recklessness of the moors than toward the romantic world we find, say, in the Gondal Poems, that remarkable cycle evolved by Emily Brontë and, possibly, by her sister Anne. Much more typical is Ellen Dean's complaint that "The curate might set as many chapters as he pleased for Catherine to get by heart and Joseph might thrash Heathcliff till his arm ached; they forgot everything the minute they were together again: at least the minute they had contrived some naughty plan of revenge; and many a time I've cried to myself to watch them growing more reckless daily."

True, there is some Gondalizing in the novel (devoid of Emily's deadly serious intentions at certain moments in the poems), but little of it originates with Heathcliff and the elder Cathy. "You're fit for a prince in disguise. Who knows but your father was the

Emperor of China, and your mother an Indian queen." These lines do appear in the book, but they are recited by Ellen Dean, not by Cathy. Again, in the novel, Ellen relates the following incident:

> Catherine came to me, one morning, at eight o'clock, and said she was that day an Arabian merchant, going to cross the Desert with his caravan; and I must give her plenty of provision for herself and beasts: a horse, and three camels, personated by a large hound and a couple of pointers.

But the charming proposal is made by the *young* Cathy, not by her mother.

What is the result of bestowing these twin attributes, romanticism and a desire for aggrandizement, on Cathy in the movie version? The effect is to force Emily Brontë's story into a conventional Hollywood mold, the story of the stable boy and the lady. The convention ought to be reasonably familiar. A lady bred in respectable surroundings finds herself torn between one of her "own kind" and an attractive stranger. The first is effete, wealthy, uninteresting, and kind; the second is rebelliously masculine, poor, passionate, and rough. For romantic and sexual reasons, the lady clearly prefers the outsider. If the lady is not willing to run away with the stranger (as in Capra's *It Happened One Night*), she sets out to make him respectable, to improve his table manners as well as his income (as in Hitchcock's *Rear Window*). In *Wuthering Heights*, the story takes a tragic turn due to a run of bad luck. First, Heathcliff does not carry through his initial resolve to run away and get rich. Then he does not stay long enough to hear Cathy's profession of love. And later, when he finally does return, a sartorial and financial success, Cathy is already married to Edgar Linton. The film's denouement revolves around Cathy's refusal to submit to Heathcliff because of conventional scruples. This conflict is made quite explicit in the scene where Cathy comes to protest Heathcliff's loveless conquest of Isabella. Heathcliff responds by crying out, "If your heart were only stronger than your dull fear of your God and the world, I would live silent and contented in your shadow." He moves to take her, but Cathy backs away. Heathcliff flares up, "But no. . . . You must destroy me with that weakness you call virtue. You must keep me tormented with that cruelty you think so pious." Apparently, if Cathy were not too scrupulous to try it, Heathcliff would be satisfied with an adulterous affair. But now, rebuffed, nothing remains to him but an undeviating policy of revenge, with Isabella as his first victim. The story as it stands, then, is a tragedy of bad timing. If only Heathcliff had transformed himself *sooner*.

This addition constitutes a major revision in Emily Brontë's intentions. None of the dialogue I have just alluded to appears in the novel. The film, to be sure, retains the contrast between Cathy's affection for Edgar and her stronger passion for Heathcliff. To Ellen, she describes her feelings for Edgar in conventional clichés: "I love the ground under his feet and the air over his head and everything he touches." But the moment Heathcliff gallops off, stung to anguish by what he has heard, Cathy goes on to articulate her impassioned love for Heathcliff: "He's more myself than I am. Whatever our souls are made of, his and mine are the same—and Linton's is as different as frost from fire—My one thought in living is Heathcliff—Ellen, I *am* Heathcliff . . . Oh, Ellen, if everything in the world died and Heathcliff remained, life would still be full for me."

In spite of the carry-over, the theme of spiritual identity which, by later implication, cannot be fully realized until the soul is free of corporeal entrapment, is not sustained in the film version. A line in which Cathy explains that it would be degrading to marry Heathcliff is retained in the film's edited print. But a line which appears in the original script and which was to come closer to Emily Brontë's meaning, has been omitted. Originally, when Ellen asks Cathy why she seems to have reservations about marrying Edgar, Cathy was to have replied, touching her heart, "The obstacle is here or wherever the soul lives." Whatever the motives of the film-makers (and there are dozens which always arise in the normal process of film production), their choice indicates a conflict of intentions. The significant thing, for us, is that at this point in Cathy's explanation the social obstacle takes precedence over the spiritual.

For Emily Brontë, on the other hand, the central conflict rages not between the world of the stable boy and the world of the gentry but between the animals and harebells and birds of the moors, and the elegant trappings of Thrushcross Grange, between nature and society in general. For Emily Brontë, the conflict is irreconcilable. It is irreconcilable because the passionate love of kindred souls, the only real love for her, cannot hope to survive in this world. It cannot survive because, as we shall see in Emily Brontë's own terms, life exists on a principle of destruction. Beatitude can be found only in a private kind of afterlife, in the soul's liberation beyond the grave.

If the second half of the novel proves anything, it is precisely that worldly devices to redeem love are doomed to failure. Heathcliff's economic conquests, as we have seen, are devastatingly complete, since no one can resist his will. His destruction of everything responsible for keeping Catherine from him during her lifetime turns, ironically, upon himself. For at the moment when his boiling rage begins to turn to physical violence, to threaten young Cathy and Hareton (the only living survivors of the Earnshaw-Linton clans), when his destruction is about to become complete, his will suddenly snaps. He loses his desire to live. He has seen the presence of the dead Cathy in both the children's eyes and knows now that every one of his earthly deeds is mockingly empty. For while he lives, he can neither possess Cathy nor forget her. He tells Ellen, "I get levers and mattocks to demolish two houses, and train myself to be capable of working like Hercules, and when everything is ready, and in my power, I find the will to lift a slate off either roof has vanished!" The loss of will (not power) is the immediate antecedent to death, for it is only in death that he can live again. Even a conquered world cannot bring back his love. Social destruction thus becomes a preface to self-destruction.

If young Catherine and Hareton find happiness at the end, it is on grounds different from those which Heathcliff and the elder Cathy had sought. It is a more diluted, more conventional kind of love, the only kind one can have and still live in this world. Cathy and Heathcliff fell in love on the wind-tossed moors, the wild terrain. Hareton and the young Cathy fall in love over a book. Where Heathcliff and Cathy's passion was too consuming for the social world of West Riding, Hareton and young Cathy will make their peace with it.

It cannot be argued that the film's new direction was overlooked by the author of the novel. Emily Brontë might have chosen the film's more explicitly social theme. In spite of the dismal insularity of Haworth parsonage, the Brontë sisters were not ignorant of contemporary social and economic tensions. The story is often told about Miss Wooler, the schoolmistress at Roe Head, who used to beguile the girls with stories of the Luddite riots which had taken place in the local factories. One of these factories was even visible from the schoolhouse windows.[5] We know that the sisters were aware of the industrialization of southern England, of the railroads pushing out like a net across the country, even as far as West Riding where the girls' brother, Branwell, tried to hold down a job as a ticket agent. We know, too, that Charlotte Brontë used a number of these social conflicts in her novels; for example, the conflicts between the cotton workers and mill owners of Yorkshire in *Shirley*.

Phyllis Bentley points out that where Charlotte's world is full of factory towns and railroad tracks and social climbing, Emily's world is restricted to moors and animals and anguished love.[6] Seen from a distance, the Hollywood product more closely approximates Charlotte's world than Emily's. It was not that the realities of economic aggrandizement and social climbing were unknown to Emily; it was simply that for her they held little interest. Private reality was foremost in her consciousness. Anguished love, relieved only by the stark beauty of the moors, was more central to her cosmos than all the property in Yorkshire. If it is true, as Ralph Fox suggests, that *Wuthering Heights* "is the most violent and frightful cry of human suffering which even Victorian England ever tore from a human body,"[7] it is also true that Emily Brontë never attributed the cause to national or social repression. In her world, the cause is love's inevitable defeat. A destructive universe cannot abide a Heathcliff and a Cathy. Pas-

---

[5] Lawrence Hanson and E. M. Hanson, *The Four Brontës* (London, 1950), revised edition, p. 27.

[6] Phyllis Eleanor Bentley, *The Brontë Sisters*, for the British Council and National Book League (New York, 1950), a supplement to *British Book News*.

[7] Ralph Fox, *The Novel and the People* (New York, 1945), p. 60.

sionate love is impossible because the body, the agent of *this* world, simply cannot sustain it. Death is the redeemer, not station.

Such additions and deletions as I have ascribed to the film-makers are bound to influence the purely pictorial effects which we see on the screen. And if we grant the film-makers their respective choices, we may go on to test the effectiveness of those choices by cinematic standards. Here we find even further evidence that the collective unit responsible for making the film, however honorable its intentions, seriously shifted the meaning of Emily Brontë's book. Many of the alterations we find here follow logically, or at least plausibly, from the deletions and additions already mentioned, and from the reorientation that always accompanies a change in medium.

But there is another group, aside from these, which bears analysis, the type of alteration which results from what might be called the principle of Hollywood Aristotelianism. According to this always operative, rarely articulated principle, all elements of the film—spectacle, diction, character, and certainly thought—must be subordinated to plot, the prime arbiter. Parker Tyler has pointed out the dangers inherent in "the nonchalant assumption of the usual commercial film that the only necessary formal element is *plot* and that merely conventional 'framing' and clear photography are required for plastic values."[8] While *Wuthering Heights* exhibits certain exceptions to the usual result—what Tyler calls "the vulgar journalistic look and formlessness of standard movie products"—it does omit a number of promising pictorial effects which appear both in the novel and in the original script. These effects, if integrated into the film's total composition, might have supported the drive of sheer incident which the film now has. As it stands, the film is overloaded with medium shots, relieved only occasionally by long shots of the "Castle" or the Heights. In spite of the storms and brooding moors, the physical set-ups of the landscape and the characters are only occasionally allowed to endorse the dramatic event.

For example, the novel presents all the Earnshaws as dark; all the Lintons as light. The Earnshaw children, Hindley and Cathy,

[8] Parker Tyler, "The Film Sense and the Painting Sense," *Perspectives USA*, No. 11 (Spring, 1955), p. 104.

are wild and passionate, not a little irresponsible; the Linton children, Edgar and Isabella, are tame and controlled, victims of their own weakness. Heathcliff suddenly appears among them, a surly waif, both strange and familiar, as dark as the Earnshaws in hair and eye. His passions and will, it is suggested, become mere extensions of tendencies already inherent in the Earnshaw character. In the novel, this contrast in pigmentation is played on frequently. Heathcliff tells Nelly in a moment of envy that he wishes he had "light hair and a fair skin like Edgar Linton." Young Cathy has both "yellow curls combed back behind her ears, as plain as a quaker," and her mother's dark, flashing eyes. By combining the coloring of both families, as well as their conflicting qualities, Cathy escapes the curse of both. This obviously pictorial motif does not appear in the film. Merle Oberon and Laurence Olivier are dark, but David Niven and Geraldine Fitzgerald as the Lintons are not contrastingly fair. Their faces, it is true, are finer, more subdued, more weakly delicate than Sir Laurence's or Miss Oberon's, and at one point Cathy even lashes out at Edgar, "I hate the look of your milk-white face. I hate the touch of your soft, foolish hands." But the contrast remains verbal rather than visual.

During Cathy's growing delirium in the novel, she performs a remarkable piece of dramatic business which indicates the turmoil within her. She rends a pillow, and then, as Ellen Dean tells us, she seems to find childish delight in pulling out the feathers and ranging them on the sheet before her. As she performs this rite, she speaks distractedly:

That's a turkey's . . . and this a wild duck's; and this a pigeon's. Ah, they put pigeon's feathers in the pillows—no wonder I couldn't die! Let me take care to throw it on the floor when I lie down. And here is a moor-cock's; and this—I should know it among a thousand—it's a lapwing's. Bonny bird; wheeling over our heads in the middle of the moor. It wanted to go to its nest, for the clouds had touched the swells, and it felt rain coming. This feather was picked up from the heath, the bird was not shot; we saw its nest in the winter, full of little skeletons. Heathcliff set a trap over it, and the old ones dare not come. I made him promise he'd never shoot a lapwing after that, and he didn't.

Yes, here are more! Did he shoot my lapwings, Nelly? Are they red, any of them? Let me look.

The passage is reminiscent of the mad Ophelia; the feathers are Cathy's rosemary and columbine. But the scene, which ought to have delighted Mr. Goldwyn because it reads "just like a scenario" does not appear in the film. The film, in fact, is content merely with establishing the fact that Cathy is ill. Her condition is quite casually reported by Dr. Kenneth, who has come to Wuthering Heights for another purpose entirely. The significance of Cathy's self-imposed death, the *rendition* of it, which runs to some sixty pages in the novel, appears nowhere in the final movie version.

The strain of sacrificing pictorial comment to exigencies of plot may be further illustrated by the number of discrepancies between the shooting-script and the movie's final print. Not only are many of Emily Brontë's cinematic details abandoned but also many that were originally proposed by the screen writers. That Hecht and MacArthur may have wanted to pay minimum obeisance to Emily Brontë's passion for bird symbolism is indicated in the original draft of the film's closing shot. A view of Heathcliff, his flesh frosted in death, was to dissolve to a view of the moors, as Cathy and Heathcliff had beheld them in happier days, and end with a shot of two birds hovering over the castle before flying off into the winter sky. Instead, following Dr. Kenneth's remarking on the mystery of finding only a single set of tracks in the snow, we see a brief shot of the moors and the disembodied wraiths of Cathy and Heathcliff walking along hand in hand. We cannot be sure that the original shot, as proposed in the shooting-script, would have been any less artificial than the present one. But as it stands the shot is visually static, two wraiths haunting a papier mâché set. The writers had at least attempted to find a rough equivalent to that image of peace and beatitude which closes the novel. But with the shot's imaginative failure, Emily Brontë's magic is gone.

Similarly, in the ball scene following Heathcliff's return, during which Heathcliff professes his love for Cathy, the script calls for a black fan as part of Cathy's ensemble. The fan, poised against Cathy's resplendent gown, might have been precisely the jarring note which was needed to reinforce the premonition of disaster. In her wedding scene, Cathy had felt a cold wind. Before Heathcliff reappears at the Linton house, transformed now by elegance and wealth, Cathy feels chilled and asks that another log be added to the fire. The fan, fluttering nervously like a bird, combining the qualities of blackness and cold, might have been a more telling clue to Cathy's feelings than the merely prosaic dialogue we have now ("I'm another man's wife and he loves me—and I love him.") In the final editing, however, the fan is barely recognizable—the camera does not focus upon it; it is indistinguishable from the color of Cathy's gown; it retreats into the anonymity of the general setting.

As a final example, consider the scene which occurs shortly after Cathy has begun seeing Edgar regularly. Emily Brontë has Heathcliff complain by pointing to a calendar on which he has recorded the days she has spent with the Lintons and those she has spent with him. The calendar is a precise and graphic chart of Cathy's current favors. The calendar, too, does not appear in the scene's movie rendition. Heathcliff's challenge remains strictly verbal.

If, then, the film-makers transmute brief clues in the narrative into pictorial and dramatic cinema, they also sacrifice, in their insistence on an absolutely clear line of development, the kind of detail which would lend density and control to their filmic images.

Such alterations, additions, and deletions point up the surgical tendencies of the Hollywood Aristotelians. The story conference becomes a kind of autopsy designed to uncover the skeletal outlines of the plot. William Wyler must still frame his shots, alternate Olivier's brooding face with medium shots of the room, leave enough footage for graceful dissolves, but the question to which all subsidiary components must finally answer is still, "Will the story line be clear?"

Some of these alterations are, of course, inevitable. The major part of Emily Brontë's novel is narrated from Ellen Dean's point of view. But in the film, the camera is omniscient. The film does copy the opening device, as we have seen, retaining essentially the same entree into the story proper: Lockwood's visit to the Heights; his brusque treatment; his curiosity at the strange assembly before the fire; his question to Ellen Dean, who then proceeds with her recapitulation of events. The novel, however, retains

Ellen's voice throughout. Except for the passages which Lockwood narrates on his own behalf, Ellen is everywhere in control. Even when she is reporting events at which she was not present, it is she who is always there to receive the news—Isabella's letter relating the horrors of life at Wuthering Heights, Heathcliff's account of Cathy's mishap at the Lintons, Zillah's picture of young Cathy and Hareton, the two Cathys' reports of encounters with Heathcliff. All these are filtered through Ellen Dean's sensibility, for at every point she recounts them to Lockwood. The narrative is full of Ellen's interpolations, interjections, and moral judgments, judgments which constitute a kind of norm against which the various characters are measured. Ellen represents stability, reason, common sense, a suggestive but not officious Christian conscience (as opposed to Joseph's cant and Bible-quoting). She gauges the flight of that excess and perversity which ends by snuffing out lives as well as happiness.

But the density which Emily Brontë achieves by having Ellen function both as narrator and as actor at one and the same time is impossible in the film. When the aged Ellen begins telling Lockwood her story in Goldwyn's movie, her face dissolves to a shot of Wuthering Heights as it looked many years before. But it is a shift in space, not time. We have not dipped into Ellen's memory; we have merely replaced the spatial image of her face with the spatial image of Wuthering Heights. In the process, Ellen's voice is lost. Henceforth it will not matter whether Ellen appears in a given scene. The camera has preëmpted the narrator's role.

If the removal of Ellen Dean's angle of vision is inevitable, as it must be whenever a fiction told from a single point of view is translated into images of physical reality (unless the camera eye becomes the eye of a character, as in *Lady in the Lake*), it does not follow that alterations in character are equally inevitable. Heathcliff, for example, is modified in such a subtle way that his filmic function and characterization shift considerably. Through the persistent use of attributive adjectives and metaphor, Emily Brontë creates a much more devastating portrait than the one which Olivier portrays in the film. The motif of demonism and violence which pervades the book is almost unrelieved. With increasing intensity, Heathcliff is variously presented as having "a diabolical sneer," "eyes like devils' spies," and "sharp, cannibal teeth"; as being "an imp of Satan," "a devil," "a cruel man," "an unreclaimed creature," "a fierce, pitiless, wolfish man," "a lying fiend," "a monster," "a madman," "a savage beast," "an evil genius," and "a goblin, ghoul or vampire." Within the general atmosphere of violence (even Hindley tries to pry a knife between Ellen's teeth), Heathcliff is specifically responsible for shoving a tureen of hot apple sauce in Edgar's face; threatening to crush Edgar's ribs "like a rotten hazel-nut"; hanging Isabella's dog, Fanny; throwing a kitchen knife at Isabella; dashing his head against the knotted trunk of a tree; pummeling young Cathy with his hands. In addition, he is forever threatening violence. It was this kind of undeviating propensity for physical violence that prompted Charlotte Brontë to argue that if Heathcliff had not been redeemed by his affection for Hareton and by his half-implied esteem for Nelly Dean, we should say he was "child neither of Lascar nor gypsy, but a man's shape animated by demon life—a Ghoul—an Afreet." [9]

It is granted that many of these details would seem absurd on the screen. Raw brutality, literally transposed, loses the cushioning effect of language. We have seen, however, that used with prudence, the single incident in which Heathcliff slaps Cathy can work effectively as a symbol of his guilt, despair, and suffering. But the film writers were not solely concerned with the absurdity of violence boldly presented. Wisely using passion rather than brutality to advance their story-line, they were also confronted with the problem of how to transform the demonic Heathcliff into a conventional hero.

This troubling concern is indicated in a scene in which an incidental switch transforms Heathcliff into the sinned against instead of the sinner. In the film, the immediate cause of Heathcliff's swearing to avenge himself on Hindley occurs when (a) Hindley demands Heathcliff's horse, (b) Heathcliff refuses, (c) Hindley strikes Heathcliff with a rock. In the book, this episode is more evenly weighted. Here, (a) it is Heathcliff who demands Hindley's horse, and (b) Hindley who refuses, (c) though a mo-

---

[9] Charlotte Brontë, "Editor's Preface to the 1850 Edition of *Wuthering Heights*," in Emily Brontë's *Wuthering Heights*, World Classics Series (London, 1944), p. xxx.

ment later Hindley does knock Heathcliff off his feet. Since, then, the only diabolical acts we see Heathcliff commit in the film are his conquest of Isabella, his acquisition of Wuthering Heights (neither of which is presented directly), his eventual humiliation of Isabella, and his striking of Cathy, his revenge, we feel, is not wholly in excess of his injuries. It is an altogether less savage affair. Heathcliff loses that very exaggeration which Virginia Woolf saw as the source of his power: "He is impossible, we say, but nevertheless no boy in literature has so vivid an existence as his."[10] In the movie image, Heathcliff's diabolism disappears; only his anguish remains.

When Emily Brontë was a student at M. Héger's Pensionat de Demoiselles, in Brussels, she wrote an essay called "The Butterfly." The essay became a kind of credo:

> Nature is an inexplicable puzzle, life exists on a principle of destruction; every creature must be the relentless instrument of death to the others, or himself cease to live. Nevertheless, we celebrate the day of our birth, and we praise God that we entered the world.[11]

The statement will serve as a paraphrase of Emily Brontë's worldview as it emerges in her poems and in her book. Pain will be transformed to "happiness and glory" when "sin and death" are spent. The phrasing is another version of the theme which was to ring out in her best poems:

> No coward soul is mine,
> No trembler in the world's storm-troubled sphere!
> I see Heaven's glories shine,
> And Faith shines equal, arming me from Fear.

This was about as far as Emily Brontë could ever go toward affirming and celebrating the corporeal world. Redemption through death, spiritual affirmation in the teeth of anguish and hell—this remains the root-idea of the book, not as in the film, that star-

[10] Virginia Woolf, " 'Jane Eyre' and 'Wuthering Heights,' " *The Common Reader* (New York, 1948), p. 227.
[11] Emily Jane Brontë, *Five Essays Written in French*, trans. Lorine White Nagel (Univ. of Texas Press, 1948), p. 17.

crossed lovers, if their love is strong enough, may find each other after death. In reducing the severity of the sin, the film-makers have forfeited the impact of that final repose, that peace which is at last granted "the sleepers in that quiet earth."

It takes tremendous courage to praise the works of God in a predatory universe. It takes less courage to show the tragedy of marrying for conventional comfort instead of for love. True, both in the Goldwyn production and in Emily Brontë's novel, bad luck dogs the lovers' tracks. But where Emily Brontë's lovers, given the intensity of their passions, could never hope to find happiness in this life, Hollywood's lovers, it is clearly implied, might have been compatible if Heathcliff had only settled down.

Thus, in one way, the novel is more positive in its outcome than the film, for not only are the lovers convincingly at peace in their graves but Hareton and young Cathy have been reconciled. Unwilling to probe the face of hell, as Emily Brontë did, Hollywood could not hope to render that final image of rest and sublimity.

Yet, in spite of these serious alterations, the Goldwyn production has achieved a certain critical and even financial success. In 1955, there were several revivals in a number of urban theaters throughout the country. In Italy, the production continues to be revived under the title, "*La Voce Nella Tempesta.*"[12] And one writer argues that William Wyler should have received the 1939 Academy Award for direction instead of Victor Fleming.[13]

How can we account for this success in spite of the consequences which follow from the film's deletions, alterations, and additions? One cannot, in the last analysis, argue with a film-writer's prerogative to take liberties with his literary models, since these are, in any event, inevitable. One can, if he wishes, argue with alterations which change the novelist's intention and meaning. But the final standard, the one to which we must always revert, is whether, regardless of thematic, formal, and medial mutations, the film stands up as an autonomous work of art. Not whether the film-maker has respected his model, but whether he

---

[12] *New York Times Theater Section* (May 1, 1955), p. 5.
[13] Reggie Hurd, Jr., "Academy Award Mistakes," *Films in Review*, VI (May, 1955).

has respected his own vision. I have tried to show how the film *Wuthering Heights* stands up *qua* film, where the plastic imagination fails and where it succeeds, and how the cinema version alters, without obliterating, the book's final meaning. We are further obliged to account for the film's persistent impression on competent judges.

Consider John Gassner's justification for the inclusion of *Wuthering Heights* in his *Twenty Best Film Plays:*

> ... the screenplay of *Wuthering Heights* is distinctive because for once passion—from adolescence to adulthood—has been presented without adulteration. In some respects the film play even improves upon the novel by concentrating upon the central drama in the lives of the possessed lovers and dispensing with some of the Gothic hugger-mugger and exaggerations of the book that was born in the fevered brain of a brilliant recluse.[14]

At first glance, the conclusion to be drawn seems obvious: even diluted Brontë is so far superior to the standard Hollywood product that it commands our attention. But if the researches of C. P. Sanger and others prove anything, it is that Emily Brontë foreswore "Gothic hugger-mugger and exaggerations," that the woman's passions were at every moment under the artist's control. After a close reading, one agrees that the contours of the book, seen from a distance, are "hard, bright, clean." "For all its strangeness," write the Hansons, "it is a well-balanced, unhysterical novel,"[15] and this writer readily concurs.

The virtues of economy and condensation, then, are not what lend effectiveness to Samuel Goldwyn's film. For even if director, producer, and writers had been able collectively to solve their plotting problem, and solved it to perfection, there would remain perhaps equally troubling difficulties. Margaret Kennedy has published a sensitive discussion of the problems inherent in making comprehensible to one culture films originally designed for another.[16] In spite of the tendency of the film to respond to its mass

[14] *Twenty Best Film Plays*, ed. John Gassner and Dudley Nichols (New York, 1943), p. xix.

[15] Hansons, p. 233.

[16] Margaret Kennedy, *The Mechanized Muse* (London, 1942).

audience by finding low common denominators, it cannot hope, indeed would be ill-advised, to obliterate cultural differences between peoples. For while it remains a special cinematic triumph to find Charlie Chaplin and Greta Garbo as enthusiastically received in Hamburg as in Liverpool, we would be remiss to overlook the adjustments that must be made when films designed for the Germans are shown to the British. One has only to note in passing the almost insoluble problem of dubbing English words to Latin gestures (although certainly the reverse is not always true), or finding adequate subtitles for French and Italian idioms, in order to remember the thousands of *small* adjustments that are constantly taking place. But Miss Kennedy's account of how an "English ending" was tacked onto the German print of Leontine Sagan's *Maedchen in Uniform* illustrates what may happen in areas where conflicting conventions are not reconcilable.

If Miss Kennedy illustrates the problem of attuning conventions between European countries, how much more difficult is it to make the leap when not only alien countries but alien centuries are involved. It was difficult for the English to accept *Maedchen in Uniform;* how much more difficult, then, for twentieth-century America to orient itself to nineteenth-century England. Emily Brontë, of course, could not speak for all of England, let alone for her entire century. But as a sensitive observer she could organize the mores and conventions of mid-century Yorkshire into her special lyric vision. If we read her book at all today, it is because we can, to some extent, project ourselves into her world, into that very private *weltanschauung* which makes her book unique. E. M. Forster was very wise in pointing out that *Wuthering Heights* has no mythology beyond what the characters of Cathy and Heathcliff provide: "no book is more cut off from the universals of Heaven and Hell. It is local, like the spirits it engenders . . . ."[17] Moreover, if what emerges from this novel is at once a reflection of Victorian repressions and a cry of private anguish, the impossibility of love in a predatory universe, the redemption of love through death, then we are close to the central idea of "The Butter-

[17] Forster, p. 210.

fly," close to the mystical view of Emily Brontë proposed by Virginia Moore.[18]

This combination of local mythology and mystical insight endows the book with an extremely complex set of values. But given this complexity, we are more prone to understand the changes which occur in the film version of the book. It is too much to expect that a mass audience will be able to accept conventions which time and distance have made remote, let alone the peculiar intricacies of Emily Brontë's private world. Add all the additional changes that a new medium demands, and it becomes all but impossible to effect a "faithful" rendition. If nothing else, the impossibility of retaining Emily Brontë tropes would make the shift inevitable. The cinema cannot retain the metaphor which depicts a "vinegar-faced Joseph"; the allusion which compares the incoherence of Lockwood's threats to the "virulency" that "smacked of King Lear"; the simile which shows how Heathcliff's anguished cry is "like a savage beast getting goaded to death with knives and spears." In abandoning language for the visual image, the film leaves behind the author's most characteristic signature, her style.

Clearly it is not Emily Brontë as we know her that endows the film with substance. What, then, is it? We are forced to conclude that it is precisely those additions which the film-makers have written into their story, the entire network of additions, deletions, alterations which are characteristically theirs and not Emily Brontë's. By heightening status-motivation in Cathy's character; by making her the gadfly to Heathcliff's self-improvement; by changing Heathcliff from a demon into a lovesick stable boy; by eliminating the theme of virtual suicide; by dropping the conditions under which Hareton and young Cathy escape their parental curse—by all these changes the film-makers have made the events comprehensible to a twentieth-century mass audience. In conjunction with those spare situational remnants which are left over from the novel, and the film's handling of composition, music, acting (henceforth the face of Laurence Olivier will be inseparably bound up with our image of Heathcliff), the various additions of the

[18] Virginia Moore, *The Life and Eager Death of Emily Brontë* (London, 1936).

production unit are what give the film its value. Samuel Goldwyn, William Wyler, Ben Hecht, and Charles MacArthur are being revived in American and Italian theaters, not Emily Brontë. Emily Brontë provided only the occasion, the initial impulse from which everything else followed.

This process is at work whenever the film version of a novel is being prepared, but particularly when the novel is incomprehensible for reasons of spatial and temporal distance. But so general is the process, so much a part of the film industry's methods, so widely accepted as movie protocol, that it is rarely, if ever, questioned. The film-makers still talk about "faithful" and "unfaithful" adaptations without ever realizing that they are really talking about successful and unsuccessful films. Whenever a film becomes a financial or even a critical success, the question of "faithfulness" is given hardly any thought. If the film succeeds on its own merits, it ceases to be problematic. The film-makers are content with the assumption that they have mysteriously captured the "spirit" of the book. The issue goes no farther.

This stubbornly casual, persistently uncritical approach to the problem of film adaptation may help to explain a curious phenomenon. In Ben Hecht's six-hundred-page autobiography, of which a hundred are devoted to a devastating account of a screen writer's life in Hollywood, there appears not a single reference to his best literary adaptation, Samuel Goldwyn's *Wuthering Heights*.[19]

[19] Ben Hecht, *A Child of the Century* (New York, 1954).

4   *Pride and Prejudice*

TO SPEAK OF JANE AUSTEN'S *Pride and Prejudice* is to speak of contradiction, of a scheme in which the claims of conflicting tendencies are ultimately adjusted through a process of moral education. Jane Austen criticism has slowly but surely been working its way from an appreciation of Jane Austen's realism to a recognition of the moral conflicts which inform her ironies. Regardless of the terms of those contradictions, almost every recent commentator proposes a pattern of opposing value-systems which begin in hostility and end in reconciliation. Edwin Muir discusses the plot in terms of "its strict interior causation,"[1] placing it along a general scale of freedom and necessity. Mary Lascelles derives the "war within her" from Jane Austen's irony, "the critical faculty that would not be quieted," and goes on to quote Metcalfe's extension of this principle: "A *rational* woman, exceptional in intellect, unique in wit, found herself in circumstances which were always meagre, and at times *irrational;* and endowed with *fastidiousness on the one hand and enjoyment on the other,* she employed her experience creatively in the service of Comedy"[2] (italics mine). In his brief remarks, R. W. Chapman

[1] Edwin Muir, *The Structure of the Novel* (New York, 1929), p. 45.
[2] Mary Lascelles, *Jane Austen and her Art* (Oxford, 1939), p. 21.

argues that "the subject of her art is not individuals but their inter-action."[3] Samuel Kliger places the antitheses against the wider background of eighteenth-century controversies over "art" and "nature": "Art and reason are the terms on one side of the antithesis; nature and benevolence are the terms on the other side,"[4] and, with particular reference to the shifting relationship between Elizabeth and Darcy, "the partial capitulation of each to the other makes clear that each recognizes that every quality has its corresponding defect."[5] Andrew H. Wright, attempting a survey of the critical literature, concludes that it is most fruitful to approach Jane Austen's irony as a world view centered upon the juxtaposition "of two mutually incompatible views of life."[6]

For C. S. Lewis, Jane Austen's moral irony is derived from a disparity between a moral norm and a deviation from that norm: "Unless there is something about which the author is never ironical, there can be no true irony in the work."[7] Lionel Trilling finds in the novels a troubling terror beneath the skin of Jane Austen's world arising from an exhausting conflict between rest and motion, between life and a kind of vegetable death, reaching its logical outcome in *Mansfield Park*.[8] And finally, Frank O'Connor argues that the essential conflict resides in a continuing opposition between imagination and judgment, with imagination as the spur and judgment the constant rein, until Jane Austen's last published work, *Persuasion*, becomes "the revenge of her imagination on her judgment."[9]

These antitheses are advanced with cogency, an often sensitive practice of hermeneutics, and even with passion. But regardless of their particular content, we find again and again the impulse to

[3] Robert W. Chapman, *Jane Austen: Facts and Problems* (Oxford, 1948).
[4] Samuel Kliger, "Jane Austen's *Pride and Prejudice* in the Eighteenth Century Mode," *University of Toronto Quarterly*, xvi (July, 1947), 359.
[5] *Ibid.*, pp. 366–67.
[6] Andrew H. Wright, *Jane Austen's Novels* (London, 1953), p. 24.
[7] C. S. Lewis, "A Note on Jane Austen," *Essays in Criticism*, iv (October, 1954), 370.
[8] See Lionel Trilling, "Mansfield Park," *Partisan Review*, xxi (September–October, 1954), 504 ff.
[9] Frank O'Connor, "Jane Austen and the Flight from Fancy," *Yale Review*, xlv (Autumn, 1955), 42.

range one set of principles against another. Always the polarities, always the interpenetration of opposites, always the poles attracting each other toward a more or less agreeable center.

It is a curious fact that of the eight statements quoted above, six have appeared since the end of World War II, almost none before. Recent criticism, then, has shown an unusual awareness of the contradictions at the heart of Jane Austen's world, an awareness which is only occasionally apparent in earlier valuations. There has been, on the other hand, a surprising lack of awareness of the film version of *Pride and Prejudice*, released by Metro-Goldwyn-Mayer in 1940, which faithfully embodies the dialectics of Jane Austen's central ironies. What will concern us here, therefore, is how these contradictions, manifested in Jane Austen's structure and stylistics, were transferred to a cinematic version of the novel. That Aldous Huxley received a screen writer's credit, in collaboration with Jane Murfin, for scripting Hunt Stromberg's production, leads us to suspect that the script, embodying the difficult metamorphosis from word to image, received more than the usual care. The reviewers, to be sure, praised the casting and suggested that the actors had made Jane Austen's characters come alive.[10] But none had time to analyze the adaptational process. How was it done?

To begin with, *Pride and Prejudice*, given the special attributes of its style, possesses the essential ingredients of a movie script. Although a film scenario, in the last analysis, provides the rough notations which guide the director, Dore Schary is right when he argues that the screen writer's task is "to sit down and by word create images."[11] John Gassner and Dudley Nichols have shown that the shooting-script, devoid of technical jargon and with literary embellishment, can be profitably read as a separate form.[12] But even in its technical form, the shooting-script, the manual from which the director must build his frames, is an arrangement of words bearing certain characteristics. These characteristics have a

---

[10] See, for example, *Time*, xxxvi (July 29, 1940), 45.

[11] Dore Schary, "Speech Before the National Council of Teachers of English" (MS, November 27, 1953), p. 8.

[12] See John Gassner and Dudley Nichols, *Twenty Best Film Plays* (New York, 1943).

remarkable resemblance to the components of Jane Austen's style —a lack of particularity, an absence of metaphorical language, an omniscient point of view, a dependency on dialogue to reveal character, an insistence on absolute clarity. When Aunt Gardiner suggests a trip to the Lake country, Elizabeth Bennet says, "We *will* know where we have gone—we *will* recollect what we have seen. Lakes, mountains, rivers shall not be jumbled together in our imaginations; nor when we attempt to describe any particular scene, will we begin quarreling about its relative situation." Regardless of locale, Elizabeth tries, with varying degrees of success, to see things clearly. So insistent is the principle that, by the end of the novel, this penchant for clarity has become an ethical as well as an aesthetic standard. "We *will* know where we have gone." Elizabeth's proposal is the hidden motto behind every movie's story-conference.

Yet in Jane Austen, as in the script, clarity is not the same as particularity. Any number of commentators have pointed out the absence of minute physical detail which accompanies Jane Austen's absolute fidelity to the psychological timbre of her characters. Léonie Villard suggests the distinction when she writes:

> If there flows on each page a fragrance of youth and of feminine grace, if we always know, and in their most subtle nuances, the color of the thought and mood of an Elizabeth or an Emma, we know nothing of the elegance of their attire or the color of their gowns.[13]

That the exclusion of physical minutiae like the color of Elizabeth's gown was deliberate has been sufficiently demonstrated by Miss Lascelles,[14] and by Jane Austen herself. In her famous letter to Cassandra, following her visit to a painting exhibition in Spring Gardens, Jane Austen writes of finding "a small portrait of Mrs. Bingley [Jane Bennet] . . . " but none of Elizabeth. With a typical combination of whimsy and seriousness, she goes on to elucidate her discovery: "Mrs. Bingley is exactly herself—size, shaped face,

---

[13] Léonie Villard, *Jane Austen: Sa Vie et Son Oeuvre* (Thèse pour le Doctorat-ès-Lettres, l'Université de Paris, 1914), p. 300. The translations from Miss Villard are my own.

[14] Lascelles, p. 112 ff.

features, and sweetness; there never was a greater likeness. She is dressed in a white gown with green ornaments, which convinces me of what I had always supposed, that green was a favourite colour with her. I dare say Mrs. D. will be in yellow."[15]

What is the effect of this rigid suppression of particular detail? On one level, Miss Villard suggests that what we lose by not knowing the color of Elizabeth's clothing is more than compensated for by what we *do* know about the color of her thought. But in order to explore the appropriateness of this technique for film adaptation, we must examine its characteristics in more detail.

We need hardly labor the point that physical descriptions in *Pride and Prejudice* are generalized. The great houses at Netherfield, Rosings, Pemberly are never rendered with the exact brush strokes of the painter. At our first glimpse of Rosings, we are told "It was a handsome modern building, well situated on rising ground." The kind of sudden detail which appears in our first view of Mr. Collins' Parsonage—"the green pales, and the laurel hedge"—is so rare that it underscores the general absence of color and greenery.

That the physical descriptions of the characters are equally bare of color and texture is also evident. Bingley "was good looking and gentlemanlike; he had a pleasant countenance, and easy, unaffected manners." Darcy, on his first appearance, draws the attention of the room "by his fine, tall, person, handsome features, noble mien . . . . The gentlemen pronounced him to be a fine figure of a man, the ladies declared he was much handsomer than Mr. Bingley . . . ." Lady Catherine de Bourgh is presented as "a tall, large woman, with strongly marked features, which might once have been handsome." Yet the sparse detail in no way diminishes the imaginative force of the characterization, for, as we shall see, personality achieves a density of its own which, if not pictorial, is nonetheless highly effective. Through a kind of thorough psychological delineation, through a fidelity to "the color of the thought," Jane Austen's characters, to borrow E. M. Forster's definition, are seen in the "round."

The absence of metaphorical language goes hand in hand with

[15] William and Richard Arthur Austen-Leigh, *Jane Austen: Her Life and Letters* (New York, 1913).

the lack of particularity. Jane Austen never revealed the reasons for her strategy here, but Miss Lascelles has suggested that if Jane Austen's style is devoid of metaphor, then hackneyed figures of speech, on the other hand, are constantly attributed to characters whom we are intended to dislike. Miss Lascelles speculates on the possibility that Jane Austen was wary of the figure's tendency to "fossilize" once it had served its immediate emotional purpose. Whether or not hackneyed words and phrases cropped up in the conversation she heard around her or in the phraseology of contemporary novelists, Jane Austen seems to have been repelled by "a general and insidious misuse of language in the interests of an ugly smartness," which produces "much the same sort of unpleasant sensation as seeing a tool misused."[16] Whatever else we may say of it, her style is *clean*. And when an occasional figure does appear—like the concealed simile, "time and her aunt moved slowly"—it strikes with unusual force.

At first glance, this poverty of specific detail would seem to handicap the film-maker. But, paradoxically, it ends by working in his favor. In the first place, he is not troubled by the loss of style which we find, for example, when one adapts Emily Brontë and Liam O'Flaherty to the screen, since the metaphoric language on which these authors depend cannot be transmuted into the film medium. When an author depends on resemblances as an organizing principle, a large part of himself is inevitably left behind once the plastic replaces the literary mode. In the second place, the film-maker, given only clues in the narrative, is forced to fall back on his own resources, to invent his details for himself. In adapting Jane Austen to the screen, the wardrobe, coiffure, and art departments were able to fulfill their offices with an unusually clear conscience. Since setting, clothing, and styles are almost invariably given more loving care in Hollywood than formal pictorial composition, the studio research departments often turn in more authentic sketches of physical reality than their colleagues do of psychological or social reality.

Pride and Prejudice, as we shall see, manages to retain Jane Austen's human insights, but her plot line is constantly reinforced in the film by images of physical reality which the M-G-M pro-

[16] Lascelles, p. 114.

duction crew had to imagine for itself. Not only did it have to dig back into its files for authentic styles, costumes, architecture, props, garden arrangements, but it had to supply aural details as well. In the novel, we never learn the names of the books which fill the library at Pemberly, nor the selections which Elizabeth plays on the pianoforte, nor the tunes which Mary sings at Nether-field. But if on the screen the books can remain anonymous, the music cannot. Here the research department reveals its talent for historical accuracy. Probably taking its clue from a single line in the novel which has Miss Bingley singing a few Scotch airs, the film-makers have Mary singing "Flow Gently, Sweet Afton." This song is a shrewd choice, since it combines proper sentimentality with historical probability. Its author, Robert Burns, died in 1796, the very year in which Jane Austen began writing her *First Impressions,* what ultimately became the first draft of *Pride and Prejudice.* The film is filled with dozens of similar details which the film-makers, given free rein by Jane Austen's spatial generalities, were at liberty to supply.

Jane Austen's novel further resembles a shooting-script in that its point of view is omniscient. Only in rare instances has the camera narrated a series of events from a single point of view; that is to say, from an angle where the camera eye is identical with the eye of a character. Traditionally, the camera has resembled the narrative mind in Tolstoy, say, where we move from one point of view to another, rather than Lambert Strether's unitary vision in *The Ambassadors.* The camera, like Jane Austen, to use Wright's formulation, "is by turns omniscient and ignorant, humble and sententious, direct and oblique, the dramatist and the teller of tales."[17] The book opens with the classic conversation between Mr. and Mrs. Bennet which reveals the arrival of the new tenants at Netherfield Park. Elizabeth, who is mentioned in Chapter I, does not make her appearance until Chapter II. It is true that from this point on, Lizzy's is the dominant sensibility, since we rarely know more than she does about Wickham or Darcy or Bingley. Yet, when it suits her purpose, Jane Austen is not above moving inside another character's mind: "Darcy had never been so bewitched by any woman as he was by her. He really believed, that were it not

[17] Wright, p. 36.

for the inferiority of her connections, he should be in some danger." Though Jane Austen, like the camera's point of view, is generally observing events through Elizabeth's eyes, she often sees Elizabeth as she appears to other characters (as in our example of Darcy). The film has no difficulty approximating this method.

Finally, the novel resembles the scenario in its heavy reliance on dialogue to advance plot and reveal character. Frank O'Connor observes the subtlety with which hints and suggestions in the opening chapters reveal essential details. We are given the conversation between Mr. and Mrs. Bennet, then between Elizabeth and her parents; random comments by the other girls as one by one they make their appearance; narrative summary depicting the courtesy calls by Bingley and Mr. Bennet; the first Assembly Ball; the discussion with the Lucas clan, following the ball, in which Darcy and Bingley's behavior are weighed and judged—until, by Chapter VI, we are surprised to discover that almost without our knowing it, we have acquired all the pertinent data we need about the *dramatis personae* of Netherfield and Longbourn. The dialogue throughout serves to advance the plot, heighten character, provide comments on the action, set up ironies and reversals.

So much of the dramatic revelation occurs in dialogue that it was not very difficult for Helen Jerome to cull enough Jane Austen lines to use intact in her stage adaptation of the novel, the adaptation which provided the immediate model for the filmmakers.

In 1942, Margaret Kennedy, gently deploring the division of labor to which screen writers had been subjected, speculated on what it would be like to bring *Pride and Prejudice* to the screen:

Jane Austen, had she lived today, might have been asked to supply the "story" of *Pride and Prejudice* without any of the characterization, any of the idiomatic touches, which lie in her dialogue. *Mr. Collins proposes to Elizabeth* would have been thought sufficient. No more from her, as an artist, would have been required. And the actual proposal of Mr. Collins might then have been written by Mr. Ernest Hemmingway [sic].[18]

18 Margaret Kennedy, *The Mechanized Muse* (London, 1942), p. 25.

If Miss Kennedy had seen the production directed by Robert Z. Leonard, released just two years before the appearance of her book, she would doubtless have recognized that she had sold Aldous Huxley and Jane Murfin short, not to speak of Mr. Hemingway. With few exceptions, as we shall see, the dialogue which appears in the film is Jane Austen's own. It was, in fact, the screen writers' respect for it which prompted one reviewer to praise the film for "some of the most literate dialogue ever spoken on a sound track."[19]

If, then, Jane Austen suppresses her specific knowledge of what Jane Bennet looks like, an image which she could find exactly delineated in a portrait at the Spring Gardens exhibition, she is entirely scrupulous about permitting the reader to imagine Jane for himself. But where the reader can fill in his own portrait, the film-maker must render the scene in every detail. Paradoxically, the absence of pictorial effects in the novel, as we have seen, encourages "plastic thinking," in Pudovkin's sense of the term. Léonie Villard clearly summarizes the aesthetic advantages of Jane Austen's technique:

> The delicacy of her composition would become a useless merit if the characters were not detached from a simplified and neutral background. When the artist, working on a canvas of restricted dimensions—and here it is necessary to remember the primitives —minutely studies his figures and wishes to center upon them all the interest, he deliberately subdues the background. A novelist who imposes upon himself very narrow limits ought to follow the same procedure.[20]

Obviously, the film-maker, bound by the demands of photographic realism, cannot really approximate the method of the primitive painters. When he shows a character in close-up, to be sure, the background for the moment blurs and becomes indistinct, but his characters are always acting before a setting in which the details are not "neutral and simplified," but absolutely precise. Yet, ever since Charlotte Brontë, critics have pressed the analogy be-

[19] See note 10 above.
[20] Villard, p. 334.

tween Jane Austen's methods and the methods of painting. Charlotte Brontë, no champion of her predecessor's work, nevertheless found in *Pride and Prejudice* an "accurate daguerrotyped portrait of a commonplace face," and "a Chinese fidelity."[21] But we have already seen that Jane Austen gives us few details which can be considered painterly. We can only conclude that Jane Austen somehow rendered the psychological pressure of her characters with such intensity that for generations—from Sir Walter Scott and Charlotte Brontë to the film reviewers who swore that the characters of *Pride and Prejudice* had jumped full blown onto the screen—readers have retained powerful *physical* images of Jane Austen's characters. That these characters leave so persistent a sensory impression would seem nothing less than a remarkable act of conjuring, were not Jane Austen's intentions so serious. How does she achieve this effect? How, in Virginia Woolf's phrase, does she stimulate us "to supply what is not there?"[22]

Much of the answer can be elicited by reverting to our earlier statements about Jane Austen's irony. Without rehearsing the intricacies of a familiar plot, we may remind ourselves that *Pride and Prejudice* is essentially the story of Fitzwilliam Darcy and Elizabeth Bennet, the first embodying the principle of pride, the second the principle of prejudice, each of which endows its protagonist with the flaw of moral blindness. The lovers proceed through a series of misunderstandings and revelations which culminate in the two central climaxes of the book—Elizabeth's rejection of Darcy, completing the initial movement of the lovers away from each other; and Elizabeth's acceptance of Darcy, completing the final movement of the lovers toward each other. Elizabeth primarily, but Darcy, too, receives a moral education through the shock of continual reversal, which brings her to an understanding of what Darcy is really like. Wickham's deception, Bingley's departure from Netherfield, the visit to Rosings, Darcy's letter, the visit to Pemberly, Darcy's role in Lydia's elopement—all reveal aspects of Darcy about which Elizabeth has been mistaken. For each of the lovers, the veils of appearance are drawn back, one by one, to reveal the other's reality. Misunderstanding gives way to

---

[21] Quoted in Wright, p. 7, p. 8.
[22] Quoted in Lascelles, p. 134.

understanding. Of Jane's feelings for Bingley, Darcy writes: "I remained convinced from the evening's scrutiny, that though she received his attentions with pleasure, she did not invite them by any participation of sentiment." But in the same letter, he reveals that Wickham, when Georgiana was fifteen, so far recommended himself to her "whose affectionate heart retained a strong impression of kindness to her as a child, that she was persuaded to believe herself in love, and to consent to an elopement . . . Mr. Wickham's chief object was unquestionably my sister's fortune . . . ." If Darcy in his pride was mistaken about Jane, Elizabeth in her prejudice was mistaken about Wickham. "You taught me a lesson," Darcy tells his betrothed at the end, but the moral education has been mutual.

Now this process has been appraised from several points of view, has been given a number of varied interpretations—the shifting conflict between appearance and reality; insincerity and sincerity; complexity and simplicity; moral blindness and moral awareness; rest and motion; economic coercion and individual choice; art, reason, control, *vs.* nature, feeling, spontaneity; judgment and imagination—all encompassing a wide range of epistemology, ethics, and aesthetics. Yet in these contradictions, oppositions, syntheses, we find an even more general and controlling pattern which is at the heart of Jane Austen's irony. Chevalier, in his study of Anatole France, has perhaps come closest to defining it:

> Irony characterizes the attitude of one who, when confronted with the choice of two things that are mutually exclusive, chooses both. Which is but another way of saying that he chooses neither. He cannot bring himself to give up one for the other, and he gives up both. But he reserves the right to derive from each the greatest possible passive enjoyment. And this enjoyment is Irony.[23]

Lionel Trilling endorses this view when he suggests that Jane Austen caricatures Lady Bertram not so much because she dislikes what Lady Bertram represents but because she likes it too much.

[23] Haakon M. Chevalier, *The Ironic Temper: Anatole France and His Time* (New York, 1932), p. 42; quoted in Wright, p. 25.

The definition which introduces Trilling's essay echoes Chevalier: "What we may call Jane Austen's first or basic irony is the recognition of the fact that spirit is not free, that it is conditioned, that it is limited by circumstance. . . . Her next and consequent irony has reference to the fact that only by reason of this anomaly does spirit have virtue and meaning."[24]

But if this abstraction is accurate, it would be artistically worthless unless Jane Austen had found a structural analogue to embody her meaning and from which her meaning, therefore, would be indistinguishable. That such a structural pattern exists is suggested by Miss Lascelles who notes, with typical precision: "This pattern is formed by diverging and converging lines, by the movement of two people who are impelled apart until they reach a climax of mutual hostility, and thereafter bend their courses towards mutual understanding and amity."[25] To anyone thinking of the book in cinematic terms, the word "movement" is inevitably arresting. For the converging and diverging lines perceived by Miss Lascelles correspond exactly to the movements and rhythms of a dance, movements and rhythms which, I suggest, have been caught by the film.

David Daiches sees the dance movement in *Pride and Prejudice* as a kind of ritual order, a serious attempt to ward off the economic insecurities of Jane Austen's world. While Daiches does less than justice to both Karl Marx and Jane Austen in equating the two, his observations on the dance paradigm are highly suggestive. It is true that Jane Austen "exposes the economic basis of social behavior,"[26] and that there is every justification for Lord David Cecil's observation on the economic-moral paradox in Jane Austen's novels: "It was wrong to marry for money, but it was silly to marry without it."[27] But since the concepts of class struggle and labor-value are entirely alien to Jane Austen, any number of economic determinists before and since Marx could more easily

[24] Trilling, p. 492.
[25] Lascelles, p. 160.
[26] David Daiches, "Jane Austen, Karl Marx and the Aristocratic Dance," *American Scholar*, XVII (Summer, 1948), 289.
[27] See Lord David Cecil, *Jane Austen*, the Leslie Stephen Lecture, 1935 (Cambridge, 1936).

stand the comparison.[28] Yet Daiches' insight into the pattern of the "ballet movement" concretizes what many readers must feel about Jane Austen's structural rhythm.[29] "It is a stately dance on the lawn," says Daiches, "but all around there are the dark trees, the shadows . . . . We are never allowed to forget . . . what a serious business this dancing is. One false step can be fatal."

In the film sequence depicting the Assembly Ball, all the dramatic relationships are enunciated in terms of dance relationships. Since it can depict continuous motion more effectively than novels, the camera has a certain advantage when it comes to rendering dance rhythms. Ballet movements and Mozart opera are both designed for the visual as well as the aural faculties. In order to effect an imaginative link between the two, Jane Austen must alternate dialogue with narrative description, whereas the film has the advantage of simultaneity. Since the film-makers had to improvise, or rather construct, plastic images for movements which Jane Austen merely suggests, since they had to make us see "what is not there," let us look in detail at the Assembly Ball sequence.

The sequence opens with a long shot of the ballroom in which all of Meryton society is gathered. Darcy and Bingley have not yet arrived, and Mrs. Bennet (in a close two-shot) voices her concern to Mrs. Philips, since Mrs. Bennet has earlier expressed a desire to marry Jane off to Bingley. Then, when the music begins, we see Wickham dancing with young Lydia, who appears vivacious, animated, almost wild, thoroughly enjoying herself. The dance has the symmetry of a quadrille, the dancers moving alternately toward and away from each other, exchanging partners. Elizabeth is now seen dancing with Wickham, engaged in a kind of party prattle which neither takes very seriously. Elizabeth (played by Greer Garson) asks, "Shall I tell you what I thought the moment I saw you?" Before she can answer, she dances away, swept up by the intricate steps of the dance. When she returns to her partner,

[28] For example, the Utopian Socialists, Robert Owen and Comte de Saint-Simon, contemporaries of Jane Austen, in their attempts to remove economic evils through moral suasion, would more closely approximate Jane Austen's world. But there is no evidence that she was aware of their existence.

[29] Daiches, p. 291.

Wickham asks for her answer. "I'm sorry," she says, "I forget."

Before the dance is over, we see Bingley (Bruce Lester) and Darcy (Laurence Olivier) entering the ballroom, the one affable and obliging, the other distant and aloof. Sir William Lucas, Charlotte's father, makes the initial approach and officially welcomes the newcomers to the ball. Catching sight of Bingley and Darcy, Mrs. Bennet, like a nervous wardrobe mistress, goes into a flutter: "Kitty—Kitty, your dress is too *décolleté*. Lydia—Lydia, there's perspiration on your nose. Don't get so hot—it's very unladylike." Darcy, not deigning to dance with any of the eligible Meryton ladies, is seen with Miss Bingley, Charles' sister. Again, we see Lydia and Kitty, each dancing with a handsome army officer. The roving camera cuts to Mrs. Bennet and her cronies, who exchange the latest gossip, appraising Mr. Darcy's looks and lineage: "His mother was a daughter of the Marquis of Scarborough," one of the cronies whispers confidentially. Lizzy, standing with Jane, and observing Darcy, criticizes his aloofness. Sir William approaches the sisters with Bingley and formally introduces him to Jane. Jane, who possesses better looks and more poise than her sisters, is qualified to dance with Meryton's aristocrats. Lizzy, still not so qualified, dances off with Denny, an army officer. Before Bingley moves away, Mrs. Bennet manages to inject the proper note of flattery: "Mr. Bingley, we're all so delighted that you've taken Netherfield. Having it standing empty was a loss to the whole neighborhood. Like an oyster shell without an oyster in it."

Again we are treated to a shot of mothers and daughters standing about, hoping for the coveted invitation. An ugly girl is seen scratching her neck; she is sharply rebuked for being unladylike. Now Lizzy appears with Denny, then Miss Bingley with Darcy, then Jane with Charles. Of all the couples thus surveyed by the camera, Jane and Charles Bingley seem most compatible. Bingley tells Jane that he admires her because she has done an extraordinary thing: "You have talked to me about all your friends in Meryton without saying one malicious word." Why not? Jane asks, when all her friends are so pleasant. "That," says Bingley, "never prevented anyone from talking maliciously."

Now the camera cuts to a table laden with a generous display of food. Caroline Bingley approaches Jane and Charles, and draws

Jane away. Darcy is still polite and aloof, detached from the proceedings of the ballroom. Miss Bingley walks with Jane, the camera tracking along in front of them, and Miss Bingley takes advantage of the opportunity to invite Miss Bennet to Netherfield.

The next frame reveals an alcove just off the dance floor. Lizzy enters, accompanied by her friend Charlotte. Charlotte expresses her relief: in the alcove no one will notice that they have no partners. Lizzy commiserates, unconsciously indicting the exhausting strain of the dance: "Oh, why is England cursed with so many more women than men!" Just then, Bingley and Darcy approach the edge of the dance floor nearest the alcove, within earshot of Charlotte and Elizabeth. The girls cannot help overhearing Bingley encourage Darcy to dance with one of the Meryton ladies. True, Bingley argues, he has monopolized the prettiest girl in the room, but her sister Elizabeth, after all, is not unattractive, and she does have a lively wit. Darcy is unkind: "A provincial lady with a lively wit. Heaven preserve us." When Bingley presses his point, Darcy remonstrates, "I'm in no humor tonight to give consequence to the middle classes at play." Overhearing this, Lizzy grimaces, a mocking pantomime of Darcy's superior attitude. Sir William Lucas approaches Charles and Darcy. Trying to make conversation, he remarks on the excellence of the dancing, "In my opinion, it's one of the first refinements of polished society." Again, Darcy's rebuttal is cruel: "At the added advantage, sir, of being one of the first refinements of savages."

At this point, Sir William discovers Lizzy in the alcove behind the curtains. Just as he has earlier introduced Bingley and Jane, he now attempts to introduce Darcy and Lizzy. Piqued by what she has heard, Elizabeth refuses to dance with Darcy. A moment later, Wickham approaches, asks Elizabeth to be his partner. In Darcy's presence, Lizzy accepts, making her insult unmistakably clear. There is a terse sign of recognition between Wickham and Darcy. The camera pans with Wickham and Elizabeth, who now dance off to the tune of a polka mazurka. Lizzy inquires about Darcy's curt acknowledgment. Wickham explains that Darcy has harmed him. Wickham's father had been a steward on the estates of the elder Darcy. Darcy's father had been fond of Wickham as a young boy, and before his death had unofficially promised to subsidize Wickham's entering the ministry. After the death of the elder Darcy, the son had refused to make good on the promise because the understanding had never been made official. Elizabeth, now ready to believe the worst of Darcy, is shocked by the story. Wickham changes the subject by remarking that he is surprised to find that Meryton is up to date on its dance steps. Lizzy, still smarting from her encounter with Darcy, replies, "You underrate us, Mr. Wickham. Meryton is abreast with everything—everything except insolence and bad manners. Those London fashions we do not admire."

A final close-up of Darcy watching Lizzy and Wickham concludes the sequence. Just before the fade-out, we can see that Darcy's attitude has changed slightly. Humbled by Elizabeth, he is beginning tó find her more attractive.

Even the most casual reader of Jane Austen's novel will observe several significant changes in this transposition from book to screen. A number of incidents which appear at different points in the novel are here drawn together into a unified space. For example, the novel's Assembly Ball occurs in Chapter III. But the brusque encounter between Wickham and Darcy does not take place until Chapter XV, while Wickham's complaint about Darcy occurs in Chapter XVI. Elizabeth refuses to dance with Darcy not at the Assembly Ball, but at the Netherfield reception in Chapter X. In the second place, lines which have their model in the novel are often slightly altered to make them more pertinent. Darcy's line, "I'm in no humor tonight to give consequence to the middle classes at play," originally reads, "I am in no humor at present to give consequence to young ladies who are slighted by other men." In the third place, a number of lines have been added to establish continuity between the disparate events which have here been joined in a single sequence. Mrs. Bennet's strained simile, comparing Netherfield to an oyster; Bingley's comment on the absence of malicious gossip in Jane; Elizabeth's comment on the insolence and bad manners of London—these have no precedent in the book. Yet these addenda do not have the effect that often occurs in filmed novels. They do not, in this case, alter any of the essential meanings in the original. The Huxley-Murfin additional dialogue bears an unusual ring of probability. It represents the kind of thing which Jane Austen *might* have said. In other ways, Jane Bennet's lack of maliciousness, Darcy's aristocratic insolence, Mrs. Bennet's fluttery callowness are more than adequately established in the novel. In short, though these new lines do not have an exact precedent in the book, they do have reasonable equivalents. Mrs. Bennet's simile on oysters is precisely the kind of "fossilized phraseology" which, as we have seen, Miss Lascelles finds Jane Austen persistently placing in the mouths of characters of whom she disapproves.

Moreover, by combining snippets of scenes which are strung out through the first sixteen chapters, the Assembly Ball sequence achieves a flowing unity of place which is lacking in the original. Not only is the result more economical for the film-makers but it also compresses the chief plot points as subtly as the first six chapters do for Frank O'Connor. Mobilized for the rhythms of the dance, the camera dollies and cranes and pans across the ballroom, roving from couple to couple, seeing them now from one point of view, now from another, like the eye of an omniscient observer, beading the several frames on the continuous movement of the dance.

This mounting technique becomes the film's analogue for the ironic epigram. Two elements are placed in opposition to each other which in combination form a *tertium quid*. "But do you always write such charming long letters . . . Mr. Darcy," asks the novel's Caroline.

"They are generally long; but whether always charming it is not for me to determine," replies Darcy. Just as Darcy's syntax replaces the continuity of "charming long" with a new and revealing opposition, the film-makers break up the continuity of the dance with a medium shot of Wickham and Lizzy, say, and a close shot of the rejected, and dejected, Darcy.

There is hardly a dramatic and psychological relationship in either the film or novel's opening events which is not realized here in terms of a dance relationship. Jane and Bingley's meeting and coming together; Kitty and Lydia's preference for handsome soldiers; Mrs. Bennet's nervous grooming of the girls for the marriage block; Charlotte's feeling of inadequacy in the social game; maternal competition for the eligible males; Elizabeth's hostility to

Darcy's snobbishness; her consequent willingness to become blinded by Wickham's prevarication; her retaliatory snub in declining Darcy's first offer—all these are carried out in terms of dance ritual—the taking, refusing, and searching out of partners, the ceremonial rhythms which join couples and cast them asunder. Moreover, the analogy becomes an accurate forecast of narrative events. Giving credence to Wickham's story, Lizzy will, in fact, refuse Darcy's first offer of marriage; following the ruse of sending Jane to Netherfield in the rain, Jane and Bingley will actually fall in love; after a number of flirtations, Lydia will really elope with a soldier. Everything is here except Mr. Bennet's sardonic wit, and Mr. Collins, who is held in reserve for the novel's next major movement. For the moment, choreography becomes an exact analogue of the social game.

Aside from the recurrence of actual parties, balls, formal entertainments, the novel provides ample grounds for using the device in this way. References to the accomplishments of dancing (as well as to the other social graces) appear frequently: "It would surely be much more rational if conversation instead of dancing were made the order of the day."

"Much more rational, my dear Caroline, I dare say," replies Charles, "but it would not be near so much like a ball."

Mr. Collins' dancing is exactly suited to his character: "awkward and solemn, apologizing instead of attending, and often moving wrong without being aware of it. . . . The moment of her release from him was ecstasy." This, in a nutshell, is Lizzy's dramatic relationship to Collins as it unfolds in both the book and film.

By extension, the pattern of the dance applies to the formal modes of walking, standing, performing. In the garden at Netherfield, Miss Bingley tries to slight Elizabeth by obstructing her walk, thus breaking up the graceful picture she presents. When Darcy tries to effect a more courteous arrangement, Lizzy cries out, "No, no; stay where you are. You are charmingly grouped, and appear to uncommon advantage."

The formal demands are exacting, even exhausting, the extremes parodied in Caroline Bingley's prescription for the accomplished lady: "A woman must have a thorough knowledge of music, singing, drawing, dancing, and the modern languages, to deserve the word; and besides all this, she must possess a certain something in her air and manner of walking, the tone of her voice, her address and expressions, or the word will be but half-deserved." When Darcy adds, "the improvement of her mind by extensive reading," Elizabeth retorts, "I am no longer surprised at your knowing *only* six accomplished women. I rather wonder now at your knowing *any*."

It may be objected, of course, that what the sequence of the dance gains in compression and plastic clarity, it loses in pace. Jane Austen would doubtless have been disturbed by the *speed* with which the conventional limits of the film demand that her story be told. Samuel Kliger points out the significance of the banter between Darcy and Bingley on the speed of Bingley's writing habits: "As the banter grows, it becomes clear that Darcy reproves 'precipitance' (it is his own word) in letter-writing and in social conduct."[30] The issue takes on social import only because "the period correlated art with morals." Jane Austen's way is much more akin to Darcy's careful pace than to Bingley's facility (though Darcy's letter to Lizzy, like the novel itself, proves that careful workmanship can give the effect of ease and polish).

But the film, by convention, is bound to Bingley's way. True, Elizabeth's mind evolves slowly. Her perceptions are like a lambent pool over which the light of experience plays quietly. In spite of her vivacity, her moral education proceeds slowly. She must meditate upon and savor each new aspect of experience, and the stronger her regard for Darcy grows, the greater becomes her introspection. But where the novel's Elizabeth can stop to meditate on a letter or conversation, the film's Elizabeth must hurtle forward with the looping progress of the visual action. The film's final criteria must be cinematic, however, not linguistic; in these terms, the entire film is as carefully modulated as our one example of the Assembly Ball. Since the film cannot adequately render the quality of thought, we see, instead, an Elizabeth who is in constant motion. Yet even here the film-makers have done no violence to that aspect of Elizabeth which balances her meditative side. "We think of Elizabeth Bennet as in physical movement," says Lionel Trilling, "her love of dancing confirms our belief that she moves

[30] Kliger, p. 360.

gracefully . . . ."[31] Again, in spite of the necessarily quickened pace of film narrative, the film-makers have succeeded in preserving an essential ingredient of Miss Austen's novel.

We are now in a position to understand how the characters appear in the "round," how Jane Austen renders "the color of the thought" with such compelling density that it takes on, through a kind of coalescence, an almost physical reality. The novel, among other things, patterns its drama on the intricacies of the dance, thus suggesting an identity between psychological and physical movement. We come to know Lizzy's mind so well that, like Charlotte Brontë and the film-makers, we think we also know her face and form. In such an organic process, dance and dancers, form and content, can no longer be distinguished.

We have seen, then, the stately dance in its transmuted filmic form. But where are the shadows, the dark trees, of which David Daiches speaks? They are not in the photography or sets. These are lit with confidence and assurance, as if in this world there were no night. Then where are they? They are in the eyes of the actors —in Olivier's Darcy, in Karen Morley's Charlotte, in Edmund Gwenn's Mr. Bennet. *Pride and Prejudice*, like all Jane Austen's other novels, ends happily for a pair of lovers who are at first driven apart by moral flaws. Like Fanny Price and Catherine Morland and Elinor Dashwood and Emma Woodhouse, Elizabeth is finally reconciled to her elegant young man in such a cloud of moral felicity that one hardly dares examine the alternatives. Yet the shadow of alternatives does hover over the shifting fate of the lovers, and we must attend to it.

What would happen if the lucky turns, proper accidents, and right revelations did not eventuate to support that "strict interior causation" which Edwin Muir sees? What happens to the girl who cannot dance? To the man who does not find a woman he loves? The results are everywhere for Elizabeth to see. For the ugly, scratching girl at the ball, the fate of a wallflower, doomed to stand outside the circle of dancers. For Mr. Bennet, the fate of an intelligent man married to a woman he cannot respect. Aware of his position, but powerless to escape it, he is reduced to ironic comment on a game which he cannot change. For Charlotte, a

[31] Trilling, p. 497.

morally repellent marriage to Mr. Collins, and the dogged, loveless credo which she persuades herself to accept in order to survive. In the film, as in the book, Charlotte attempts to answer Lizzy's disturbing objection to her loveless match: "Happiness, Lizzy? In marriage happiness is just a matter of chance. . . . Where ignorance is bliss, Lizzy, if one's to spend one's life with a person, it's best to know as little as possible of his defects. After all, one will find them out soon enough." For Lydia, a fugitive life with an irresponsible spouse: "They were always moving from place to place in quest of a cheap situation, and always spending more than they ought." For Darcy, a life of loveless decorum. Or, as in real life for Jane and Cassandra Austen, a spinster's loneliness.

It is often easy to forget that Jane Austen was not ignorant of these perils. Preferring spinsterhood to loveless marriage, Jane and her sister Cassandra never married after the men they loved died sudden and premature deaths. Jane Austen had unmarried friends who lived the shabby genteel lives of governesses in prosperous homes. And Jane's aunt, Philadelphia Austen, was packed off to India for a dismal marriage to an Army surgeon. Small wonder that Elizabeth Bennet, caught up in trying to meet the requirements of a rigorous dance, like so many of Jane Austen's other heroines, often verges on sheer exhaustion: "The more I see of the world," she says to Jane, "the more am I dissatisfied with it; and every day confirms my belief of the inconsistency of human characters, and of the little dependence that can be placed on the appearance of either merit or sense." And later, to Aunt Gardiner, she says of men in general, "I am sick of them all." She welcomes the prospect of relief in the more natural surroundings of the lake country, where the formalities of the dance may be dispensed with: "Adieu to disappointment and spleen! What are men to rocks and mountains?"

The film retains these overtones—in the conversations between Elizabeth and Charlotte; in the constant pressure of formal occasions; in Charlotte's marriage to the insufferable Mr. Collins; but most of all in Laurence Olivier's face. We see the shadow in Darcy's utter boredom, in his solitary acts of standing alone or writing letters, in his dancing with Caroline, for whom he has no regard, in his proposing to Elizabeth when, for the first time, through his formal pride, there show glimmers of pain and tenderness. By the end we know that without Lizzy, Darcy is doomed to a life of proud and granite-like loneliness. It is a tribute to the director Robert Z. Leonard, and the men responsible for casting, that the same actor was chosen to play Darcy who just a year before had played Heathcliff with equal success. Behind the stiff formality of Darcy's face and dress, there smolders the anguish of Emily Brontë's stable boy.

In rendering the quality of Jane Austen's intentions, in finding cinematic equivalents for what Jane Austen, by choice, merely implied, the film-makers successfully rethink the material in terms of their own medium. The screen writers, reading closely, find the same converging and diverging lines as Miss Lascelles and, like David Daiches, divine the meaning of Jane Austen's aristocratic dance.

From the film-makers' technique of establishing an identity between the movements of the dance and the pattern of the plot, and the consequent fusing of theme and medium, follows everything else that one may say about the additions, deletions, and alterations which occur in the mutation from book to film. On the whole, the additions bind together disparate events and lend them visual and aural density; the deletions tighten the story line and drop peripheral characters or meditative passages; alterations emend the inevitable discrepancies which result from the first two. Yet, with few exceptions, these mutations, like those in the Assembly Ball sequence, do not alter the meanings of Jane Austen's novel.

At first glance, the two opening sequences—Mrs. Bennet gathering up her brood in Meryton, and the carriage race with the Lucases—seem to be mere appendages. The scene in the drapery shop, in which the proprietor suggests either the "shell pink gossamer muslin, or the figured damask"; the discovery of Darcy and the Bingleys drawing up in their carriage to the inn across the street; Aunt Philips' breathless arrival with the news that Bingley and Darcy, the new tenant at Netherfield and his guest, are both rich and available; the unwelcome appearance of Lady Lucas to buy damask for Charlotte's new gown; the competitive chatter between Lady Lucas and Mrs. Bennet (Lady Lucas to Charlotte:

"You may not have beauty, my love, but you have character—and some men prefer it." Mrs. Bennet: "How true, Mrs. Lucas. That's why girls who have both are doubly fortunate. Come, my dears."); the rush to collect the other girls so that Mrs. Bennet can return at once to urge Mr. Bennet to call on Mr. Bingley; picking up the bespectacled Mary, who is reading Burke's *Of the Sublime and Beautiful* in a bookshop window; then Lydia and Kitty, who are watching a Punch and Judy show with the soldiers, Denny and Wickham; the hustling of Mrs. Bennet's bevy into the family carriage—all these precede the conversation between Mr. and Mrs. Bennet which, in the novel, initiates the action.

On closer examination, however, we find that the sequence is not so much an addition as a transposition of incidents. We learn later in the book that the girls are in the habit of going to Meryton three or four times a week. We learn that Mrs. Lucas and Mrs. Bennet will have their daughters competing for the favor of Bingley and Darcy. We discover that Mary is bookish and slightly affected, that Lydia and Kitty are flighty and flirtatious. On the other hand, while some of the dialogue is derived from later conversations, some of it is new, but the two are blended so skilfully that we are not aware of a clash in style. The Punch and Judy show is added, but it is precisely the kind of entertainment at which one would normally find the girls with two soldiers on leave. Like Lizzy's comment on the insolence of London in the Assembly Ball sequence, these additions are credible because they lie entirely within the probabilities of Jane Austen's world.

Similarly, the carriage race between the Bennets and the Lucases on the open country road does not appear in the novel. And yet it has more than a merely capricious function. First the Lucas carriage overtakes the Bennet carriage. Stung by the gesture, Mrs. Bennet, never one to be left behind, orders her coachman to storm ahead, until the Bennet carriage is again well in the lead. The visual competition becomes an exact forecast of what is to come. At first, the Lucases will take the lead in the social contest when Charlotte marries Collins, entailing the Longbourn estate away from the Bennet clan. But in the end, with the betrothal of Jane to Bingley and Elizabeth to Darcy, the Bennets will emerge with an unshakable social advantage. Again, the screen writers have been able to "see" what is not there.

In a similar fashion, image and sound are consistently worked into the dramatic texture of the film. Like the carriage race, there are other scenes which do not appear in the novel. In both book and film, Darcy, becoming convinced that Jane does not care for Bingley, persuades his friend to go with him to London. But then we are shown a scene in which Darcy and Bingley are playing billiards. Charles, preoccupied with thoughts of Jane, accidentally runs his cue through the billiard green. Thus his distraction is rendered visually. Again, when Collins condescendingly offers to marry one of the Bennet girls, Lizzy strikes a discordant note on a harp. Her disturbance is rendered acoustically. When the Bennets are preparing to leave Longbourn following Lydia and Wickham's scandalous elopement, the younger girls are seen arguing irresponsibly over taking their personal things—one insists on her music box, the other on her parrot. A moment later, Lady Catherine appears for her interview with Lizzy. She is made ridiculous by sitting on the music box, which begins to play, and by the parrot, which begins to squawk. Here the incongruity is rendered by a *combination* of sound and image.

The most remarkable addition, however, is the garden party at Netherfield, which occurs midway through the film. Probably to avoid visual monotony, the screen writers changed both the locale and the time of day. Since the lovers will reach their closest understanding yet before the end of this sequence, the lighting is bright, the time afternoon. The camera maintains the same mobility and dance movements as in the Assembly Ball sequence, but it catches a number of physical details which are the sole creations of the film writers. Since the relationship between the characters has shifted, the camera dwells on a series of new physical realities. Darcy, who has been humbled, is no longer caustic about Meryton society. Now it is Caroline who plays the role of the snob: "Entertaining the rustics is not as difficult as I had feared. Any simple childish game seems to amuse them excessively."

Kitty and Lydia are now seen in adjoining swings being pushed by the soldiers, Denny and Carter, repeating the movements of the dance, first toward, then away from each other. Collins, who has been pursuing Lizzy romantically, now pursues her literally—out of the house and across the terrace, down the terrace and over the lawn, as graceless and awkward in his running as we have seen him in his dancing. Now Darcy, attracted by Elizabeth's spirit and independence, literally rescues her from Collins, just as he will, in a more serious sense, rescue her from a loveless marriage. When Collins asks Darcy if he has seen Miss Elizabeth Bennet, Darcy misdirects him to another corner of the park, leaving Lizzy alone with him. As they once again begin their cautious conversational sparring, Darcy invites Elizabeth to some practice in archery. He has still not divested himself of pride, however, for he assumes at once that his skill is superior. He offers to instruct Lizzy in the proper handling of the bow and arrow. When Lizzy takes the bow, she proceeds to score three bulls'-eyes in a row. Again Darcy has underestimated her. Again she has proved that she needs no instructions. Echoing the roster of accomplishments which Caroline and Darcy had earlier proposed, Lizzy's archery skill graphically demonstrates her ability to compete with Darcy on an equal level. At that moment, Miss Bingley approaches to ask that Darcy instruct her, too. Darcy's reply is prophetic: "I give no more instructions to young ladies. Hereafter they give instructions to me." Like the carriage race, this scene foreshadows a future relation. Darcy and Lizzy have drawn closer than ever. The arrows have been aimed not only at the target but at Darcy as well.

These contrivances are so artfully accomplished that they never become obtrusive. Moreover, they beguile the spectator into forgetting that the girls on the swings, Collins chasing Lizzy across the lawn, and the play on archery never appear in the novel. The arrangements of physical reality are invented by the screen writers to render the chiaroscuro of dramatic complexity. They have a rightness which seems wholly appropriate to Jane Austen's intentions.

The garden party ends indoors, following another brief exchange between Elizabeth and Darcy on the terrace outside the drawing room. Here they enunciate the central theme of both the book and film: "You're very puzzling, Mr. Darcy. At this moment it's difficult to believe that you're so—*proud*," to which Darcy replies, "At this moment it is difficult to believe that you're so *prejudiced*. Shall we not call quits and start again?" Immediately, the camera moves in out of this temporary sunlight. Lizzy's sisters, the cause of Darcy's earlier discontent, displace the lovers, acting up in a manner which becomes embarrassing to Lizzy. Kitty is getting high on punch; Lydia is giggling foolishly with the soldiers. And Mr. Bennet has already had to stop Mary's tasteless singing. Back in the more subdued light of the drawing room, Collins approaches to ask Elizabeth to dance. As the scene fades, Darcy must again stand alone, watching Lizzy with another partner, as he had stood earlier at the Assembly Ball watching Lizzy dance away with Wickham. The time for Elizabeth and him to dance together has not yet come.

Once again we can see how the screen writers and director, by taking liberties with Jane Austen's text, by imagining what she has not told them, have managed to render her meanings, almost as if destroying the book were a precondition for its faithful resurrection.

If additions reveal a process of rethinking, the deletions and alterations prune what is not pictorial and adjust resulting discrepancies. Deletions fall into two general classes—minor characters, and scenes which are either too meditative or fail to advance the story line. Georgiana, Darcy's sister, and the Gardiners, Mr. Bennet's kin in London, are mentioned but do not appear on the screen. We miss Aunt Gardiner more than Georgiana, since in the novel Aunt Gardiner provides a common-sense antidote to Elizabeth's unhappiness. But since Aunt Gardiner's main function is to accompany Lizzy to Pemberly, and since the entire Pemberly episode is dropped in the film, the loss is not as great as we might at first expect. In the first place, everything we need to know about the taste and luxury of Darcy's life we learn from the physical trappings at Lady Catherine's house in Hunsford. We have already seen the similarities in the descriptions of Pemberly and Rosings. But the differences Elizabeth finds between Darcy's Pemberly and Lady Catherine's Rosings are all but negligible: "Elizabeth saw, with admiration of his taste, that it was neither gaudy nor uselessly fine; with less splendor, and more real elegance, than the furniture of Rosings." The difference is so fine that it would undoubtedly be missed in a casual comparison on the screen. Not only do the film-makers save themselves the trouble of building or finding another set, but they economize on dramatic incident as well. In the second place, a good part of the narrative in chapters XLIII through XLV is taken up with Lizzy's meditations through which she comes to a better appreciation of Darcy's virtues. Not only is she attracted by his taste, not only does she imagine herself as mistress of Pemberly, but she is also deeply moved by Darcy's subsequent courtesy to the Gardiners and by the housekeeper's praise of her master. When Mrs. Reynolds says, "Some people call him proud; but I am sure I never saw anything of it," Elizabeth understandably takes it to heart, for, she thinks, "What praise is more valuable than the praise of an intelligent servant?"

Nevertheless, the decisive act which distills Elizabeth's love for Darcy is his intervention on Lydia's behalf in order to save the Bennets from scandal. This event, inadvertently reported in the film by Lady Catherine, is the last significant scene before the finale. The bald revelation of Darcy's act, held in reserve until the very last moment, draws back the final veil of appearance, bringing the film to its logical conclusion. As in the Assembly Ball sequence, what the film loses in the luxury of subtle shading, it gains in the shock of dramatic reversal.

In a similar fashion, dialogue and minor characters who are not immediately grounded in dramatic incident are dropped in the movie. The aesthetic-moral repartee, gravitating around conflicting styles in music, landscaping, and letter-writing, rightly suggests for Samuel Kliger the crucial dichotomy between nature and art. But it rarely appears on the screen. Rather than talk, the film-makers prefer to *show* conflicts in style through sound and image. Similarly, characters not absolutely essential to the central conflicts are either dropped or relegated to the background. In the novel, Bingley has two sisters; in the film he has one. In the novel, he brings an entourage of socialites from London to help him arrange his ball; in the film, only Bingley, Darcy and Caroline seem to be in residence at Netherfield.

We are able to discover only two alterations and one addition which in any way shift Jane Austen's intentions: the suppression of the fact that Mr. Collins is a clergyman; the conversion of Lady Catherine; and the neat and blissful ending. The first of these was doubtless a surrender to the Production Code which expressly forbids the presentation of clergymen in an unflattering light. But since Jane Austen was not to become preoccupied with the theme of ordination until *Mansfield Park*, and since Mr. Collins holds his sinecure only by the good graces of Lady Catherine, the loss is not serious. In both book and film, Mr. Collins' affectation is social, not clerical.

Not so with Lady Catherine. In the novel, Lady Catherine has always assumed that Darcy would eventually marry her homely daughter, Ann. She is bitterly opposed to Darcy's liaison with Elizabeth, and she does everything in her power to stop it, including a visit to Longbourn to try, unsuccessfully, to dissuade Elizabeth. She is rude, officious, autocratic to the end. In an epilogue, however, we are told that Lady Catherine finally comes to a grudging acceptance of the marriage. In the film, on the other hand, Lady Catherine undergoes a metamorphosis which reveals a heart of gold beneath the gruff exterior. As in the novel, she visits Elizabeth to attempt to dissuade her from marriage. She even mysteriously acquires the power of Darcy's purse and threatens to cut him off without a cent if Lizzy persists. Although Elizabeth has not yet been asked by Darcy a second time, she rebuffs Lady Catherine, refusing to promise anything. But all is well, however, for it turns out that Lady Catherine is really acting as an emissary for Darcy to test Elizabeth's affection and character. Outside the Longbourn house, we see Darcy sitting in a carriage, waiting for his aunt. When she emerges, Lady Catherine reports, after some verbal play, that Lizzy, "being positively obstinate, merely refused to refuse to marry you." Darcy is overjoyed. The way is now clear for him to make a proper proposal and for Lizzy to accept. Lester Asheim suggests that Lady Catherine's conversion may have been effected to accommodate the role with which Edna Mae Oliver had long been associated.[32] It may be closer to the truth, however, that the film-makers wanted an unequivocally happy ending. Since Lady Catherine ultimately ac-

[32] Lester Asheim, "From Book to Film" (Ph.D. dissertation, University of Chicago, 1949), pp. 118–119.

cepts the marriage in the novel, why not show it in the film's denouement?

A similar tendency is revealed in the very last scene of the film. Now that Jane and Elizabeth are safely betrothed to Bingley and Darcy, and Lydia is married to Wickham, only two unmarried daughters remain. Mr. and Mrs. Bennet swing open the doors of the drawing-room, and the camera trucks in to reveal: Mary at the piano, singing the perennial "Flow Gently, Sweet Afton," a bespectacled young man standing over her shoulder, accompanying her on the flute; Kitty and Denny standing together, looking pleasantly happy. Mrs. Bennet immediately sizes up the situation and urges Mr. Bennet to find out their financial status. "Colonel Forster can tell you about Denny. Sir William knows all about Mr. Witherington. . . . Oh, think of it! Three of them married, and the other two just tottering on the brink!" thus pulling the shutters closed on the twin motifs of money and matrimony. Mrs. Bennet's final flourish may betray a confidence more apparent than real, for in the novel we do not learn what happens to Mary and Kitty. Yet here again, the screen writers might properly defend their choice. Chapman tells us that Jane Austen, in her rigid method of selection, often knew more than she chose to make public. Some additional information has been handed down, however. "In this traditionary way," the *Memoir* tells us, "we learned that . . . Kitty Bennet was satisfactorily married to a clergyman near Pemberly, while Mary obtained nothing higher than one of her uncle Philip's clerks, and was content to be considered a star in the society of Meriton [sic] . . . . "[33] It would indicate a marvelous scrupulosity if the screen writers had gone this far in finding a textual basis for their last scene. But that they should come so close to the image Jane Austen had in mind, providing Kitty with the affable Denny (if not her clergyman), and Mary with the gentle Mr. Witherington, indicates a remarkable power of projection into Jane Austen's artistic sensibility.

Given, then, the ironies, misunderstandings, illusions, and contradictions of Jane Austen's world, and the way this constant pressure of opposite tendencies becomes embodied in comic incongruity, moral education, and epistemological clarity; given the

[33] Quoted in Chapman, p. 123.

structural dance pattern which the film enunciates in plastic terms; and given the transmutation of psychological complexity and bare narrative style into the most detailed kind of sensory experience— one problem still remains. Much has been made of Jane Austen's modernity. Of Asheim's twenty-four specimens of filmed novels, *Pride and Prejudice*, in spite of the additions, deletions and altera- tions we have suggested, shows the least percentage of deviation from its original—11 per cent. Why?

In spite of the glamor which is traditionally associated with showing the clothes, habitat, and manners of the well-to-do to a mass audience, Jane Austen's preoccupations are still very much with us. The world of *Pride and Prejudice* meets the require- ments of Hollywood's stock conventions and, at the same time, allows a troubling grain of reality to enter by the side door. It depicts a love story which essentially follows the shopworn for- mula of boy meets girl; boy loses girl; boy gets girl. It presents rich people in elegant surroundings. It seems to allow for social mobility. Instead of the shop girl marrying the boss's son, a daughter of the gentry marries an aristocrat. It offers an individual solution to general problems. Good looks and luck are the touch- stones which make it possible for Elizabeth and Jane both to marry for love and improve their station. If wickedness is not punished, virtue at least is rewarded. Neither the upper-class nor the middle-class worlds are all white or all black. Darcy is just as ashamed of Lady Catherine as Lizzy is of her mother. Above all, the story has a happy ending.

On the other hand, Jane Austen, as we have been told again and again,[34] was not ignorant of the economic and political realities of her time. She had two brothers who eventually became ad- mirals in the British Navy. Cassandra lost her fiance, Rev. Thomas Fowle, an Army chaplain in the West Indies, to tropical fever. Jane's cousin, Eliza de Feuillide, was married to a French aristo- crat who died at the guillotine in the French Revolution. Nor is this unrest wholly alien to the world of her novels. Wickham, Denny, Carter and Colonel Forster, attached to a regiment of militia camped first in Hertfordshire and later in Brighton, are,

[34] See Laura M. Ragg, "Jane Austen and the War of her Time," *Con- temporary Review*, CLVIII (November, 1940), 544-49.

after all, soldiers on leave from the Napoleonic Wars. Town gossip casually includes the information that "a private had been flogged." Jane Austen, like the film-makers and audience of 1940, lived in a time of wars and preparation for wars. If war does not figure as a major theme in *Pride and Prejudice*, it is not because Jane Austen was ignorant of war. It is because she took war so much for granted. Every family she knew had a son in the service.

Against these troubling realities, Jane Austen's novels may be viewed as a rear-guard action to consolidate a moral system against the erosions of changing times. For her, as for us, economic and moral coercion were often indistinguishable. Today, as in 1940, and again in 1813, we are aware of the perils of the dance, of the penalties inherent in failing to play the economic or social game. With the same juggler's skill and actor's finesse as those possessed by the characters in Jane Austen's novel, we continue the exhausting task of performing roles.

Yet, in spite of the film's effectiveness, *Pride and Prejudice* has not had the reputation it deserves. Its survival neither as a box-office hit nor a *succès d'estime* is rather puzzling. The men who received credit for the film did not go on to maintain a steady level of work. Although Greer Garson, Laurence Olivier, Edmund Gwenn, and others in the cast have continued as movie stars, and Hunt Stromberg was one of M-G-M's highest salaried producers in 1938, the key men have not been so fortunate. Robert Z. Leonard, though he is at present more active than Stromberg, has done little serious work. Aldous Huxley, after attempting to write a screenplay about the Curies for Greta Garbo (rejected by Madame Curie's daughter, so the story goes, because she was afraid Garbo would overshadow any actor who attempted to portray Monsieur Curie), finally abandoned Hollywood. Jane Murfin was rarely heard from before her death in 1955.

A more central reason, however, may reside in one of the film's main virtues, its "literate dialogue." The *New Republic* reviewer, for example, suggested the difficulty when he anticipated objections "to the two-hour-long talkiness of this Regency conversation piece."[35] Critics more sensitive to literary than to cinematic effects would tend to miss the quiet plastic accomplishments of

[35] Philip T. Hartung, *New Republic*, xxxii (August 2, 1940), 34.

the M-G-M production; they would overlook the fact that the understatements of the camera are exactly suited to those epigrammatic understatements we have come to associate with Jane Austen's style. The pictorial excellence is so subtly transcribed that until now it has gone unnoticed. Yet, in another way, the film may have had a more extensive influence than even the film-makers are aware. In June, 1940, in direct response to the film's premier, Pocket Books brought out a soft-cover edition of *Pride and Prejudice*. By 1948, just eight years later, Jane Austen's novel had gone into twenty-one printings.

5   *The Grapes of Wrath*

IN HIS COMPACT LITTLE STUDY OF CALI-
fornia writers, *The Boys in the Back Room*, Edmund Wilson
comments on the problems inherent in the close affiliation between
Hollywood and commercial fiction:

> Since the people who control the movies will not go a step of
> the way to give the script writer a chance to do a serious script,
> the novelist seems, consciously or unconsciously, to be going
> part of the way to meet the producers. John Steinbeck, in *The
> Grapes of Wrath*, has certainly learned from the films—and not
> only from the documentary pictures of Pare Lorentz, but from
> the sentimental symbolism of Hollywood. The result was that
> *The Grapes of Wrath* went on the screen as easily as if it had
> been written in the studios, and was probably the only serious
> story on record that seemed equally effective as a film and as a
> book.[1]

Indeed, not only did Steinbeck learn from Pare Lorentz; he also
received, through Lorentz, his first introduction to Nunnally
Johnson, the screen writer who did the movie adaptation of his

[1] Edmund Wilson, *The Boys in the Back Room* (San Francisco, 1941),
p. 61.

novel.[2] And Bennett Cerf, the publishing head of Random House, must have had none other than Steinbeck in mind when he wrote, "The thing an author wants most from his publisher these days is a letter of introduction to Darryl Zanuck."[3] For if Steinbeck was fortunate in having Pare Lorentz as a teacher and Nunnally Johnson as a screen writer, he was one of the few who earned the coveted letter to Darryl Zanuck, the producer of *The Grapes of Wrath*. Add Gregg Toland's photography, Alfred Newman's music, and John Ford's direction, and one sees that Steinbeck had an unusually talented crew, one which could be depended upon to respect the integrity of his best-selling book.

Lester Asheim, in his close charting of the correspondence between twenty-four novels and films, seems to corroborate Edmund Wilson's conclusion about the easy transference of Steinbeck's book to John Ford's film. According to Asheim's analysis, the major sequences in the novel bear more or less the same ratio to the whole as the corresponding sequences do in the film:

	per cent of whole	
sequence	*book*	*film*
Oklahoma episodes	20	28
Cross-country episodes	19	22
General commentary	17	—
Government camp episodes	15	18
Hooverville episodes	10	13
Strike-breaking episodes	9	16
Final episodes	10	3
	100	100

And when Asheim goes on to explain that, if one ignores the major deletions which occur in the transference and considers only those episodes in the novel which appear in the film, the percentage of both book and film devoted to these central events

[2] In conversation with Mr. Johnson.

[3] In *Hollywood Reporter* (January 9, 1941), p. 3; quoted in Leo C. Rosten, *Hollywood: The Movie Colony, The Movie Makers* (New York, 1941), p. 366.

would be virtually identical, his observation seems, at first, to be providing indisputable proof for Wilson's claim.[4]

Yet, to follow through Wilson's primary analysis of Steinbeck's work is to come at once on a contradiction which belies, first, his comment on the ineluctable fitness of the novel for Hollywood consumption and, second, his implication that Steinbeck, like the novelists whom Bennett Cerf has in mind, had written with one eye on the movie market. For it is central to Wilson's critical argument that the "substratum which remains constant" in Steinbeck's work "is his preoccupation with biology."[5] According to Wilson's view, "Mr. Steinbeck almost always in his fiction is dealing either with the lower animals or with human beings so rudimentary that they are almost on the animal level."[6] Tracing the thematic seams that run through Steinbeck's prose, Wilson notes the familiar interchapter on the turtle whose slow, tough progress survives the gratuitous cruelty of the truck driver who swerves to hit it. This anticipates the survival of the Joads, who, with the same dorsal hardness, will manage another journey along a road, emerging like the turtle from incredible hardships surrounded by symbols of fertility, much like the turtle's "wild cat head" which spawns three spearhead seeds in the dry ground. And Wilson notes, too, the way in which the forced pilgrimage of the Joads, adumbrated by the turtle's indestructibility, is "accompanied and parodied all the way by animals, insects and birds," as when the abandoned house where Tom finds Muley is invaded by bats, weasels, owls, mice, and pet cats gone wild.

This primary biological analysis seems to contradict Wilson's more casual statement on the film, since the screen version, as evolved by Nunnally Johnson and John Ford, contains little evidence of this sort of preoccupation. And when Asheim concludes, after a detailed comparison, that to one unfamiliar with the novel there are no loose ends or glaring contradictions to indicate that alterations have taken place,[7] we begin to uncover a series of dis-

[4] Lester Asheim, "From Book to Film" (Ph.D. dissertation, University of Chicago, 1949), pp. 55–56.
[5] Wilson, p. 42.
[6] *Ibid.*, pp. 42–43.
[7] Asheim, p. 161.

parities which, rather than demonstrating the ease of adaptation, suggests its peculiar difficulties. We are presented in the film with what Asheim calls "a new logic of events," a logic which deviates from the novel in several important respects. Tracing these mutations in some detail will illuminate the special characteristics of book and film alike. The question immediately arises, how could *The Grapes of Wrath* have gone on the screen so easily when the biological emphasis is nowhere present?

Undeniably, there is, in the novel, a concurrence of animal and human life similar to that which appears in the work of Walter Van Tilburg Clark, another western writer who transcends regional themes. Even from the opening of the chapter which depicts the pedestrian endurance of the turtle, creature and human are linked:

> The concrete highway was edged with a mat of tangled, broken, dry grass, and the grass heads were heavy with oat beards to catch on a dog's coat, and foxtails to tangle in a horse's fetlocks, and clover burrs to fasten in a sheep's wool; sleeping life waiting to be spread and dispersed, every seed armed with an appliance of dispersal, twisting darts and parachutes for the wind, little spears and balls of tiny thorns, and all waiting for animals and for the wind, for a man's trouser cuff or the hem of a woman's skirt, all passive but armed appliances of activity, still, but each possessed of the anlage of movement.

Here, the central motifs of the narrative are carefully, but inobtrusively enunciated, a kind of generalized analogue to the coming tribulations of the Joads: a harsh, natural order which is distracting to men and dogs alike; a hostile, dry passivity which, like the dormant blastema, is at the same time laden with regenerative possibilities. From the opening passages ("Gophers and ant lions started small avalanches . . .") to the last scene in which an attempt is made to beatify Rose of Sharon's biological act, the narrative is richly interspersed with literal and figurative zoology. Tom and Casy witness the unsuccessful efforts of a cat to stop the turtle's slow progress. In the deserted house, Muley describes himself as having once been "mean like a wolf," whereas now he is "mean like a weasel." Ma Joad describes the law's pursuit of

Pretty Boy Floyd in animal terms: "they run him like a coyote, an' him a-snappin' an' a-snarlin', mean as a lobo." Young Al boasts that his Hudson jalopy will "ride like a bull calf." In the interchapter describing the change, the growing wrath triggered by the wholesale evictions of the tenant farmers, the western states are "nervous as horses before a thunder storm."

Later, Ma Joad savagely protests the break-up of the family: "All we got is the family unbroke. Like a bunch of cows, when the lobos are ranging." Later still, Tom tells Casy that the day he got out of prison, he ran himself down a prostitute "like she was a rabbit." Even the endless caravans of jalopies are described in terms which echo the plodding endurance of the turtle. After a night in which "the owls coasted overhead, and the coyotes gabbled in the distance, and into the camp skunks walked, looking for bits of food . . . " the morning comes, revealing the cars of migrants along the highway crawling out "like bugs." After the relatively peaceful interlude of the Government Camp, Al comments on the practice of periodically burning out the Hoovervilles where the dispossessed farmers are forced to cluster: ". . . they jus' go hide down in the willows an' then they come out an' build 'em another weed shack. Jus' like gophers." And finally, toward the end, Ma expresses her longing to have a settled home for Ruth and Winfield, the youngest children, in order to keep them from becoming wild animals. For by this time, Ruth and Winnie do, indeed, emerge from their beds "like hermit crabs from shells."

The persistence of this imagery reveals at least part of its service. In the first place, even in our random selections, biology supports and comments upon sociology. Sexual activity, the primacy of the family clan, the threat and utility of industrial machinery, the alienation and hostility of the law, the growing anger at economic oppression, the arguments for human dignity, are all accompanied by, or expressed in terms of, zoological images. In the second place, the presence of literal and figurative animals is more frequent when the oppression of the Joads is most severe. The pattern of the novel, as we shall see, is similar to a parabola whose highest point is the sequence at the Government Camp. From Chapter XXII to the middle of Chapter XXVI, which covers this interlude, the animal imagery is almost totally absent.

Densely compacted at the beginning, when Tom returns to find his home a shambles, it recurs in the closing sequences of the strike-breaking and the flood. The point is that none of this appears in the film. Even the highly cinematic passage depicting the slaughtering of the pigs, in preparation for the journey, is nowhere evident in the final editing. If the film adaptation remains at all faithful to its original, it is not in retaining what Edmund Wilson calls the constant substratum in Steinbeck's work. It is true, one may argue, that biological functions survive in the Joads' elementary fight for life, in the animal preoccupation with finding food and shelter, in the scenes of death and procreation, but this is not what Edmund Wilson has in mind. In the film, these functions are interwoven so closely with a number of other themes that in no sense can the biological preoccupation be said to have a primary value. This type of deletion could not have been arbitrary, for, as Vachel Lindsay showed as early as 1915, animal imagery can be used quite effectively as cinema. Reviewing Griffith's *The Avenging Conscience*, Lindsay is describing the meditations of a boy who has just been forced to say goodbye to his beloved, supposedly forever. Watching a spider in his web devour a fly, the boy meditates on the cruelty of nature: "Then he sees the ants in turn destroy the spider. The pictures are shown on so large a scale that the spiderweb fills the end of the theater. Then the ant-tragedy does the same. They can be classed as particularly apt hieroglyphics...."[8] More recently, the killing of the animals by the boy in *Les Jeux Interdits* shows that biology can still effectively support cinematic themes. In the particular case of *The Grapes of Wrath*, however, the suggestions of the book were abandoned. If, then, we are to understand the mutation, to assess the film's special achievement, we must look elsewhere.

Immediately, a number of other motifs strongly assert themselves in Steinbeck's model: the juxtaposition of natural morality and religious hypocrisy; the love of the regenerative land; the primacy of the family; the dignity of human beings; the socio-political implications inherent in the conflict between individual

[8] Vachel Lindsay, *The Art of the Moving Picture* (New York, 1915), p. 124.

work and industrial oppression. Consider Casy's impulsive rationalizations in the very early section of the book where he tries, like the Ancient Mariner, to convince his listener and himself at the same time, that his rejection of religious preaching in favor of a kind of naturalistic code of ethics is morally acceptable. Tortured by his sexual impulses as a preacher, Casy began to doubt and question the assumptions which he had been articulating from his rough, evangelical pulpit, began to observe the discrepancy between theoretical sin and factual behavior. He repeats his conclusions to Tom, "Maybe it ain't a sin. Maybe it's just the way folks is. Maybe we been whippin' hell out of ourselves for nothin'. . . . To hell with it! There ain't no sin and there ain't no virtue. There's just stuff people do. It's all part of the same thing. And some of the things folks do is nice, and some ain't nice, but that's as far as any man got a right to say."

Casy retains his love for people, but not through his ministry, and later this love will be transmuted into personal sacrifice and the solidarity of union organization. This suspicion of a theology not rooted in ordinary human needs continues to echo throughout the novel. When Casy refuses to pray for the dying Grampa, Granma reminds him, quite offhandedly, how Ruthie prayed when she was a little girl: " 'Now I lay me down to sleep. I pray the Lord my soul to keep. An' when she got there the cupboard was bare, an' so the poor dog got none.' " The moral is clear: in the face of hunger, religious piety seems absurd. After Grampa's death, the inclusion of a line from Scripture in the note that will follow him to his grave is parodied in much the same way, but Casy's last words at the grave echo his earlier statement: "This here ol' man jus' lived a life an' jus' died out of it. I don't know whether he was good or bad, but that don't matter much. He was alive, an' that's what matters. An' now he's dead, an' that don't matter. . . . if I was to pray, it'd be for the folks that don' know which way to turn." Ma Joad expresses the same kind of mystical acceptance of the life cycle when she tries to tell Rose of Sharon about the hurt of childbearing:

They's a time of change, an' when that comes, dyin' is a piece of all dyin', and bearin' is a piece of all bearin', an bearin' an' dyin' is two pieces of the same thing. An' then things ain't lonely any more. An' then a hurt don't hurt so bad, 'cause it ain't a lonely hurt no more, Rose-asharn. I wisht I could tell you so you'd know, but I can't.

Because Ma is so firm in her belief in the rightness of natural processes, she becomes furious at the religious hypocrites who plague the migrants. At the Hoovervilles and in the government station, the evangelists whom Ma characterizes as Holy Rollers and Jehovites are grimly present, like camp followers. Beginning with polite acceptance, Ma becomes infuriated when one of these zealots works on Rose of Sharon, scaring her half to death with visions of hellfire and burning. Ma represents the state of natural grace to which Casy aspires from the beginning.

Just as the novel reveals a preoccupation with biology, it is also obsessed with love of the earth. From the opening lines of the book, "To the red country and part of the gray country of Oklahoma, the last rains came gently, and they did not cut the scarred earth," to the last scene of desolation, the land imagery persists. The earth motif is woven into the texture complexly, but on the whole it serves two main functions: first, to signify love; and second, to signify endurance. Tom makes the sexual connection when, listening to Casy's compulsive story, he idly, but quite naturally, draws the torso of a woman in the dirt, "breasts, hips, pelvis." The attachment of the men for the land is often so intense that it borders on sexual love. Muley's refusal to leave, even after the caterpillar tractors have wiped him out, looks ahead to Grampa's similar recalcitrance. At first, Grampa is enthusiastic about the prospect of moving to a more fertile land, and he delivers himself of words verging on panegyric: "Jus' let me get out to California where I can pick me an orange when I want it. Or grapes. There's a thing I ain't ever had enough of. Gonna get me a whole big bunch a grapes off a bush, or whatever, an' I'm gonna squash 'em on my face, an' let 'em run offen my chin." But when the moment for departures arrives, Grampa refuses to go. His roots in the ground are too strong; he cannot bear to tear them up. Very soon after the family leaves its native soil, Grampa dies of a stroke. And when Casy says to Noah,

"Grampa an' the old place, they was jus' the same thing," we feel that the observation has a precision which is supported by the texture of the entire novel. When the Joads get to California, they will, of course, find that the grapes which Grampa dreamed of are inaccessible, that the grapes of promise inevitably turn to grapes of wrath. The land, one interchapter tells, has been possessed by the men with a frantic hunger for land who came before the Joads. And the defeated promise is bitterly dramatized in the last scene, when a geranium, the last flower of earth to appear in the novel, becomes an issue dividing Ruthie and Winfield, and results in Ruthie's pressing one petal against Winfield's nose, cruelly. Love and endurance have been tried to their utmost. When the land goes, everything else goes, too; and the water is the emblem of its destruction.

Love of family parallels love of the earth. During the threatening instability of the cross-country journey, Ma Joad acts as the cohesive force which keeps her brood intact. Whenever one of the men threatens to leave, Ma protests, and sometimes savagely. When she takes over leadership of the family, by defying Pa Joad with a jack handle, it is over the question of whether or not Tom shall stay behind with the disabled car. Even after Connie, Rose of Sharon's husband, and Noah, one of the brothers, desert the family, the identity of the clan remains Ma Joad's primary fixation. After half a continent of hardship, Ma articulates her deepest feelings. She tells Tom, "They was a time when we was on the lan'. They was a boundary to us then. Ol' folks died off, an' little fellas came, an' we was always one thing—we was the fambly— kinda whole and clear. An' now we ain't clear no more." The deprivation of the native land, and the alienation of the new, become more than economic disasters; they threaten the only social organization upon which Ma Joad can depend. The fertility of the land and the integrity of the clan are no longer distinct entities; both are essential for survival.

Closely bound up with this theme of familial survival is the theme of human dignity. Clearly, the exigencies of eviction and migration force the problem of brute survival upon the Joads. But just as important is the correlative theme of human dignity. The first time the Joads are addressed as "Oakies," by a loud-mouthed deputy who sports a Sam Browne belt and pistol holster, Ma is so shocked that she almost attacks him. Later, Uncle John is so chagrined by Casy's sacrificial act (deflecting from Tom the blame for hitting the deputy, and going to prison in his stead) that he feels positively sinful for not making an equal contribution. At the Government Camp, a woman complains about taking charity from the Salvation Army because "We was hungry— they made us crawl for our dinner. They took our dignity." But it is Tom who makes the most articulate defense of dignity against the legal harassment to which the Joads have been sub- jected: " . . . if it was the law they was workin' with, why, we could take it. But it *ain't* the law. They're a-workin' away at our spirits. . . . They're workin' on our decency." And the final image of Rose of Sharon offering her breast to the starving farmer is in- tended as an apotheosis of the scared girl, recently deprived of her child, into a kind of natural madonna.

In short, if the biological interest exists, it is so chastened through suffering that it achieves a dignity which is anything but animal, in Edmund Wilson's sense of the word. The conflicts, values, and recognitions of the Joads cannot, therefore, be equated with the preoccupations of subhuman life. The biological life may be re- tained in the search for food and shelter, in the cycle of death and procreation, but always in terms which emphasize rather than oblit- erate the distinctions between humans and animals. When Stein- beck reminisces about his carefree bohemian days in Monterey, he is just as nostalgic about the freedom of assorted drifters, his "interesting and improbable" characters, as he is about Ed Ricketts' "commercial biological laboratory."[9] Steinbeck's novel may be read, then, as much as a flight from biological determinism as a representation of it. The story of the pilgrimage to the new Canaan which is California, the cycle of death and birth through which the Joads must suffer, becomes a moral, as well as a physical, trial by fire.

The socio-political implications of the Joad story, more familiar than these correlative themes, serve to counterpoint and define the

[9] John Steinbeck, "Dreams Piped from Cannery Row," *New York Times Theater Section* (Sunday, November 27, 1955), p. 1.

anger and the suffering. Throughout the novel, the Joads are haunted by deputies in the service of landowners, bankers, and fruit growers; by the contradiction between endless acres in full harvest and streams of migratory workers in dire straits; by unscrupulous businessmen who take advantage of the desperate, westbound caravans; by strike-breakers, corrupt politicians, and thugs. At first, the Joads must draw from their meager savings to pay for gas and half-loaves of bread; but as they draw West they must even pay for water. In California, they cannot vote, are kept continually on the move, are bullied by the constabulary, and must even watch helplessly as one of the Hoovervilles is burned out. The only time they earn enough money to eat comes when they are hired as strike-breakers. Gradually, there is the dawning recognition that the only possible response to these impossible conditions is solidarity through union organization, precisely what the fruit growers and their agents dread most. In order to overcome the fruit growers' divisive tactics, Casy becomes an active union organizer and gets killed in the process by a bunch of marauding deputies. At the end, Tom, in his familiar farewell to Ma Joad, is trembling on the verge of Casy's solution. "That the end will be revolution," one reviewer writes, "is implicit from the title onwards."[10] Steinbeck ultimately withdraws from such a didactic conclusion, as we shall see in a moment, but that the didactic conclusion is implicit in the narrative can hardly be denied:

> . . . the companies, the banks worked at their own doom and they did not know it. The fields were fruitful, and starving men moved on the roads. The granaries were full and the children of the poor grew up rachitic, and the pustules of pellagra swelled on their sides. The great companies did not know that the line between hunger and anger is a thin line. And money that might have gone to wages went for gas, for guns, for agents and spies, for blacklists, for drilling. On the highways the people moved like ants and searched for work, for food. And the anger began to ferment.

[10] Earle Birney, "The Grapes of Wrath," *Canadian Forum*, xix (June, 1939), 95.

Hence the symbolism of the title. Clearly woven through the novel, and therefore inseparable from Steinbeck's prose, we find these sharp political overtones. Besides being a novel, writes one reviewer, *The Grapes of Wrath* "is a monograph on rural sociology, a manual of practical wisdom in times of enormous stress, an assault on individualism, an essay in behalf of a rather vague form of pantheism, and a bitter, ironical attack on that emotional evangelistic religion which seems to thrive in the more impoverished rural districts of this vast country. . . ."[11]

Along the highways, a new social order is improvised, a fluid but permanent council in which the family is the basic unit, an order reaching its almost utopian operation at the Government Camp. According to this scheme, the governing laws remain constant, while the specific counters are continually replaced, one family succeeding another, a sort of permanent republic which can accommodate a populace in constant motion:

> The families learned what rights must be observed—the right of privacy in the tent; the right to keep the past black hidden in the heart; the right to talk and to listen; the right to refuse help or to decline it; the right of son to court and daughter to be courted; the right of the hungry to be fed; the rights of the pregnant and the sick to transcend all other rights. . . .
>
> And with the laws, the punishments—and there were only two—a quick and murderous fight or ostracism; and ostracism was the worst.

Within such a scheme, Ma Joad's fierce maintenance of the family becomes more clear. For without the integrity of the clan, survival is all but impossible. The alternatives are death, which does, in fact, snip the Joad family at both ends, claiming both the grandparents and Rose of Sharon's baby, or, on the other hand, militant struggle through union organization.

If the biological motifs do not appear in the film, these correlative themes are adopted with varying degrees of emphasis. The religious satire, with a single exception, is dropped entirely; the political radicalism is muted and generalized; but the insistence

[11] James N. Vaughan, "The Grapes of Wrath," *Commonweal*, xxx (July 28, 1949), 341–342.

on family cohesion, on affinity for the land, on human dignity is carried over into the movie version.

In the film, the one remnant of tragi-comic religious satire occurs in Tom's first talk with Casy on the way to the Joad house. Casy's probing self-analysis is essentially the same as in the book, and its culmination, "There ain't no sin an' there ain't no virtue. There's just what people do," is a precise copy from the novel. Once the theme is enunciated, however, it is underplayed, recurring almost imperceptibly in the burial scene. Ma's anger at the evangelical camp followers is dropped entirely.

The film-makers must have known that the film was political dynamite. After a difficult decision, Darryl Zanuck began what turned out to be, thematically speaking, one of the boldest films in the history of the movies. The secrecy which surrounded the studios during production has become legend. Even as the film was being shot, Zanuck reportedly received 15,000 letters, 99 per cent of which accused him of cowardice, saying he would never make the film because the industry was too closely associated with big business.[12] And yet, fearful that the Texas and Oklahoma Chambers of Commerce would object to the shooting, on their territory, of the *enfant terrible* of the publishing world, the studio announced that it was really filming another story innocuously entitled, *Highway 66*.[13] It was precisely this fear of criticism, of giving offense to vested interests that was responsible for muting the film's political implications. Lester Asheim has pointed out how the film scrupulously steers clear of the book's specific accusations. Many small episodes showing unfair business practices, for example, were cut from the film version.[14] While the reference to the handbills which flood Oklahoma, luring an excess labor force out West, is carried over into the film, most of the corresponding details are dropped. The complaint about the unfair practices of used-car salesmen; the argument with the camp owner about overcharging; the depiction of the company-store credit racket; the dishonest scales on the fruit ranch; and even the prac-

[12] Frank Condon, "The Grapes of Raps," *Collier's* (January 27, 1940), p. 67.
[13] *Ibid.*, p. 64.
[14] Asheim, p. 277.

tice, on the part of an otherwise sympathetic luncheon proprietor, of taking the jackpots from his own slot machines—none of these was ever even proposed for the shooting-script. Similarly, all legal authority is carefully exempt from blame. In Tom's angry speech about the indignities foisted upon the family by the local constabulary, everything is retained except his bitter indictment of the deputies, and his line, ". . . they comes a time when the on'y way a fella can keep his decency is by takin' a sock at a cop."[15] In Casy's discourse on the progress of the fruit strike, the line, "An' all the cops in the worl' come down on us" is deleted. Casy's announcement that the cops have threatened to beat up recalcitrant strikers is retained, but the film adds, "Not them reg'lar deputies, but them tin badge fellas they call guards. . . ."

In spite of the revolutionary candor of the interchapters, whenever the film raises questions about whom to see or what to do for recourse or complaint, the novel's evasive answers are used in reply. When Tom asks the proprietor of the Government Camp why there aren't more places like this, the proprietor answers, "You'll have to find that out for yourself." When Muley wants to find out from the City Man who's to blame for his eviction, so that he can take a shotgun to him, the City Man tells him that the Shawnee Land and Cattle Company is so amorphous that it cannot be properly located. The bank in Tulsa is responsible for telling the land company what to do, but the bank's manager is simply an employee trying to keep up with orders from the East. "Then who do we shoot?" Muley asks in exasperation. "Brother, I don't know . . . " the City Man answers helplessly. To add to the mystification, the film supplies a few clouds of its own. In the scene where Farmer Thomas warns Tom and the Wallaces about the impending raid on the Government Camp, the recurring question of "red" agitation comes up again. The "red menace" has become the *raison d'être* for attacks against the squatter camps. Tom, who has heard the argument before, bursts out, "What is these reds anyway?" Originally, according to the script, Wilkie Wallace was to have answered, cribbing his own line from the novel, that according to a fruit grower he knew once, a red is anyone who "wants thirty-cents an hour when I'm payin' twenty-

[15] *Ibid.*, p. 256.

five." In the final print, however, Farmer Thomas answers Tom's question simply but evasively, "I ain't talkin' about that one way 'r another," and goes on to warn the men about the raid.

Even Tom's much-quoted farewell to Ma Joad, retained in the film, is pruned until little remains but its mystical affirmation. And the final words, backing away from Casy's conscious social commitment, are carried over intact.

Ma: "I don' un'erstan . . . ."

Tom: "Me neither, Ma. . . . It's jus' stuff I been thinkin' about. . . ." In the world of the Ford-Johnson film, the politico-economic tendency is merely an urge in search of a name it is never allowed to find. And yet because of the naked suffering, the brute struggle to survive, devoid of solutions in either church or revolution, John Gassner finds that more appropriate than the image of God "trampling out the vintage where the grapes of wrath are stored," from which the title is derived, are the lines, "And here in dust and dirt . . . the lilies of his love appear,"[16] which connote neither religion nor politics. According to Gassner, bedrock is reached in this film, "and it proves to be as hard as granite and as soft as down."

If the religious satire is absent and the politics muted, the love of land, family and human dignity are consistently translated into effective cinematic images. Behind the director's controlling hand is the documentary eye of a Pare Lorentz or a Robert Flaherty, of the vision in those stills produced by the Resettlement Administration in its volume, *Land of the Free* (with commentary by Archibald MacLeish), or in Walker Evans' shots for *Let Us Now Praise Famous Men* (with commentary by James Agee), which, like Lorentz's work, was carried on under the auspices of the Farm Security Administration. Gregg Toland's photography is acutely conscious of the pictorial values of land and sky, finding equivalents for those haunting images of erosion which were popularized for the New Deal's reclamation program and reflected in Steinbeck's prose. The constant use of brooding, dark silhouettes against light, translucent skies, the shots of roads and farms, the fidelity to the speech, manners and dress of Oklahoma farmers—

[16] John Gassner, *Twenty Best Film Plays,* ed. John Gassner and Dudley Nichols (New York, 1943), p. xxvi.

all contribute to the pictorial mood and tone. I am told that some of these exteriors were shot on indoor sound stages at the studios,[17] but even this has worked to the advantage of the film-makers. In the studio, Ford was able to control his composition by precise lighting, so that some of the visuals—Tom moving like an ant against a sky bright with luminous clouds, the caravans of jalopies, the slow rise of the dust storm—combine physical reality with careful composition to create striking pictorial effects. Finally, generous selections of dialogue, culled from the novel, echoing the theme of family affiliation with the land, appear in the final movie version. Grampa's last minute refusal to go, as he clutches at a handful of soil, necessitates Tom's plan to get him drunk and carry him aboard by force. And, as Muley, John Qualen's apostrophe to the land, after the tractor has ploughed into his shack, is one of the most poignant anywhere in films.

In the same fashion, the central episodes depicting Ma Joad's insistence on family cohesion, and Tom's insistence on dignity, are either presented directly or clearly suggested. Ma, to be sure, is made a little less fierce than she is in the novel. Tom still tells Casy the anecdote about Ma's taking after a tin peddler with an ax in one hand and a chicken in the other, but the scene in which she takes a jack handle after Pa, originally scheduled according to the script, is deleted. We never see Ma physically violent.

Tracing through these recurring themes, comparing and contrasting the emphasis given to each, gives us all the advantages of content analysis without explaining, finally, the central difference between Steinbeck's artistic vision and that of the film-makers. This difference does emerge, however, when we compare the two structures.

Some deletions, additions, and alterations, to be sure, reflect in a general way the ordinary process of mutation from a linguistic to a visual medium. On the one hand, the characteristic interchapters in the novel are dropped entirely, those interludes which adopt the author's point of view and which are at once more lyric and less realistic than the rest of the prose. The angry interludes, the explicit indictments, the authorial commentary do not appear, in-

[17] In an interview with Mr. Ford.

deed would seem obtrusive, in the film. Translated into observed reality, however, and integrated into the picture within the frame, certain fragments find their proper filmic equivalents. For example, the interchapters are mined for significant dialogue, and, in fact, Muley's moving lines, "We were born on it, and we got killed on it, died on it. Even if it's no good, it's still ours. . . . " appear originally in one of these interludes. In the second place, the themes of one or two of these interchapters are translated into a few highly effective montages—the coming of the tractors, the caravans of jalopies, the highway signs along route 66. As Muley begins telling his story, over the candle in the dimly lit cabin, the film flashes back to the actual scene. A series of tractors looming up like mechanical creatures over the horizon, crossing and criss-crossing the furrowed land, cuts to the one tractor driven by the Davis boy, who has been assigned the task of clearing off Muley's farm. Later, as the Joads' jalopy begins its pilgrimage, we see a similar shot of scores and scores of other jalopies, superimposed one upon the other, making the same, slow, desperate cross-country trek. Finally, the central episodes of the trip are bridged by montages of road signs—"Checotah, Oklahoma City, Bethany," and so on to California. These devices have the effect of generalizing the conflicts of the Joads, of making them representative of typical problems in a much wider social context. In every reversal, in every act of oppression, we feel the pressure of thousands.

If the film carries these striking equivalents of Steinbeck's prose, it is partly due to the assistance which Steinbeck offers the film-maker, partly to the visual imagination of the film-maker himself. Except for the freewheeling omniscience of the interchapters, the novel's prose relies wholly on dialogue and physical action to reveal character. Because Steinbeck's style is not marked by meditation, it resembles, in this respect, the classic form of the scenario. Even at moments of highest tension, Steinbeck scrupulously avoids getting inside the minds of his people. Here is Ma right after Tom has left her, and probably forever:

> "Good-by" she said, and she walked quickly away. Her footsteps were loud and careless on the leaves as she went through the brush. And as she went, out of the dim sky the rain began

to fall, big drops and few, splashing on the dry leaves heavily. Ma stopped and stood still in the dripping thicket. She turned about—took three steps back toward the mound of vines; and then she turned quickly and went back toward the boxcar camp.

Although this is Steinbeck's characteristic style, it can also serve as precise directions for the actor. There is nothing here which cannot be turned into images of physical reality. Critics who seem surprised at the ease with which Steinbeck's work moves from one medium to another may find their explanation here. Precisely this fidelity to physical detail was responsible, for example, for the success *Of Mice and Men* first as a novel, then as a play, then as a film. And yet, in *The Grapes of Wrath*, the film-makers rethought the material for themselves, and frequently found more exact cinematic keys to the mood and color of particular scenes in the book. Often their additions are most effective in areas where the novel is powerless—in moments of silence. Casy jumping over a fence and tripping, after the boast about his former preaching prowess; Ma Joad burning her keepsakes (the little dog from the St. Louis Exposition, the old letters, the card from Pa); the earrings which she saves, holding them to her ears in the cracked mirror, while the sound track carries the muted theme from "Red River Valley"; the handkerchiefs which Tom and Casy hold to their mouths in the gathering dust; Tom laboriously adding an "s" to "funerl" in the note which will accompany Grampa to his grave; the reflection of Al, Tom, and Pa in the jalopy's windshield at night as the family moves through the hot, eery desert—all these, while they have no precedent in the novel, make for extraordinarily effective cinema. The images are clean and precise, the filmic signature of a consistent collaboration between John Ford and his cameraman.

The deletions, on one level, are sacrifices to the exigencies of time and plot. The dialogue is severely pruned. Most of the anecdotes are dropped, along with the curse words. And the leisurely, discursive pace of the novel gives way to a tightly knit sequence of events. The episodes involving the traveling companionship of the Wilsons; the desertions of Noah and Connie; the repeated warnings about the dismal conditions in California from bitterly disappointed migrants who are traveling home the other way; and countless other small events do not appear in the film story, though a few of them, like Noah's desertion, appeared in the script and were even shot during production. But the moment we go from an enumeration of these deletions to the arrangement of sequences in the final work, we have come to our central structural problem.

As I indicated earlier, the structure of the book resembles a parabola in which the high point is the successful thwarting of the riot at the Government Camp. Beginning with Tom's desolate return to his abandoned home, the narrative proceeds through the journey from Oklahoma to California; the Hooverville episodes; the Government Camp episodes; the strike-breaking episodes at the Hooper Ranch; Tom's departure; the flooding of the cotton pickers' boxcar camp; the last scene in the abandoned farm. From the privation and dislocation of the earlier episodes, the Joads are continually plagued, threatened with dissolution, until, through the gradual knitting of strength and resistance, the family finds an identity which coincides with its experience at the Government Camp. Here they are startled by the sudden absence of everything from which they have been running—dirty living conditions, external compulsion, grubbing for survival, brutal policemen, unscrupulous merchants. They find, instead, a kind of miniature planned economy, efficiently run, boasting modern sanitation, self-government, co-operative living, and moderate prices. After their departure from the camp, the fortunes of the Joads progressively deteriorate, until that desolate ending which depicts Rose of Sharon's stillborn child floating downstream. The critical response to Steinbeck's shocking ending was almost universally negative. Clifton Fadiman called it the "tawdriest kind of fake symbolism."[18] Anthony West attributed it to the novel's "astonishingly awkward" form.[19] Louis Kronenberger found that the entire second half of the book "lacks form and intensity . . . ceases to grow, to

[18] Clifton Fadiman, "Highway 66—A Tale of Five Cities," *New Yorker,* xv (April 15, 1939), 81.
[19] Anthony West, "The Grapes of Wrath," *New Statesman and Nation,* xviii (September 16, 1939), 404–405.

maintain direction,"[20] but did not locate the reasons for his dissatisfaction. Malcolm Cowley, in spite of general enthusiasm, found the second half less impressive than the first because Steinbeck "wants to argue as if he weren't quite sure of himself."[21] Charles Angoff was one of a small minority who defended both the ending and the "robust looseness" of the novel as squarely in the narrative tradition of Melville, Cervantes and Thomas Hardy.[22]

Contrast these objections with the general approval of the film's structure. Thomas Burton becomes adulatory over Ford's "incessant physical intimacy and fluency."[23] Otis Ferguson speaks in superlatives: "this is a best that has no very near comparison to date. . . . It all moves with the simplicity and perfection of a wheel across silk."[24] Why did the film-makers merit such a sharply contrasting critical reception? Simply because they corrected the objectionable structure of the novel. First, they deleted the final sequence; and second, they accomplishd one of the most remarkable narrative switches in film history. Instead of ending with the strike-breaking episodes in which Tom is clubbed, Casy killed, and the strikers routed, the film ends with the Government Camp interlude. This reversal, effected with almost surgical simplicity, accomplishes, in its metamorphic power, an entirely new structure which has far-reaching consequences. Combined with the deletion of the last dismal episode, and the pruning, alterations, and selections we have already traced, the new order changes the parabolic structure to a straight line that continually ascends. Beginning with the desolate scene of the dust storm, the weather in the film improves steadily with the fortunes of the Joads, until, at the end, the jalopy leaves the Government Camp in sunlight and exuberant triumph. Even a sign, called for in the original script,

---

[20] Louis Kronenberger, "Hungry Caravan: The Grapes of Wrath," *Nation*, CXLVIII (April 15, 1939), 441.

[21] Malcolm Cowley, "American Tragedy," *New Republic*, XCVIII (May 3, 1939), 382.

[22] Charles Angoff, "In the Great Tradition," *North American Review*, CCXLVII (Summer, 1939), 387.

[23] Thomas Burton, "Wine from These Grapes," *Saturday Review of Literature*, XXI (February 10, 1940), 16.

[24] Otis Ferguson, "Show for the People," *New Republic*, CII (February 12, 1940), 212.

which might have darkened the rosy optimism that surrounds the departing buggy, does not appear in the cut version. The sign was to have read, "No Help Wanted." As in the novel, Tom's departure is delayed until the end, but the new sequence of events endows his farewell speech with much more positive overtones. In place of the original ending, we find a line that appears at the end of Chapter XX, exactly two-thirds of the way through the book. It is Ma's strong assurance, "We'll go on forever, Pa. We're the people." On a thematic level, as Asheim points out, the affirmative ending implies that action is not required since the victims of the situation will automatically emerge triumphant. "Thus the book, which is an exhortation to action, becomes a film which offers reassurance that no action is required to insure the desired resolution of the issue."[25] But the film's conclusion has the advantage of seeming structurally more acceptable. Its "new logic" affords a continuous movement which, like a projectile, carries everything before it. The movie solution satisfies expectations which are there in the novel to begin with and which the novel's ending does not satisfactorily fulfill. Hence the critics' conflicting reaction to the two endings. Where the book seems to stop and meander in California, the film displays a forward propulsion that carries well on beyond the Colorado River.

Is such an inversion justified? Nunnally Johnson reports that he chose Ma's speech for his curtain line because he considered it the "real" spirit of Steinbeck's book.[26] This might seem at first like brazen tampering. But Johnson further reports that from Steinbeck himself he received *carte blanche* to make any alterations he wished. Steinbeck defended his position on the grounds that a novelist's final statement is in his book. Since the novelist can add nothing more, the film-maker is obliged to remake the work in his own style. If Steinbeck's awareness of the adaptational process is not enough, we may also find internal justification for the filmmakers' brilliantly simple reversal. We have seen how the production crew effected alterations which mute the villainy of cops and tradesmen; underplay the religious satire; cloud over the novel's political radicalism. But part of this withdrawal has precedent in

---

[25] Asheim, p. 157.
[26] In an interview with the author.

the novel itself. The city man's portrayal of the anonymity of the banks; the proprietor's evasive answer to Tom in the Government Camp; Ma and Tom's mystical faith—these are all Steinbeck's. So is the fact that from the beginning Tom is on parole, which he technically breaks by leaving the state. Already he is outside the domain of legal ordinance. Tom is a fugitive who *has* to keep running. If the film's conclusion withdraws from a leftist commitment, it is because the novel does also. If the film vaporizes radical sociology, the novel withdraws from it, too, with Rose of Sharon's final act. The familial optimism of the one and the biological pessimism of the other are two sides of the same coin.

The structural achievement of the cinematic version may account, paradoxically, for the film's troubling reputation. On the one hand, acclamation, box-office success, critical enthusiasm; Jane Darwell winning an Academy Award for her portrayal of Ma Joad; the casting and acting of Henry Fonda, John Carradine, Charlie Grapewin, John Qualen, Frank Darien, Grant Mitchell, and the others, generally considered flawless; Nunnally Johnson sporting a gold plaque on the wall of his studio office in recognition of a fine screenplay; and one reporter poking fun at the grandiose premiere of the film at the Normandie Theater in New York, which was attended by glamorous stars adorned in jewels and furs, and, like a "Blue Book pilgrimage,"[27] by the representatives of the very banks and land companies that had tractored the Joads off their farms. Zanuck and his entourage must have known that the filmic portrait of Steinbeck's book was no serious threat.

On the other hand, the industry's discomfort. *The Grapes of Wrath* came as close as any film in Hollywood's prolific turnout to exposing the contradictions and inequities at the heart of American life. A new thing had been created and its implications were frightening. In spite of its facile conclusion, the film raises questions to which others, outside the fictive world, have had to supply answers. The film's unusual cinematographic accomplishments, its structural unity, its documentary realism, combine to fashion images, embodying those questions, which one may review with profit again and again. If the novel is remembered for its moral

[27] Michael Mok, "Slumming with Zanuck," *Nation*, CL (February 3, 1940), 127–28.

anger, the film is remembered for its beauty. And yet the industry has been a little embarrassed by its success. That success and that embarrassment may help explain why Nunnally Johnson has accomplished so little of lasting interest since his work on this film, and why he was last seen completing the scenario for Sloan Wilson's *The Man in the Gray Flannel Suit*, a book of a very different kind! It may explain why John Ford never lists *The Grapes* as one of his favorite films, and why Ford himself offers perhaps the best explanation for the film's unique personality. Tersely, but with just the slightest trace of whimsy and bravado, John Ford remarks, "I never read the book."[28]

[28] In an interview with the author.

6   The Ox-Bow Incident

ASKED HIS OPINION OF THE 1943 FILM
version of his novel *The Ox-Bow Incident*, Walter Van Tilburg
Clark once replied that as far as he could remember only two
changes had occurred in the mutation from book to film: Gil's
reading of the letter in the last sequence, and Sparks' singing of
the spiritual following the hanging.[1] Clark's judgment is indicative
of what most readers of the book have found to be true, that William Wellman's production of *The Ox-Bow Incident* is, on the
whole, a faithful cinematic rendition of the original. What has
never been sufficiently explained is how the film-makers, rethinking their verbal source in plastic terms, produced a rendition that
has won a unique place for itself in American film history.

Director William Wellman, writer and producer Lamar Trotti,
actors Henry Fonda and Dana Andrews created, if not a financial
success for Twentieth Century-Fox, then at least a critical coup
in the American cinema. Wherever films are taken seriously, *The
Ox-Bow Incident* consistently appears as one of the industry's significant events.[2] Except for a few precursors like John Ford's

[1] In conversation with the author.
[2] The scenario is included in John Gassner and Dudley Nichols, *Best Film
Plays: 1943-44.* See also John Howard Lawson, *Theory and Technique of*

Stagecoach and James Cruze's *Covered Wagon, The Ox-Bow Incident* became the first western to treat a moral theme with the high seriousness of tragedy. It is entirely possible that without the bold innovations of Wellman's film, later productions which carried on the tradition of the serious western (*Red River, Yellow Sky, The Gunfighter, High Noon, Shane*) would not have been possible. We will first enquire, therefore, into the manner in which Wellman's unit, going outside the pale of convention, achieved a cinematic equivalent of Clark's literary model; and second, into the subsidiary reasons for the film's commercial failure.

The Ox-Bow Incident is the story of a lynching which takes place in the Nevada cattle town of Bridger's Wells in 1885. The events of the narrative, grim as they are, would not of themselves qualify either book or film as a special achievement. But if we examine the structural arrangements of Clark's novel, closely followed in the Wellman-Trotti film, we shall be in a better position to assess both its unified artistic effect and the ways in which it achieves the devastating power of an allegory permeated with moral and social overtones.

Clark's story, on the screen as in the novel, breaks through a number of conventions which we traditionally associate with the western. But perhaps the most telling innovation of all is the density the book achieves through a careful balancing of moral ambiguities. Like a morality play, Clark's characters become embodiments of virtues and vices who wage rhetorical, ethical, and even physical war with each other. But unlike a morality play, Clark's characters are endowed with complex motives. The answer to the general question "What is justice?" hinges on two subsidiary questions which inform the narrative at every moment: "What is real?" and "Who is guilty?" The final comment on these questions, setting *The Ox-Bow Incident* off from the traditional genre whose burden it is forced, unfortunately, to accept, does not appear until almost the very last page of the book, the very last shot of the film.

From the book's innocent first line, "Gil and I crossed the

Playwrighting and Screenwriting (New York, 1949), pp. 431-32; Roger Manvell, *The Film and the Public*, Penguin Books (London, 1955), pp. 146-49.

eastern divide about two by the sun," the events, characterizations, and conflicts mount in tension until, by the hard light of morning, the men turn and ride back to town. The cumulative effect of the narrative can best be seen, perhaps, from the way in which diversified characters are carefully played off against each other, each member of the posse balanced against at least one other, and each with virtues and vices contending within himself. The voices which favor lynching are represented first of all by Major Tetley, the steely-minded sadist who rallies the posse in its moment of weakness; Jeff Farnley, Kinkaid's friend, who is honestly outraged by the news of the murder; Bartlett, the demagogue, an old rancher who provides the traditional justification for lynching: if we let them get away with this, nothing, not even our women, will be safe; Monty Smith, the town drunkard, an amoral sensualist who goes along looking for much the same kind of thrill he finds in liquor; Ma Grier, the defeminized woman, who runs the town boarding house, joining the posse as another sign of her masculinity; Mapes, the brutalized deputy, who makes a mockery of his semi-legal office by swearing in the posse; Winder, the tough stagecoach driver; and Gabe Hart, his giant, simple-minded crony. Among the hunters, then, we find a scale of culpability. All the men are guilty, but most damnable of all is Tetley, the sadist parading in robes of impartiality, dragging out the execution in order to enjoy the suffering of the men. Farnley is guilty, too, but his motive is at least an honest one, simple vengeance for a friend who has been murdered. After discovering that Kinkaid is alive, Farnley is relieved when Risley, the Sheriff, picks him to go back and tend to the dead men: "Farnley was mean with a grudge, but he was honest. If he didn't like Risley right then, he liked himself a lot less." Not only are we shown the separate faces in the crowd, but we are allowed to distinguish the varieties of human motivation.

Arraigned against the lynchers is the ineffectual opposition: Davies, the storekeeper, who continually urges the men to bring the suspects back for a fair trial; Sparks, the Negro handyman and former preacher, whose moral simplicity and gaunt presence become the posse's silent conscience; Gerald Tetley, the Major's son, whose sensitive nature is completely revolted by the hunt in which he has been forced to participate. Just as we are given degrees of culpability among the lynchers, so we can calibrate degrees of weakness among the opposition. Davies continues to plead for the return of the men until the last moment, though in his final confession to Art Croft, for reasons which we will examine later, he is the most tormented of all. Sparks and young Tetley make no active attempt, aside from their voting, to resist the lynching, but each with differing results. Sparks is the silent, grieving witness to the abomination, the rustic Christian conscience who accepts the sin in man, but who, in the pacific strength of his own piety, can do little more than pray for the victims. Gerald, on the other hand, recognizes the cowardice in his motives, and, unlike Sparks, who will endure because he has gone by choice to act as the mob's conscience, Gerald ends by suicide, a victim of his own weakness. Both Gerald and Sparks are allied with Davies in opposition to the lynching, but in their contrasting motives yield quite different moral results.

In between the active killers and the active detractors are the neutral spirits, Gil Carter and Art Croft, the outsiders who have no sympathy with the mission, and yet, in order to protect themselves, do not vote against the hanging. One of the few alterations in the film, we shall see, shows Gil and Art joining Davies, Sparks, and a handful of others for the negative vote, but since in the novel Gil and Art are suspicious of the leadership, and since Gil in fact breaks into open conflict with Tetley and Farnley, the switch of vote in the film has a probability which is quite convincing.

In much the same way the victims, though united in death, differ in response to their common, tragic fate. Donald Martin of Pike's Hole is outraged by the tactics of the lynchers, unashamedly scared, deeply concerned about the survival of his family. His first helper, Alva Hardwick, the feeble-minded old man, has only one surviving sense, a vestigial will to live. Martin's second helper, the Mexican, has lived by contrivance and deception; Martin, so far as we know, by instinctive honesty; but in the final showdown the Mexican is more frightened. In spite of the Mexican's bravado, it is Martin who meets death bravely.

Finally, we have the set of characters who play no direct part in the lynching, but who shape and highlight the central episode.

Included in this category are Judge Tyler, who inadvertently contributes to the lynching by his pompousness, his ineffectual moralizing, which the men do not respect; Sheriff Risley, who unwittingly contributes by appointing a bully like Mapes as his deputy; Rose Mapen, who has rejected Gil to marry the urbanite from San Francisco, and who functions mainly as the feminine antithesis to Ma Grier.

Yet this delicate interplay of conflicting forces does not in itself explain the density of character, the controlled workmanship of the book, what Clifton Fadiman calls its "cabinet-worker precision."[3] The appreciative reviewer who wrote, "there is not a completely drawn character in the book. There is only enough of each one to satisfy the needs of this particular situation,"[4] told some of the truth, but not all of it. For while it is true that we never learn everything about any one of the characters, we are willing to accept all of them as fully rounded individuals. The magic behind this illusion deserves further exploration. For while the *dramatis personae* include no less than two dozen central characters, each one not only remains distinct in our minds, but at every moment plays a consistent role in the drama.

A good measure of this accomplishment is due, first, to the impingement of the past on the characters' present, and second, to the relationships between the characters as manifested in the hunt. Before the story begins, the men of Bridger's Wells already know each other. In this small, homogeneous community, they have had ample opportunity to learn each other's flaws and weaknesses. The lynching bee becomes merely the latest public occasion for the exhibition of typical roles. Characterization is achieved on one level by familiarity, by the continual comments of one character upon another. Farnley is immediately hostile to Davies' familiar temporizing; Mapes to Judge Tyler's scrupulosity about the forms of due process; Smith to Sparks' religious piety. Through these persistent references to past traits and habits, the protagonists achieve a kind of immanent historicity. The past impinges on the present, lending it credibility.

[3] Clifton Fadiman, "The Ox-Bow Incident," *New Yorker* (October 12, 1940), p. 84.
[4] Max Gissen, "The Ox-Bow Incident," *New Republic*, CIII (December 2, 1940), 764.

Even the victims are characterized in this manner. Bartlett thinks he recognizes the Mexican as a gambler and murderer whom he has known before. When Donald Martin, in his interview with Tetley, explains that he is a newcomer to Pike's Hole, one of the riders, who knows the town, is called up to corroborate his story. The men's dubious pasts reinforce the posse's present suspicions.

Through this slow accumulation of details, giving each character a point of reference outside the present action, the narrative achieves a dimension it would not otherwise have. This attribute is particularly appropriate to the film, since the film, ordinarily locked in a continual present, has difficulty rendering the presence of the past in current events. The historicity of the characters is strengthened, moreover, by the way in which the conflicting personalities become attuned to the exigencies of the hunt. Each character, it turns out, has a personal stake in riding out after the rustlers. At the lowest level, we have the bullies who possess no capacity for leadership, but are content to follow the strong men in order to prove their manly courage. Mapes and Smith are typical of the strong, amoral, and even degenerate men who become fodder for Bartlett's harangue. For the more dominant characters, the stake is even stronger. Tetley rides out to satisfy his sadistic cravings by forcing a spurious form of manhood on his son; Farnley to avenge the death of his friend; Davies to justify his notions of justice; Gil and Art to keep suspicion from devolving upon them; Ma Grier to prove that she is one of the boys. For each rider, communal role and private conflict combine to make of the chase a more or less personal quest.

In addition to the complex juxtaposition of motives, the narrative is further compacted by the ambiguity of reality as it unfolds for the various characters. Not only are the men in constant conflict among themselves, but the reality they unfold is ambiguous. As the posse collects, we are never quite sure of what has really happened. Greene, the young kid who acts as courier, reports that Kinkaid has been killed and his cattle stolen, but it soon becomes clear that the only detail Greene is sure about is the time of day Kinkaid's body was found, and even this, it turns out, is false. The story is unreliable because Greene has had the story from another rancher. He has not seen the body himself, and yet no one bothers to check his story, just as no one will bother to check Martin's. Farnley is immediately off in a rage to collect his pack. Even after the victims have been taken prisoner, we are still not certain about their guilt. The circumstantial evidence weighs too heavily against them. But Art Croft, who narrates the story, tells us, "The Mexican's courage, and even, in a way, young Martin's pride in the matter of the letter, had won them much sympathy, and I think we all believed now that the old man was really a pitiful fool, but whatever we thought, there was an almost universal determination to finish the job now." Some of the truth has been revealed and even accepted by the men, but not until the Sheriff's revelation after the lynching can the reader be absolutely sure of Martin's innocence. The evidence, as Art points out, has been too incriminating. Martin has fifty head of Kinkaid's cattle; he has no bill-of-sale; the man from Pike's Hole does not know him; the old man blubbers out an accusation against the Mexican; the Mexican seems to have a criminal past; and after his abortive attempt to escape, the Mexican turns up with Kinkaid's gun. There is no final justification, of course, for the crimes of the posse, but the claims of circumstance do reinforce the men's fatal error. Reality is elusive and makes for ambiguity.

Furthermore, the men have a kind of instinctive suspicion of legal processes. Judge Tyler is presented as an ineffectual magistrate, and, it is implied, he has allowed rustlers to slip through his fingers in the past.

The effect of these complexities and ambiguities, then, is to inform the narrative with a kind of resistless necessity which we find only in well-constructed tragedy. The effect of Clark's careful balancing of factors is to give his narrative the precision of a formula. For while our disapprobation rests heavily on Tetley, we understand fully how the other men come round to his point of view. Given this combination, no other result was possible. If the accidents of circumstance had been just a little less incriminating, if Tetley had been a little less iron-willed, or Davies a little more violent, the victims might have survived.

At the same time, understanding cannot be converted to approval. The tale clearly suggests that none of these mitigating circumstances in any way justifies the posse's crime. On the contrary, the complex circumstances serve only to increase the men's responsibility. Any one of the protagonists could have resisted Tetley if, for example, Martin had been able to produce a bill-of-sale. But the situation as it develops calls for a truly great display of courage, and no member of the posse is able to provide it. Ethical and ontological complexity are no excuse for murder.

Up to a point, the critic can discuss the structure of Clark's book and Wellman's film without distinguishing between them because up to a point everything that one may say of the novel may be said of the movie. Yet, in spite of the very close resemblance between Clark's narrative and Trotti's screen play, a number of differentiating traits assert themselves.

To be sure, much of Clark's technique simplifies the job of script writer. The reviewer who described the novel as an attempt "to adapt the manner of Hemingway to the manner of somebody like Joseph Conrad,"[5] understood the combination, in Clark's work, of sensory experience and moral preoccupation. With a precision that is characteristic of Clark's prose, each character in the drama is described in sufficient detail not only to make casting and costuming easy but also to give the reader insight into his personality as well. Here is Davies:

> an old man, short and narrow and so round-shouldered he was nearly hunchback, and with very white, silky hair. His hollow, high-cheeked face, looking up at Farnley, was white from indoor work, and had deep forehead lines and two deep, clear lines each side of a wide, thin mouth. The veins made his hollow temples appear blue. He would have been a good figure for a miser except for his eyes, which were queerly young, bright and shining blue, and usually, though not now, humorous.

The passage is rendered with a simplicity that tends to hide its narrative skill, the way, for example, in which the history of the man is suggested at the same time that his features are being sketched. Davies' face is white "from indoor work"; the detail reveals his occupation. Furthermore, dramatic action does not stop while the figure is being delineated. The face acts even in the

[5] Fred T. Marsh, "The Ox-Bow Incident," *New York Times Book Review* (October 13, 1940), p. 6.

process of revealing itself. The "hollow, high-cheeked face" is "looking up at Farnley." The subjunctive clause, "He would have been a good figure for a miser . . . " even in the process of preparing us for Smith's later taunt about Davies' profit motive, expresses a condition contrary to fact. The physical world, deeply lodged in narrative events, becomes a clue to present action. The eyes are "usually, though not now, humorous," and the phrase joins an habitual trait with its present deviation. In the face before us, we see the imprint of the past. To anyone who has read this description, the appearance on the screen of Harry Davenport as Davies strikes with the impact of recognition. He comes as close as movies can to rendering literary characters.

In a similar fashion, Clark makes use of physical setting to heighten the emotional content of his scenes. Clark has remarked that where some writers find their root-idea in a specific character, and some in a specific incident, he most often derives his initial impulse from a specific place.[6] The way in which setting, weather, and time of day in *The Ox-Bow Incident* are consistently grounded in dramatic conflict, without ever becoming obtrusive, would seem to bear out Clark's contention.

Consider the opening passage in which Gil and Art ride into Bridger's Wells:

> When we came onto the last gentle slope into the valley, we let the horses out and loped across the flat between the marshes where the redwing blackbirds were bobbing the reeds and twanging. Out in the big meadows on both sides the long grass was bending in rows under the wind and shining, and then being let upright again and darkening, almost as if a cloud shadow had crossed it. With the wind we could hear the cows lowing in the north, a mellow sound at that distance, like little horns.

Here again, as in Clark's character descriptions, the details of natural setting are lodged in active events. The scene is not static. This is the way the slow pitch of the valley would look to a

[6] In a reading at the State University of Iowa of his story, "The Indian Well." For an interesting study of space and loneliness themes in Clark's work, see the article by Herbert Wilner in *The Western Review*, xx (Winter, 1956).

horseman riding into town at a leisurely lope. Furthermore, the dominant tone is one of serenity. The gentle agitation of birds and animals occurs within the frame of a general stillness. Yet there is the barest suggestion of foreboding, like the storm motif in Rossini's *William Tell Overture*, the quiet warning of the trouble to come. In the image of the meadow grasses shining and darkening "as if a cloud shadow had crossed it," we have our first premonition of impending evil. Just a moment before, Art has watched Gil sitting restless in his saddle, watched him take off his sombrero, push back his sweaty hair, then return the hat, "the way he did when something was going to happen." The shadow on the grass picks up the shadow in Gil's gesture. The forecast is accurate. The next time Gil and Art hear the sound of cattle it will come through the darkness of the Ox-Bow. For very quickly they both become involved in the fever of the lynching party. With the acceleration of the plot, the weather and the time of day also change. As the posse collects, the warm afternoon gives way to a cold twilight, and as the men ride out toward the mountain trail, the ominous twilight turns to pitch darkness, the cold weather to thick snow.

On the way up the trail to the Ox-Bow, Art says,

> I looked for a meadow lark. Usually about sunset you can see them playing, leaping up and fluttering for a moment, and then dropping again, suddenly, as if they'd been hit. . . . But there was too much wind. Probably all over the big meadow they were down flat in the grass and ruffled. They could feel the storm coming too.

Just as expectations are raised about Tetley's frailty, and Davies' miserliness and good humor, which then turn into their contraries, the expectation of leaping birds is here met with its opposite reality. As we saw earlier in our review of structural ambiguities, reality is elusive, norms are continually abandoned, expectations continually reversed. Yet the signs of natural storm in the above passage are accurate signs of the approaching moral storm. And when the darkness finally does set in, it becomes an analogue for ethical as well as perceptual confusion. Not until moral and physical order are restored, through the suicides and retribution at the end of the novel, do we find the reappearance of the bird symbolism. A meadow lark sounds off in the distance, "And then another, even farther off, teenk-teenk-a-leenk." Drawn by the sound, Art and Gil bend their thoughts away from the town and its horror.

Before serenity is restored, however, the cowhands must endure the rigors of the night. In the darkness, the men begin to mistake each other. One of the riders warns Art to put out his cigarette, but Art never discovers who it is. At first he thinks it is Winder. Sparks thinks it is Bartlett. The film identifies him as Farnley. The driver of the stagecoach mistakes the posse for a holdup gang and almost cracks up in his lunge to escape. In his confusion, the driver's helper shoots wild, accidentally wounding Art in the shoulder. And at the precise moment when the riders close in toward their sleeping victims, this confusion becomes complete: "In a moment you couldn't tell which was riders and which was trees. The snow blurred everything . . . ." The dark, then, is a moral dark. And the snow confounds the riders, much as, in *The Track of the Cat*, Clark's most recent novel, Curt Bridges is sensorially confounded by the snow storm. In an earlier story, "The Wind and Snow of Winter,"[7] snow accompanies Mike Braneen's confused sense of time.

This close unity between action, character and setting is easily transmuted to the screen because so much of the narrative is visual to begin with. In the single composition of the frame, event and thing are inseparable. Arthur Miller's photography and William Wellman's set-ups render cinematically everything we have noted about the appearance of Davies, Tetley, and the other riders, about the weather and time of day, about the correlation between character and setting in physical action. In the film, Gil and Art ride into town in the baleful light of late afternoon. The slight agitation suggested by the birds and lowing cattle is caught in the film by a solitary dog who crosses the riders' path as they come down a street cut with dry wagon ruts. On the screen, the lighting changes with the storm, the darkness and the snow closing in on the men in the pass, rendering faithfully that emotional and physical separa-

[7] In *The Watchful Gods and Other Stories* (New York, 1950). The stories referred to below all appear in this edition.

tion we have already seen in the book. Finally, at the end, Gil and Art ride away into the restored gray light that fans out over the town, just as they came in, the solitary dog again their only witness.

Wellman's pictorial devices so closely parallel the verbal devices of the book that one reviewer was able to describe the camera work in almost literary terms: the "pace is slow, monosyllabic and stolid, it drills persistently into the scene. . . ."[8] Again, Wellman's directorial skill has been described in words which could apply as easily to Clark's technique: "If good acting must seem spontaneous, good direction must seem like no direction at all. Bill's [Wellman's] whole effort is to wipe away all traces of his own participation so that the eventual scene looks as though a roving camera had poked in and caught the people unaware."[9] Appropriately enough, *The Track of the Cat*, the only other work by Clark to be adapted to the screen, was directed by William Wellman.

Just as the novel's dramatic tension mounts through a slow, carefully controlled accumulation of details, the film achieves the same effect through the accumulation of monitored images. Wellman, for example, makes skillful use of close-ups to render certain passages in the book. Silence is used as carefully as speech. In the sequence where Tetley interviews Martin, the camera alternates between Tetley's face, showing his cold, sadistic pleasure; Martin's face, showing his fear, confusion, indignation; and the faces of the men, showing their anxiety, curiosity, cruelty, hatred, doubt—each commenting on the other, creating a dimension which is lacking in the individual shot.

Finally, the screen writer and director were aided by a tight plot which needed little pruning to fit the standard limits of commercial running time. Clark's narrative is divided into three broad movements corresponding roughly to an Aristotelian structure: a beginning in which the posse is formed; a middle in which the men are caught and hung; an end in which the retribution of the

[8] Manny Farber, "Let Us Now Praise Movies," *New Republic*, cvii (May 17, 1943), 670.
[9] Dore Schary, *Case History of a Movie*, as told to Charles Palmer (New York, 1950), p. 104.

protagonists is worked out. The first movement takes place in the changing twilight of the town; the second in the darkness of the mountains; the third in town the following day. All three are faithfully followed in the film.

Yet, in spite of the close correspondence between script and novel, a number of alterations occur which shift the meaning of the book even more, perhaps, than Clark suspects.

Some of these alterations, arising from the exigencies of translating one medium into another, do no damage to the textural impact of the novel. For example, the book is told entirely in the first person from Art Croft's point of view. But unlike Ellen Dean, in *Wuthering Heights*, Croft centers steadily on physical events, only rarely indulges in reminiscence or meditative comment. Unlike Ellen Dean, he is not the sole norm of reason and common sense which measures the deviations of demonic characters. Art is, rather, only one point in a complicated system of co-ordinates, less culpable than Tetley, less guilt-ridden than Davies, less impulsive than Gil. As a relative outsider, he possesses no vital information which does not eventually emerge in the ordinary revelations of speech. Almost every one of Art's attitudes is made sufficiently clear through action and its attendant dialogue. Furthermore, Art's sensibility is highly inferential. Through external signs, he is constantly reading the quality of internal states, a method which is exactly analogous to the revelations of the camera-eye. In the stagecoach scene, for instance, Swanson keeps staring at Gil "like he wanted to remember everything about him." At the Ox-Bow, when Gil has a brush with Tetley, Art sees Gil "staring at Tetley in a way I knew enough to be scared of." And toward the end, when Art finds Davies in his room, a look of tired anguish on his face, he observes that it is not Davies' slack skin that makes him look so bad. "It was his forehead and eyes. His forehead was knotted and his eyes were too steady, like a careful drunk's, but not fogged in that way, but so bright they were mad." Art's mind, then, is analogous to the camera's angle of vision, which "drills persistently into the scene." And even though the camera preëmpts Art's role as narrator, the loss is not irreparable. In the film, we never know more at any moment than Croft or Carter.

Second, as with all literary adaptations, Wellman had to effect the necessary mutation from a verbal to a visual style. In the process some of the novel's stylistic traits had to be left behind. Clark achieves his precision, to use but one example, through the use of unusually graphic adjectives and verbs, which often carry the impact of a trope. Gerald's face has "a knife-edge, marble-white look." He is depicted as "gnawing himself inside," as a boy who "kept himself thin and bleached just thinking and feeling." That "bleached" has the surprise and shock of poetic metaphor. Similarly, the structure of the figure itself frequently appears: for Gabe Hart, "Winder was his god, and sitting was his way of worshipping"; for Art, "night's like a room; it makes the little things in your head too important." At one point, the wind blows out the horses' tails "like plumes." Judge Tyler approaches Art, holding out his hand "as if he was conferring a special favor." Sparks walks across the street, his arms hanging down, "as if he had a pail of water in each hand." Tetley was "like his house, quiet and fenced away." These tropes, like the poker hands in the opening scene, are played close to the chest. Always controlled, these images achieve an exactitude which, because they cannot be translated to the screen, must be replaced by the montage, the editing, the careful arrangement of figures and objects within the frame.

Third, since narrative summary cannot be depicted in cinematic images, much pertinent information appearing there originally is converted into dialogue. For instance, all the film dialogue covering Art's refusal to go back to town following his shoulder injury appears originally as narrative summary. Earlier in the film, Art and Gil's suspicions of Bartlett's motives in whipping up the crowd are expressed in a brief conversation between them. In the novel, the suspicion is expressed in Art's private speculation:

> Thinking about it afterward I was surprised that Bartlett succeeded so easily. None of the men he was talking to owned any cattle or any land. None of them had any property but their horses and outfits. None of them were even married, and the kind of women they got a chance to know weren't likely to be changed by what a rustler would do to them.

In the same way, unspecified songs in the novel must be supplied by the film-makers, folk tunes which, as Roger Manvell points out,[10] are dramatically counterpointed in Cyril J. Mockridge's score. In the film, the Mexican is heard singing "Jorabe Tatatio," as he removes the slug from his leg; Sparks, after the hanging, a few harsh, poignant fragments from an old hymn, "You got to go there by yourself. . . ."

The film's additions are so sparse as to be trivial. The only significant addition, aside from the ending, which we shall examine in a moment, was probably a sacrifice to audience bias. In the novel, Tetley is unmistakably an ex-Confederate cavalry officer. In the film, the detail is suppressed in favor of dissociating Tetley from his Confederate past. In the sequence on the mountain trail, Gil is complaining about the leadership in general and about Tetley in particular: "He never even saw the South till after the war—and then only long enough to marry that kid's mother and get run out of the place by her folks." When Art agrees that Tetley is queer, Gil adds, "Sure, what do you suppose he'd be doin' living in this neck of the woods if he didn't have something to hide." Since this is one of the very few additions in the film, having no precedent in the novel, we can only assume that it was written into the script in order not to offend Southern sensibilities.

Other minor alterations, bespeaking the pruning and tightening efforts of Lamar Trotti, include the conversion of the saloon-keeper's name from Canby to Darby; dropping the character of Drew, Kinkaid's boss, eliminating Kinkaid's appearance with Risley in the last sequence; dropping the character of Osgood, the ineffectual minister who tries unsuccessfully to deter the men from going (a submission to the Production Code's stricture against unflattering portraits of churchmen?). Anecdotes and dialogue not immediately pertinent to the events of the narrative are deleted, including, for instance, Winder's diatribe against railroads and Gil's story about Farnley's insane fury against the longhorn who gores his pony. The poker scene which generates the first outburst between Gil and Farnley is dropped in favor of a more direct insinuation from Farnley. And just as narrative summary is frequently translated into film dialogue, lines which are attributed to one character in the novel are often spoken by another in the film. For example, once Art's role as narrator is dropped, Gil, played by

[10] Manvell, p. 148.

Henry Fonda, becomes the more imposing character. Art's role, played by Henry Morgan, becomes that of a stalwart, level-headed friend. Where in the book Art engages in a running debate on justice with Davies, Sparks, and Gerald, in the film it is Gil who speaks most of these lines. Where it is Art who is originally entrusted with the job of fetching Judge Tyler from his home, in the film it is Gil who runs the mission for Davies. Finally, the condemnation of Tetley as a "depraved, murderous beast," and the sharp self-accusation, is given to Gerald rather than Davies.

The film contains one such transfer of dialogue, however, which is indicative of a major shift in emphasis in the third movement of the story. Clark correctly remembered that the contents of the famous letter from Martin to his wife, which Gil reads to the conscience-stricken men in the last scene, are never made explicit in the novel. All we know is that the letter's statement is honest and deeply moving in its attempt to soften the shock for Martin's wife, proof enough for Davies that the writer is incapable of willful murder, and that down in the Ox-Bow the men are reluctant, even afraid, to read it. But just as the film supplies specific songs for Sparks and the Mexican, it also makes explicit the contents of Martin's letter. This is the last part of the letter as it finally appears:

> Law is a lot more than words you put in a book, or judges or lawyers or sheriffs you hire to carry it out. It's everything people have ever found out about justice and what's right and wrong. It's the very conscience of humanity. There can't be any such thing as civilization unless people have got a conscience, because if people touch God anywhere, where is it except through their conscience? And what is anybody's conscience except a little piece of the conscience of all men that ever lived?

At first, the tone of Martin's statement seems a little improbable. It is too urbane, too polished, too carefully thought out for the character of Martin, as portrayed by Dana Andrews. And it is hard to believe that Martin as we see him in his last hours—distracted, fearful, outraged, desperate—could have been capable of so polished a performance, even to his wife. But the jarring note, made partly acceptable by the line of forlorn faces along the bar, each man aghast at what he has done, and by Henry Fonda's poignantly simple reading, becomes a little more comprehensible when we discover an exact precedent in the novel. In Chapter II of Clark's book, this statement is made, almost word for word, by Davies in a discussion with Winder. Reflecting an almost agonized concern with the problem of justice, it reveals Davies' particular obsession. Davies, it is clear, has been brooding on the problem for a long time. That is why his argument has the ring of a polished essay. His statement to Winder amounts to a passionate defense of jurisprudence as the bulwark of civilization itself. Particularly in unsettled frontier communities, where enforcement is difficult, the law becomes, for Davies, the only defense against barbarism. Davies begins by asking Winder the central question: "What would you say real justice was, Bill?" He agrees with Winder's gruff but sufficient answer, justice is "seein' that everybody gets what's comin' to him." The moral authority, which decides what is right and what is wrong, resides in the whole of society. But since men are fallible, the only way to guarantee the efficacy of the system is to make sure that the "we" which judges is all-inclusive, "so that it takes in everybody." Davies finally gets Winder to see that in the case of the rustlers it takes a bigger "we" than the handful of men in the valley to make a retributive system work. Only punishment through law, the contract to which all men have agreed, can be acceptable in the end. The system may be imperfect, but since it is the only one we have, Davies argues, we abandon it at our peril. If the posse goes through with the lynching, then "by the same law, we're not officers of justice, but due to be hanged ourselves."

"And who'll hang us?" Winder wants to know.

" 'Maybe nobody,' Davies admitted. 'Then our crime's worse than a murderer's. His act puts him outside the law, but keeps the law intact. Ours weakens the law.' " And that is the greater sin.

Davies, of course, finally realizes that he has failed with Winder, as he will eventually fail with the other men. And while it becomes clear in the novel that for Davies civilization can exist only by virtue of the law's moral authority, the precise reason for his personal torment does not emerge until the very end of the book. For against this rational statement, enunciated early in the novel, the irrational hunt assumes a tragic irony. In Davies' confession to Croft, beginning, "I killed those three men," it appears that more than anyone else, Davies was in close touch with reality. He knew from the letter that Martin was innocent; he knew that Tetley was so depraved he could not be stopped except by force; he knew, moreover, that "in their hearts the men were with me; and the right was with me. Everything was with me." But in the end, he has failed to carry through his conviction because of cowardice. Like Sparks, Davies had refused to take the proffered gun from Tetley just before the party moved in for the kill. Yet he knew that a gun was precisely what he needed to stop Tetley in the moment before the lynching: ". . . I knew Tetley could be stopped. I knew in that moment you were all ready to be turned. And I was glad I didn't have a gun." In spite of his awareness, he yields to cowardice at the crucial instant. It is through this weakness that Davies comes to share in the posse's collective guilt. In a sense, then, Davies is the most tragic figure of all. Blinded neither by Tetley's sadism on the one hand, nor Gerald's fear on the other, he fails to act responsibly. He becomes the theorist without courage, the saint *manqué*, to borrow Fadiman's phrase.[11]

In the film, by contrast, Davies' guilt is dropped. His failure there is merely a failure of tactics. In the words of one reviewer, he simply "could not find the emotional key to the situation and lost every trick to Tetley for that reason."[12] In the novel, therefore, the moral indictment is much harsher. And the concluding episodes reinforce it. Once we have the answer to the question, "What is real?" (Martin's innocence), the third movement attempts to answer, still in structural terms, "Who is guilty?" The answer to the second is as complex as the answer to the first. When Sheriff Risley arrives, he decides to let the men go. "I haven't recognized anybody here. We passed in a snowstorm, and I was in a hurry." The men are his friends, and, he seems to say, he cannot very well arrest and try the entire town. The law, then, has broken down completely, and the riders are left to the much harsher judgment of their own conscience. Gerald and Tetley commit suicide. Davies' torment we have already seen. The men

11 Fadiman, p. 84.
12 Farber, p. 669.

chip in five-hundred dollars for Martin's widow. Art and Gil, the outsiders who neither approve the crime nor actively oppose it, suffering neither the sins of the leaders nor the torment of the cowards, turn away from the town almost sardonically: "I'll be glad to get out of here," Gil says. On the whole, the final judgment is harsh, the retribution fierce.

Faithful to the first and second movements of Clark's book, the film-makers, apparently, were troubled by the bitter judgments of the third. In the first place, several passages in the original script, which would have emphasized the troubling issues that motivate Davies in the book, do not appear in the final editing of Wellman's production. Joyce, Arthur Davies' young admirer, was to have said to Gil early in the film, "Mr. Davies says lynchers always know they're wrong. That's why they never like to talk about it afterwards—and why they've always got to have a leader first—somebody they can ease their conscience by blaming it on." On the way out of town, Gerald was to have protested bitterly his own weakness as well as the hypocrisy of the men. "We're all here pretending to be so noble and superior," his line reads originally, "wishing we were somewhere else just because we're afraid someone might think we're yellow." Suffering the pangs of the damned, Gerald was to have cried out, "If we get those men and hang them, I'll kill myself." Later, according to the script, Farnley was to manifest his really brutal side: "I'd rather see those fellows hung than shot because it's a dirtier death, but if anybody's gettin' cold feet, let 'em say so and I'll bushwack all three of 'em myself." Down in the Ox-Bow, Gil was to protest the spread which Ma Grier and Smith make of the victims' provisions: "You don't eat a man's food in front of him—then hang him." A fragment of the debate noted above between Winder and Davies was to have been transferred to dialogue between Davies and Art and Gil.

"Suppose the law don't work—and lets 'em go?" Art wants to know.

"Better that—a thousand times—than commit a sin against society itself," Davies replies.

The original script, furthermore, shows Sparks discovering Gerald's body in the Tetley barn, a suicide by hanging; then Sparks reporting his discovery to Major Tetley; then Tetley flinging himself on his sword, a macabre death before the portrait of his dead wife. None of these appear in the final print.[13]

One can, in fact, make a convincing case for the alteration of the ending on the basis of filmic necessity. Davies' confession to Art at the end of the novel represents a dramatically unfeasible moral climax that extends beyond the action climax. Because the second climax verges on anticlimax, it would almost certainly have appeared anticlimactic in the film. It is conceivable, therefore, that the film-makers concern for structure and tempo had more to do with the shift of values in Davies than any deliberately different reading of Clark's resolution.

Other deletions and alterations, particularly the suicides of the Tetleys, may have been effected to keep the denouement from becoming unbearable, for as the Greeks discovered a long time ago, and as film-makers have rediscovered since, events which are cushioned by their occurrence offstage, or by their rendition in language, often become repellent when depicted directly. More central, however, is the fact that the events which finally do appear on the screen, either directly or indirectly, modify the original judgment. In contrast to the novel, Art and Gil vote with five other men against the hanging, cleansing themselves, to some degree, of responsibility. When the Sheriff finally arrives, he does not open himself to the charge of collusion by releasing the men, but on the contrary promises that justice will be done: "God had better have mercy on you, because you ain't gonna get any from me!"

Later, Gerald follows his father home, only to find that the Major has locked him out. Through the closed door, he issues a bitter indictment against the sadistic actions of the old man. Instead of seeing the death by sabre, we hear a shot offstage which allows us to deduce rather than witness Tetley's suicide. In our last glimpse of Gerald, an almost exalted look has come across his face, the look of a man shriven of his sins. As far as we know, he is not contemplating self-destruction.

[13] The author was able to check two prints of the film, one distributed by the Twentieth Century-Fox studios in Washington, D. C., and one at the George Eastman House in Rochester, New York. Both prints were alike in this respect.

Finally, instead of merely looking ahead to being rid of the town, Gil takes the letter he has just read and the money the men have raised for Martin's widow, and heads for his horse. "Where we going?" Art asks. Gil replies, in the last line of the film, "He said he wanted his wife to have this letter, didn't he? He said there wasn't anybody to look out for his kids." They mount their horses, and ride out, to make amends for the sins of the town. In the film, then, Davies, Gerald, Gil and Art stand redeemed. And since the sins in the film are less severe, the retribution becomes understandably less fatal.

That the way in which the film solves the denouement could not have been easily come by is indicated, finally, by an alternative ending which was published with Lamar Trotti's script.[14] In the rejected ending, just as Gil folds the letter and returns it to his pocket, Rose Mapen comes in with her new husband. Both are too gay, too elegantly dressed for Gil, who has been drawn out fine by the sleepless night. Immediately there is trouble in the air. When Swanson makes an objectionable remark, Gil makes a leap for him. As in the first sequence, Darby hits Gil with a bottle, buckling him. When Gil comes to, a grin spreading across his face, he looks up at the painting of the nude and says, as he does in the opening scene, "Say, ain't that guy got there yet, either?" The wheel has come full circle. Gil has returned to his original truculence; the implication is that the experience of the lynching has washed over him without any lasting effect.

While this alternative ending does come closer to the spirit of the novel, it is not appropriate to the cumulative alterations in the film which we have already traced. For once the edge of guilt is removed from Gil, Art, and Davies, the way is cleared for a more positive ending in which Gil has learned and grown from the grim incident at the Ox-Bow. The Gil who throughout the demonic hunt is given to impulsive but honest outbursts against the leadership, is consistent with the Gil whom the film-makers chose for their final shot.[15]

Taken in isolation, the novel's contrasting judgment may seem

[14] See the published scenario in Gassner and Nichols.
[15] For a discussion of the alternate ending, see Lawson, pp. 431–32.

unduly harsh, even arbitrary. But the values of the novel become comprehensible when set against the consistent world-view which emerges from the corpus of Clark's fiction. Clark's cosmos is predicated on the assumption that nature is savage and predatory. The human as well as the animal species become so caught up in the struggle to survive that at times they are indistinguishable. It is interesting to observe the frequency with which animals are personified in Clark's stories. The burros in "The Wind and Snow of Winter" and "The Indian Well," the mountain lion in *The Track of the Cat*, the purple fish in "The Fish Who Could Close His Eyes," are all personified as convincingly as the human characters. In "Hook," the entire narrative is told from a hawk's point of view. In the struggle to survive, animals and humans are of course forced to prey on each other. Still, within this predatory universe, a moral scheme is possible. For even though one must kill to live, animals and humans alike must kill mercifully, not cruelly, must take only what is necessary to survive and no more.

Within this continual zoological war, all living species may be divided into victims and killers. The killers may be further subdivided into the merciful and merciless. Only as long as the killers hunt humanely, only as long as they remain merciful, do they stand immune from moral retribution. While the merciful killers are more or less neutral, the merciless killers are morally culpable. Cruel, gratuitous, and sadistic killing becomes the sin. In the ensuing struggle, the victims are doomed by their weakness; the merciless killers by their acts. The latter must do penance, and often with their lives. Only the merciful killers, given their stoic acceptance of nature's laws, can both live and remain free of tormenting sin.

Among the victims in Clark's fictive world are Arthur Bridges in *The Track of the Cat;* Jenny, the burro, in "The Indian Well"; the deer in "The Buck in the Hills"; the rabbit in "The Watchful Gods." Among the proud or sadistic hunters, the merciless killers, are Curt Bridges, who is contemptuous of the weaknesses in man and nature; the cat who stalks the Bridges' herds, but not for food; the cougar who, having come to the well in search of antelope, kills the burro, which is not its rightful game (like all merciless killers in Clark's moral scheme, the cougar does not kill the burro at once, but tortures it to death, and feeds on it "with uncertain relish"); the boy Buck who cruelly shoots and kills a young, defenseless rabbit. Among the merciful killers are Hal Bridges, who is neither weak nor proud; Jim Suttler, who owns the burro killed by the cougar; Hook, the hawk, who kills only in order to live. The relationships between the victims and the victors are worked out in more or less complex arrangements, but the central motifs are consistent throughout. For the sins of pride or cruelty, the merciless killers are always guilty, and usually punished. If nature does not exact its revenge, then conscience does. Curt Bridges is defeated as much by his own fear as by the rigors of the snowstorm; it is only Hal Bridges, the merciful killer, who, by killing the cat, can successfully avenge the death of both his brothers, and still go on living. Jim Suttler waits through the course of an entire winter to destroy the cougar and lay its pelt over Jenny's grave. Buck, the boy in "The Watchful Gods," does penance for his sinful destruction of the rabbit by wading out into the ocean toward self-annihilation. And the Japanese farmer, like Mac in "The Buck in the Hills," becomes morally reprehensible for allowing his dog to torture the once proud but now disabled Hook instead of killing him quickly and mercifully, as his wife has urged.

In this scheme, one must proceed with a certain caution, remembering always that in Clark's world the hierarchy of human values is man-made, imposed *by man* on the natural order. In one sense, if for no other reason than that man alone makes moral judgments, the world of nature is finally amoral. But human nature at its worst is immoral, and never so immoral as when man attempts to impose his own scheme of values on nature.

In a recent letter, Clark makes this patently clear. He points out that in "The Indian Well," for instance, Jim Suttler, the killer for unnatural reasons, disturbs a whole natural pattern, but leaves unscathed. The cougar, it is true, does not care much for burro, but he does kill for hunger. In the *total pattern*, which includes man, though only too often, like Curt, man is no longer aware of it, man deems himself immune. Nevertheless, he is still subject to the forces of natural law, so that when man passes moral judgments on the animal world, he is almost always wrong:

I would say, even, moral law exists only within natural law—and among humans. Increasingly, I believe, however, man having come to dominate the world to such an unhealthy degree, that unless moral law is brought into accord with natural law, which simply cannot be broken for any length of time with immunity, which is to say, unless the moral law extends to pass judgment upon human evil where it affects other creatures, man himself will perish, via his sole concern for man, no matter how moral he may become as man to man.[16]

This special combination of Darwinian struggle and Christian sin combines to evoke an almost Biblical indictment against man's corruption. It is interesting to note the striking similarity between these moral assumptions and those of the poet Robinson Jeffers, whom Clark chose as the subject for his Master's essay at the University of Vermont. Like Jeffers, Clark explores human aberrations with a moral eye. Like Jeffers, he finds in the world of nature, the enduring rocks, the ageless sea, a superior moral order in which gratuitous violence and sadism are alien perversions. It is ironic that Buck does penance for killing the rabbit by wandering into the Pacific, a setting very similar to Robinson Jeffers' country around Big Sur. Increasingly, then, Clark's work shows a steady and growing revulsion at killing in general, at hunting in particular, so that by the time of "The Watchful Gods," Clark's most recently published work, it is a question, given the moral superiority of creatures like Hook to their human executioners, whether the killing of animals can be justified at all.

Whatever our final judgment of the details of Clark's moral search, a clear assessment of his position helps explain the unusually troubling, even anguished concern with the law which we find in *The Ox-Bow Incident.* For here, too, the pattern which is to emerge more clearly in the later novels and stories is already apparent. While the struggles of the natural world are not immediately in the foreground, the terms of the struggle do function in a kind of muted undertone. The consistent fidelity to natural setting, the appearance, disappearance, and reappearance of the birds in the descriptive passages above; the confounding of senses

---

[16] From a letter to the author, January 12, 1956.

in the snow; the affection with which Art and Gil treat their horses—all these bear witness to the horror of the lynching. Furthermore, the pursuit itself is carried out in terms of a hunt. The men read the tracks in the snow as they would in search of game. They set out, ostensibly, to avenge a gratuitous murder, as Hal Bridges sets out to avenge the death of his brothers. Farnley talks about his shot at the Mexican as impersonally as he would about his markmanship. There are, then, merciless killers among animals and humans alike, but the humans are infinitely more damnable. At their worst, they exhibit a gratuitous, even an exquisite capacity for cruelty which is rare in the animal kingdom.

The same distribution of roles which pervades Clark's moral order is also evident here. Tetley is a merciless killer; Gerald, like Martin, is a victim. And like the cougar who kills cruelly, like the burro who is doomed through weakness, Tetley, the killer, and Gerald, the victim, are both propelled to the same destructive end. The merciful killers alone are able to survive, and only then by acts of vengeance or atonement on behalf of the victims. The money that Art and Gil kick in for Martin's widow parallels Jim Suttler's long vigil in the winter snow.

If Davies, the saintly pretender, survives at the end, it is only by the thinnest margin, for like Gerald he is possessed with the impulse toward self-destruction. "Go get him," Art tells Canby when Davies stumbles from his room, "you can't leave him alone, I tell you." Only the intervention of the stronger men forestalls an end similar to that of the Tetleys.

Against the larger order of Clark's world-view, the reason for Davies' obsession with the meaning of justice becomes clear. For without the legal covenant, to which all men agree, there can be no civilization. Left to his own devices, man cannot be trusted. If a destructive cowardice possesses even men like Davies, if sins of omission make sins of commission more deadly, then how much more accessible are the ways of barbarism to ordinary men. In Clark's much anthologized story, "The Portable Phonograph" (which appeared several years before the advent of the atom bomb and the current vogue of science fiction), we are given a prophetic picture of what can happen when the compulsion of law is abandoned in favor of predatory war. Having sealed up his phonograph and books, the last vestiges of civilization in a ravaged world, the professor must still remain fearful of human thievery. It is because of man's sinful possibilities that the benign doctor must still go to sleep with his hand around "the comfortable piece of lead pipe." Law is necessary, then, because the alternatives are simply too horrible to contemplate.

Considered in these terms, the choice of the film-makers for their denouement in *The Ox-Bow Incident* constitutes a major shift in emphasis.

Yet, by a curious paradox, even the modifications which Wellman and Trotti adopted for the film were not enough to break through audience resistance to the unconventional western. Unlike John Ford's *The Informer*, *The Ox-Bow Incident* did not ultimately make a substantial return for its investors, nor did it win any Academy Awards. In spite of a warm critical reception, it remained a box-office failure. Beyond its immediate locale, the film presents so many fresh realities that all together they must have been positively baffling to spectators brought up on the stereotyped Hollywood product: Tetley frankly attempting to make sadism respectable by wearing a uniform; Jane Darwell's Ma Grier making a fetish of shedding her feminine traits, yet ending not as a comic suffragette but as a female lyncher; Anthony Quinn portraying not the conventional simple-minded, lazy Mexican, but a wily, intelligent man who speaks ten languages; Leigh Whipper performing the role not of a shuffling, grinning Uncle Tom, but of a sincerely religious man whose quiet dignity puts the lynchers to shame. The film bristles with so many of these unconventional realities and startling overtones, that again and again the label "social document" has been affixed to it.[17] When Sparks tells Gil about seeing his own brother lynched, the extension of the reference is unavoidable. Even before the cycle of serious Negro-content films following the Second World War, Leigh Whipper's portrayal of Sparks showed that it was possible, as Peter Noble points out,[18] to depict the Negro as an ordinary hu-

---

[17] See the statements in Philip T. Hartung, *Commonweal*, xxxviii (June 4, 1943), 169–70: "the most powerful social document since 'The Grapes of Wrath'"; also Farber, p. 671: "a significant moment in our culture."

[18] Peter Noble, *The Negro in Films* (London, n.d.), p. 195.

man being. Thus the circumscribed world of Bridger's Wells pours over into contemporary reality.

These overtones, in combination with Wellman's controlled mounting of plastic images, account, perhaps, for the split in the film's reputation. In Hollywood, *The Ox-Bow Incident* is still used as a term of opprobrium for "art" films that fail at the box-office. Nevertheless, the film's critical reputation has achieved for it the status of a separate genre: the classic prototype of the serious western. When the film arrived in England during the war, it was mistaken for a conventional horse opera, given a modest release in the suburbs, and deprived of a review in the daily press. Rediscovered after the war, it was given a revival run by the Academy Cinema in London, in 1946, but this time to general critical acclaim. A print of the film is now in the permanent archives at the George Eastman House in Rochester, and I am told that the Twentieth Century-Fox distributors in Washington, D. C., keep a copy in stock to meet the demand for periodic revivals. Because William Wellman and Lamar Trotti were able to accomplish cinematically what Walter Van Tilburg Clark accomplished in language, the film has shown remarkable endurance.

7 Madame Bovary

IMAGINE THE STORY OF EMMA BOVARY told within the frame of Flaubert's trial in 1857. Pinard, the public prosecutor, angrily holds up a volume of the despised book and addresses the Court: "As Public Prosecutor, I demand that further publication of this novel be forbidden and that its author, Gustave Flaubert, be found guilty of committing the misdemeanor of an outrage against public morals and established custom."

Subsequently, Flaubert himself takes the stand to answer the charge. He has, he says, "forgiven" this woman whom the prosecution contends is a disgrace to all France, who neglects her child, who betrays her husband. He does—and does not—deny the accusation. With much composure, he goes on to explain that the public prosecutor has indicted him "for the crime of forgiveness. What can I say? Forgiveness, as I understand it, is still among the Christian sentiments. I do not deny it." In clear, carefully modulated tones, he proceeds to define his position. He denies that his book is an attack on public morality. He has, he says, merely shown the vicious "so that we may preserve the virtuous." Emma was not "a monstrous creation of my degenerate imagination." On the contrary, our world created her, she may be found everywhere.

He, Flaubert, had but to draw from life to draw her truly. There are hundreds of thousands of women who wish they were Emma, and who have been saved from her fate not by virtue but simply by lack of determination (murmur in the courtroom). Now in order to understand Emma, says Flaubert, let us go back to the time she was twenty. . . .

Now imagine, from this point on, the recapitulation of Emma's story, with Flaubert as narrator, his voice intruding continually to draw the proper moral, to explain the scene transpiring before us. After depicting the wall of Emma's bedroom, papered with cut-outs from *Les Modes Illustres*, imagine him saying, "Emma Rouault. The flower beyond the dunghill. How had she grown here? The kitchen drudge who dreamed of love and beauty. What are dreams made of? Where do they come from?" Imagine, too, in the scenes unfolding before us, Charles Bovary talking to Emma in dialogue like this: "Mademoiselle, I've come into many a farmhouse kitchen at dawn. I've smelled many smells—sour milk, children's vomit—uh—I never smelled perfume before. . . ." And so on, Flaubert leading us from scene to scene, like the beadle who insists on showing Emma and Leon the virtues of the cathedral at Rouen when both would rather be doing something else. Until, finally, we are back in the courtroom, where Flaubert again asserts that he was only telling the truth, that "Truth lives forever; men do not." Imagine the Court being so impressed by Flaubert's suasion that the reaction is universally favorable (an acquittal is certain), and, in a very last line, the assurance that this "was a triumphant moment in the history of the free mind."

For Flaubert, who spent so many agonized years trying to refine himself out of his work, this retailing of Emma's story would seem appalling. Yet such a version exists. It is Vincent Minnelli's *Madame Bovary*, produced in 1949 for the Metro-Goldwyn-Mayer studios. The film exhibits such a marked failure of the pictorial imagination that it provides an excellent occasion for some concluding remarks on the differences between literary works and the cinema.

The failure of Robert Ardrey's script and Vincent Minnelli's direction is especially surprising when one considers the highly cinematic character of Flaubert's novel. Harry Levin speaks continually of the cinematic effects in *Madame Bovary*—the moment, for example, when Emma and Leon enter a curtained cab and Flaubert draws back a respectful distance, projecting "a rapid sequence of long-shots, so that—instead of witnessing their embrace—we participate in a tour of the city of Rouen, prolonged and accelerated to a metaphorical climax."[1] The metaphorical climax appears in the conclusion of Flaubert's passage: ". . . a bared hand passed beneath the small blinds of yellow canvas, and threw out some scraps of paper that scattered in the wind, and farther off alighted like white butterflies on a field of red clover all in bloom." Levin also calls our attention to the cinematic use of the great cathedral at Rouen, which bears silent witness to the adulterous act of the lovers; the breaking of Charles' barometer after his unsuccessful operation on Hippolyte; the patent leather shoe of the formerly club-footed boy; Charles' silly hat. The list could be indefinitely enlarged: Emma's tawdry bouquet of orange blossoms; the cigar case whose tobacco scent is a continual reminder of male attractions at the Vaubyessard ballroom; Rodolphe's letter, with the mock tear stain cynically rendered with a drop of water; "the close-up of a religious statuette . . . which falls from the moving-wagon into fragments on the road between Tostes and Yonville."[2]

Hence, in Levin's formulation, "every object becomes, in its way, a symbol; and the novelist seeks not merely the right word but the right thing."[3] The use of this "cinematographic manipulation of detail" may even be extended to Flaubert's method. The function of reducing Flaubert's embryonic material for the novel, which ran to some 3,600 pages, can be likened to "the cutting of a film." Needless to say, none of these central *things* (so evident in Flaubert's mounting techniques), nor the root-symbols of the cathedral and the hospital seemed, apparently, to have been of any interest to the film-makers.

[1] Harry Levin, "Madame Bovary: The Cathedral and the Hospital," *Essays in Criticism*, II (January, 1952), 6.

[2] *Ibid.*, p. 6.

[3] *Ibid.*, p. 7.

To come at this pictorial failure in another way, let us consider a passage from the book which has already been subjected to a good deal of exegesis:

But it was above all the meal-times that were unbearable to her, in this small room on the ground-floor, with its smoking stove, its creaking door, the walls that sweated, the damp flags; all the bitterness in life seemed served up on her plate, and with the smoke of the boiled beef there rose from her secret soul whiffs of sickliness. Charles was a slow eater; she played with a few nuts, or, leaning on her elbow, amused herself with drawing lines along the oilcloth table-cover with the point of her knife.[4]

Eric Auerbach uses this passage to demonstrate the manner in which Flaubert cumulatively renders the utter boredom of Emma's life at Tostes, the manner in which he continually grounds Emma's consciousness in a physical reality which is organized and given significance by that consciousness.[5] Georges Poulet modifies and extends this analysis to show a more vivid relationship between Emma's consciousness and her environment, between Flaubert's carefully balanced subjective and objective worlds.[6] By exploring the way in which the "physical motion of the words" renders "the psychic motion of the meaning," Poulet makes a convincing case for a more archetypal spatial image, the circle and its center: "the Flaubertian *milieu* appears as a vast surrounding space which spreads from Emma to an indeterminate circumference, and from the circumference to the consciousness of Emma." For the purposes of the film critic, there is still another way in which this passage can yield significant results. For it begins to suggest those elements which the film adapter may take over and successfully forge into the construct of his film, and those he cannot.

On the one hand, the basic units of physical reality which circulate on the periphery of Emma's consciousness, and even their

[4] I quote from the translation by Eleanor Marx Aveling in The Modern Library Edition of *Madame Bovary* (New York, n.d.).

[5] Eric Auerbach, *Mimesis: The Representation of Reality in Western Literature*, trans. Willard R. Trask (Princeton, 1953), p. 483 ff.

[6] Georges Poulet, "The Circle and the Center: Reality in Madame Bovary," *The Western Review*, xix (Summer, 1955), 245–260.

succession, are perfectly subservient to the camera eye: the camera can approach and withdraw, search and probe, rove and stop to the rhythms of Emma's sight and sensibility. It can show the ground-floor in a medium shot, move slowly, monotonously into the small room, catch sight of the smoking stove, pause at the creaking door, pan up or across the sweating walls, cut to a close-up of the steaming boiled beef. It can cut to a shot of Charles slowly eating, then to Emma idly drawing lines along the oil-cloth with her knife. It may be noted that the director would still have a certain amount of leeway here, that the precise direction of the movement, the precise distance from the object is suggested rather than prescribed exactly. But roughly the passage calls for a panning shot corresponding to each clause; and instantaneous cuts to bridge the gaps between clauses. Further, the camera can approximate Flaubert's technique of showing us first the figure of Emma as part of the scene, and then the content of Emma's perceiving mind as it sees the world around her. Percy Lubbock has shown us how Flaubert's style is a controlled blending of several points of view, a continual oscillation between what Lubbock calls the pictorial and dramatic modes. In the pictorial, or panoramic angle of vision, the author is somehow outside or above the action, centering his attention on the incidents of his tale. In the dramatic, or scenic, he is "regarding primarily the form and colour they assume in somebody's thought."[7] In our passage, we find exactly this shift from the pictorial to the dramatic modes. Everything we envision from the opening clause to the image of Charles is colored and organized by Emma's sensibility. It is her perceiving consciousness ranging out to the limits of a circle of indefinite circumference, the confining array of door, stove, walls, damp flags, and then contracting to the bitterness on her plate. This rush through space is precisely what gives the scene (and the film) its special power. But in the last clause (separated from its predecessor by a semicolon, as the shots might be separated by instantaneous cuts) we move out of Emma's consciousness, and see *her* as part of the setting. We have moved from the pictorial to the dramatic mode, from Emma's angle of vision to the author's, and

[7] Percy Lubbock, *The Craft of Fiction* (New York, 1947), p. 71.

yet with such consistency of texture that we feel no break in continuity. If, then, we can agree that *Madame Bovary* is "something in the nature of a drama, where the two chief players are a woman on one side and her whole environment on the other,"[8] we can understand in what manner the camera can approximate Flaubert's style.

Immediately, however, certain difficulties arise. For if our passage reveals what the camera can translate into visual terms, it also suggests what the film must leave behind. When Flaubert uses a plural noun, "meal-times," he suggests in a word Emma's habitual boredom. Through the plurality of "meal-times," supported by the particular arrangements of objects in space, the passage suggests the monotony, distraction, emptiness that possess Emma from day to day. The cinema, on the other hand, cannot show plurality in this fashion. It can only show one scene, whose habitual character we must infer for ourselves. Now it can be argued, of course, that the common transitional device of superimposing several frames, one upon the other (as in our example of the tractors and jalopies in *The Grapes of Wrath*), is the motion picture equivalent of the noun plural. But we may note that the mounting of superimposed images merely *suggests* generality (there are thousands of jalopies on the road, but even in the montage we see a bare dozen or so), or contracted time (the road signs, the snippets of highways, bridge the temporal gap from one geographical point to another). The film lacks the power of language to show habitual behavior. In the film, the monotonous repetition of events can only be suggested by the movements of a particular actor, by the way Willie Loman wearily drops his suitcases in *Death of a Salesman*, by the way the actress playing Emma doodles with her knife upon the oilcloth.

In the second place, we can only infer, but cannot see such attributive words as "were *unbearable* to her," and "*amused* herself." Nor can the camera render such abstractions and concealed tropes as those contained in "all the bitterness in life seemed served up on her plate," or in the "whiffs of sickliness" which rise with the smoke from the pot of boiled beef. The film can show the plate; it can show the steam; it can show the boiled beef. But the bitterness,

[8] *Ibid.*, p. 80.

the exhalations of disgust, and certainly the secret soul can only be suggested by juxtaposing images of physical reality.

This analysis, then, raises again one of the central problems of this study, the manner in which the attributes of language must be suppressed in favor of plastic images.

Flaubert criticism is generally agreed on the bifurcation between Flaubert's exquisitely mounted language and the relative poverty of his subject matter. While Flaubert, so the argument goes, has ostensibly refined himself out of his novel, he still manages to comment on the procession of events and characters. This he achieves by an elusive but nevertheless definable tone in which "A hint of irony is always perceptible."[9] Through this tone, Flaubert achieves a more penetrating comment on Emma, her world, and the roster of dreary characters who circulate through Tostes and Yonville and Rouen, than any explicit statement (like those of Flaubert in the film) can possibly do. In our passage, "Nothing happens, but that nothing has become a heavy, oppressive something,"[10] not because Flaubert *says* so, but because the objects depicted by his language have become impregnated with a mood of apprehension. Thus the antithesis between Emma's vagaries and that exquisitely wrought language through which Emma reaches us. The meager, futile world of the provinces is opposed to the intelligible, and intelligent, world of the prose style. That is how language comes to have "criteria for stupidity" and why it "has a part in that reality of the 'intelligent' which otherwise never appears in the book."[11] It is this very antithesis which explains why Henry James could have such split feelings about Flaubert, "the ironic painter," why in a sense the novel's very perfection is the source of its weakness. "The work is a classic because the thing, such as it is, is ideally *done*. . . . " But, "Our complaint is that Emma Bovary, in spite of the nature of her consciousness and in spite of her reflecting so much that of her creator, is really too small an affair."[12]

One example of this disjuncture between language and theme,

[9] *Ibid.*, p. 89.
[10] Auerbach, p. 489.
[11] *Ibid.*, p. 491.
[12] Henry James, *The Art of Fiction* (New York, 1948), pp. 134–135.

and of "the desperate difficulty" involved for Flaubert "in making his form square with his conception,"[13] may be found in the celebrated description of the country wedding at Bertaux:

> The table was laid under the cart-shed. On it were four sirloins, six chicken fricassees, stewed veal, three legs of mutton, and in the middle a fine roast sucking-pig, flanked by four chitterlings with sorrel. At the corners were decanters of brandy. ... Large dishes of yellow cream, that trembled with the least shake of the table, had designed on their smooth surface the initials of the newly wedded pair in nonpareil arabesques. A confectioner of Yvetot had been intrusted with the tarts and sweets. As he had only just set up in the place, he had taken a lot of trouble, and at dessert he himself brought in a set dish that evoked loud cries of wonderment. To begin with, at its base there was a square blue cardboard, representing a temple with porticoes, colonnades, and stucco statuettes all round, and in the niches constellations of gilt paper stars; then on the second stage was a dungeon of Savoy cake, surrounded by many fortifications in candied angelica, almonds, raisins, and quarters of oranges; and finally, on the upper platform a green field with rocks set in lakes of jam, nutshell boats, and a small Cupid balancing himself in a chocolate swing whose two uprights ended in real roses for balls at the top.

Now this scene is intended to comment ironically on Emma's crude initiation to marriage. But I submit that the lovely evocation of the banquet table permits no such irony, that its very fragility countermands the intended effect of rustic crudity.

Even allowing for this disjuncture, it is entirely possible to translate the portraits of provincial life into persuasive cinematic images. The camera can loop and swing and come to rest, can cut from face to face for periods of varying duration, as Carl Dreyer demonstrated once and for all in *The Passion of Joan of Arc*. It can, as in our passage depicting Emma's humdrum life at Tostes, alternate between the way Emma sees the table, the peasant guests (as Mme. Falconetti sees the faces of the Inquisitors), and the way an omniscient observer would see Emma seeing (as we see Joan's

[13] *Ibid.*, p. 141.

suffering face). What the camera leaves behind, the film-maker must imagine for himself. His task, indeed, is simplified by the necessary abandonment of Flaubert's prose style. In brief, the implication is that the film-maker who would tell Emma's story must find visual equivalents for Flaubert's language, an extraordinarily difficult task at best. It is not Emma's *story* we would primarily remember, but the lovely *rendition* of it.

This the MGM production crew has not done. Whether the film is depicting the ball at the château of the Marquis d'Andervilliers, or the agricultural fair outside the Place d'Armes, the film-makers consistently miscalculate the tone of the scene. Instead of Emma's muted wonder at the discovery, for her, of an elegant romantic world, we have a scene which ends with the smashing of windows. Instead of the ironic but controlled contrast between a kind of Rabelaisian charivari and Emma's distaste, we have a vulgar and senseless brawl. And at every point, we have James Mason, as Flaubert, intruding on the sound track to explain, in the stiffest, most conventional terms, what is going on. Indeed, it would seem that at every point where the plastic arrangement of the images was inadequate to convey the inner content of the narrative, the film unit tried to cover up by supplying a *noise*, and usually a loud one—splintering glass, raucous laughter, Flaubert's droning voice. The one or two exceptions— Jennifer Jones as Emma seeing herself in a mirror at the Château de Vaubyessard, surrounded by handsome men, as she must have seen herself countless times in her imagination; the camera quietly panning from a woodland copse to two riderless horses, then to Emma's hat and crop discarded on the grass, mutely telling us the story of her surrender to Rodolphe—these are not enough to redeem the film's general failure. For the most part, we see a procession of tired images, like an illustrated lecture. The effect is to leave us, finally, with little insight into Emma's motivations. We are told that they exist, but we never really *see* them.

Dorothy B. Jones, in an excellent little article on the content analysis of films, explains that in successful motion pictures the major character usually has one or more "wants" or values which are clearly developed scene by scene, and that "the poorer grade pictures . . . were those in which it was most difficult to analyze character 'wants.' "[14] By this standard, the film version of *Madame Bovary* is also deficient. When Van Heflin, as Charles, tells Emma at one point that he wishes he understood her, that he wishes he knew what it was she wanted, we are inclined to agree. We are moved to ask the same question.

If the film-maker, then, must abandon the essential attributes of language—plurality, metaphor, and direct references to affective states—he must also abandon those additional attributes which we normally associate with conceptual, as opposed to perceptual, thought. Without rehearsing the intricacies of her distinctions, we may adopt Susanne Langer's differentiation between discursive and presentational art, a distinction derived from the simpler juxtaposition between the visual and the verbal arts. In effecting the mutation from the language of the novel to the plastic images of the film, from the discursive to the presentational medium, certain additional alterations are necessary. The components of experiential time, mythic reference, memory, dream, must be transposed into visual equivalents which can only suggest these things.

Leo Spitzer once remarked, referring to the end of *Moby Dick*, that in the transposition from the book to the cinema something vital would inevitably be lost. As the *Pequod* sinks to its destruction, in Melville's closing passage, a bird is caught between Tashtego's hammer and the subsiding spar. Melville consciously transforms the bird into a symbol of heaven and Ahab's ship into an agent of Satan which "would not sink to hell till she had dragged a living part of heaven along with her, and helmeted herself with it." Thus the pressure of the entire Satanic myth is brought to bear on the Pequod's sinking, the added dimension endowing the conclusion with enormous power. In John Huston's film version of *Moby Dick*, as if to confirm Spitzer's speculation, this mythic element is absent simply because the cinema is incapable of rendering it. A narrator's voice reciting these lines would seem artificial (as it does in the compromised version of Huston's *Red Badge of Courage*), since it could only comment on the action from outside the physical event. In a similar fashion, the film-maker adapting

[14] Dorothy B. Jones, "Quantitative Analysis of Motion Picture Content, *Public Opinion Quarterly*, vi (Fall, 1942), 419.

Flaubert would have to leave behind such figurative allusions as the likening of Doctor Larivière to "one of the old Knight-Hospitallers," or Homais' pompous inflation to "Amphytrionic pride."

Ordinarily, the film must replace, with formative spatial images, the rendition of psychological time with which the modern novel has been so eminently preoccupied. But because it is incapable of depicting consciousness as language can, the film has not, like the novel, been tormented by the problem of psychological time in consciousness. The modern novel, confronted by the limitations of a language which is made up of units that are discrete, sequential, and irreversible (as we saw in some detail in the first chapter), has waged an endless battle to render the *durée,* in Bergson's sense of the word, or the sense of timelessness, those moments of illumination which are often indistinguishable from mystical experience. Hans Meyerhoff carefully demonstrates the way in which modern literature has been preoccupied with six aspects of psychological time: (1) subjective relativity (the distension and contraction of time in consciousness); (2) continuous flow, or duration; (3) dynamic fusion, or interpenetration, of the causal order in experience and memory; (4) duration and the temporal structure of memory in relation to self-identity; (5) eternity; (6) transitoriness, or the temporal direction toward death.[15] Auerbach summarizes the trend in another way:

> . . . in a surprising fashion unknown to earlier periods, a sharp contrast results between the brief span of time occupied by the exterior event and the dreamlike wealth of a process of consciousness which traverses the whole subjective universe. These are the characteristic and distinctively new features of the technique: a chance occasion releasing processes of consciousness; a natural and even, if you will, a naturalistic rendering of those processes in their peculiar freedom, which is neither restrained by a purpose nor directed by a specific subject of thought; elaboration of the distinction between "exterior" and "interior" time.[16]

[15] Hans Meyerhoff, *Time in Literature* (Berkeley and Los Angeles, 1955), p. 85.
[16] Auerbach, p. 538.

If these summaries are accurate, we can more easily understand why the film has not been plagued by the problem of time as literature has. Forced to deal in units of physical reality, the cinema is automatically excluded from what is essentially a non-visual, non-spatial, non-presentational problem. The "whole subjective universe," of which Auerbach speaks, is, despite dialogue, ultimately closed to the camera eye. The camera angle, as Balázs points out, *can* be subjective, but always it is a *visual* subjectivity, working in optical terms. That is why the problem of psychological time which haunts modern literature is markedly absent in our specimen studies. If the film catches the flux at all, it does so on the coattails, so to speak, of space in constant motion. Simply because cinemaphotography cannot penetrate consciousness, it naturally and systematically bends all its creative, formative efforts toward finding new and significant spatial structures. We can see how another person *sees;* but not how he *thinks.* Only language can approximate the quality of thought.

In adapting Flaubert, however, the film-maker is not yet faced with the problem of rendering the experience of psychological time which pervades so many modern novels. If, as Poulet suggests, "Flaubert is the first who builds his novels around a series of centers encompassed by their environments,"[17] and if, "For the first time in the history of the novel, human consciousness shows itself as it is, as a sort of core, around which sensations, thoughts and memories move in a perceptible space," Flaubert is still too early to be preoccupied with the fictive rendition of the *durée.* It is important to note that in Meyerhoff's study of time in literature, Flaubert is not mentioned once. For the same reason, I suspect, Poulet's essay on Flaubert in his *Studies in Human Time* is, perhaps, his most perfunctory, while his article on the *space* relationships in *Madame Bovary* is detailed and highly suggestive. If Flaubert does achieve a "depth of duration . . . that is glimpsed through a descending perspective, in which the images are spaced out like milestones, along *the whole length of life*,"[18] the specious present is still not problematic. It is germane to our discussion,

[17] Poulet, *Western Review,* p. 259.
[18] Georges Poulet, *Studies in Human Time,* trans. Elliott Coleman (Baltimore, 1956), p. 254.

I think, that one of Poulet's two concluding images, intended to catch the movement of Flaubert's fictive imagination as it relates to time, is highly spatial, almost cinematic: the image of a viewer from a shore watching a wave drawing nearer and nearer, and finally perishing at one's feet. Even in the one example Poulet draws upon to show how Flaubert endows a scene of carnal love with spatial and temporal density, through the rendition of a slower *tempo*, he omits a concluding line upon which the passage depends for its final irony. Following the sweet, sensuous, woodland scene which ends with that "prolonged cry" in the distance, we see this: "Rodolphe, a cigar between his lips, was mending with his penknife one of the two broken bridles." Nothing could be more ironically cinematic.

Time is a problem to Emma, then, only as regularity, as monotony, as the succession of one dreary moment after another. She does not wish, like Marcel, to escape from time, or to retrieve it. When the moments are pleasant, as in the ecstatic interlude with Rodolphe, she regrets their passing. Hence her attitude to time can be read almost as a copy-book maxim: good things pass; suffering endures. Emma is primarily concerned with *things* plucked from the concourse of objects around her, not with *moments* of duration. It is still space, not time, that charges *Madame Bovary* with significance.

Although the temporal dimension is not a serious problem for the film-maker (unlike the problem of language, thought, metaphor, mythic allusion), we have attempted to clarify the space-time differentia because they are still the source of considerable confusion when applied to the art of the film. When Arnold Hauser writes, "The agreement between technical methods of the film and the characteristics of the new concept of time is so complete that one has the feeling that the time categories of modern art altogether must have arisen from the spirit of cinematic form, and one is inclined to consider the film itself as the stylistically most representative, though qualitatively perhaps not the most fertile genre of contemporary art,"[19] he is, I think, mistaken in his emphasis on time as the uniquely formative element

[19] Arnold Hauser, *The Social History of Art*, II (New York, 1951), pp. 939–940.

in film. For while the film can render the common elements of distension and contraction of human time, it does not on the one hand lose "its uninterrupted continuity," nor on the other, "its irreversible direction."[20] It cannot render feelings of timelessness, mystical illuminations, because even in the celebrated flashback, the narrative continues to loop ahead with the forward motion of the film. Whatever its powers of illusion, it still holds the spectator within a system of metrically regulated time.

Similarly, Mrs. Langer's student who discovered "that photographs, no matter how posed, cut, or touched up, must *seem factual*"[21] was more correct than Robert Edmond Jones who argues that "Motion pictures . . . are our thoughts made visible and audible," because they "project pure thought, pure dream, pure inner life." Regardless of the claims made by Cocteau and the film surrealists, the movies do not justify such a conclusion. The film, as we have seen repeatedly, can render perceptions only, not "thought, dream, or the inner life." These mental states can be experienced when one is viewing a film, but only through the highly inferential motion of things in space. In the last analysis, the physical reality of the film differs from the conceptual images of consciousness both in rate and in quality. Jones forgets that the film, bound by optical laws, cannot hope to approximate the *speed* of dreams and thoughts. Even language has difficulty doing that. Try to run the reel at anything like the speed of thought, and the images become a meaningless blur. Optical capacities are severely limited in this respect. And yet it is precisely within the limits of optical laws that the film achieves its most powerful and characteristic effects. In the second place, Jones forgets that dreams and thoughts are purely mental functions. Externalized and clothed in the kind of factual reality which Mrs. Langer's student found essential in photography, dreams and thoughts lose their qualitative properties. They cease being dreams and thoughts.

These distinguishing characteristics suggest a further reason for the absence of the problems of psychological time in our specimen films. The literary figures whom Mendilow, Meyerhoff, and

[20] *Ibid.*, p. 941.
[21] Susanne K. Langer, "A Note on the Film," *Feeling and Form* (New York, 1953), p. 411, p. 415.

Poulet find most fruitful for their studies of time in literature are singularly absent from motion picture adaptations. Proust, Joyce, Laurence Sterne, Virginia Woolf, and Thomas Wolfe have never been filmed (though Paul Gregory has acquired screen rights to three of Wolfe's books); Thomas Mann unsuccessfully (Gerhard Lamprecht's 1923 production of *Buddenbrooks*); Faulkner only once (*Intruder in the Dust*—a recent television adaptation of one part of *The Sound and the Fury* was of little interest, although Jerry Wald is now reported to have offered Laurence Olivier and Vivien Leigh starring roles in a projected adaptation of the book for Twentieth Century-Fox). On the other hand, novels which have lent themselves to successful adaptation, from Jane Austen to John Steinbeck, are rarely agonized by the problem of time, are consistently characterized by their affinity to the shooting-script, by their reliance on revelation through dialogue and objects in space.

I should not like to overstate the case to the point where the contingent attributes of each medium are forgotten. For while the novel, as we have seen in Flaubert, Jane Austen, and even Emily Brontë, can be suffused with spatial elements, the film, especially since the advent of sound, is suffused with temporal traits. In spite of the formative spatial elements in cinema, the images are still in constant motion, and the flux of motion always implies a temporal extension. By the same token, the sequential, discrete and irreversible character of language survives in dialogue, while spaceless, purely temporal progression survives in music. But because neither film nor novel is "pure," because the film is suffused with temporal, the novel with spatial, effects, we should not forget the priority of each. For analytic purposes, our emphases will stand. Without visual images there would be no film. Without language there would be no novel.

While novels may be divided into those which resemble the movie scenario and those which do not, we find, increasingly, scenario-novels being taken over by the cinema, interior-subjective novels refusing such transfer. Always, in spite of its complexities, we return to that simple truth which separates the discursive from the presentational arts. The one has strong temporal referents; the other has strong spatial referents. The one deals in concepts, the other in percepts; the one in thought, the other in vision; the one in time, the other in space. Where the novelist works with a *calendar*, the film-maker works on *location*.

The film-maker, then, who would bring *Madame Bovary* to the screen must begin from the premise that, for him, Flaubert will split in two. One part the film-maker will find useful for visual mounting; the other he must inevitably discard. He will recognize that he may be discarding the most characteristic part of Flaubert himself—his language. He will recreate in his own style the verbal style which he reluctantly abandons.[22] He will keep the officious voice of Flaubert off his sound track, and strive to refine himself out of his film as Flaubert strove to refine himself out of his book. He will alternate between seeing Emma in her environment and seeing the environment through Emma's eyes. He will mount his images, shot by shot, with at least as much care as Flaubert mounted his phrases. He will be prepared to suffer the same agony of composition in heightening pictorial values as Flaubert suffered in shaping his words. He will instill his presence into the frame, but only by his use of the camera, only by the way he handles his pieces of physical reality—the wedding table, the cigar case, the broken statuette, the withered bouquet. Treating it only as raw material, he will in a sense destroy his model and create thereby a new cinematic entity. In short, to criticize Vincent Minnelli's production of *Madame Bovary* is to write a new scenario.

If the film-makers were dazzled, and therefore paralyzed by the diamond-like precision of Flaubert's prose, they may have also been repressed by an equally inhibiting thematic shock. We know that Sénard's defense of *Madame Bovary* in real life was nothing like Flaubert's defense in the film. Rather than delivering himself of a rhetorical defense of the truth, and dispersing guilt by blaming the collective "we" for making Emma what she was, Sénard (to whom the novel is inscribed) developed a shrewd legal defense calculated to play on the bourgeois sympathies of a Court

---

[22] For an illuminating account of a successful mutation from one medium to another, see Paul Goodman's account of René Clair's version of Labiche's play, "Une Chapeau de paille d'Italie," in *The Structure of Literature* (Chicago, 1954), pp. 235–245.

under the Second Empire. He argued the earnestness of Flaubert's character and the eminence of Flaubert's family; he quoted Mérimée, Chénier, and even Bossuet and Massillon to show that Flaubert did not treat love or religion with such crudity as the accusations charged; he read the passage describing Monsieur Bournisien's last rites, which Flaubert had toned down to use at Emma's death.[23] Rather than defying the court by arguing that Flaubert had told the truth, Sénard argued that it could have been a lot worse. Nor was the triumph so complete as the film makes it out to be. Though the defendants were acquitted, the book was censured.

Surely something must have deeply troubled the film-makers to move them to alter so seriously the historical facts. I suggest it was the figure of Emma herself. Is there not something familiar about Emma's entire way of looking at things? Do we not recognize the continual contradiction at the center of her world, the perpetual conflict between a romantic ego and besetting facts, between exotic dreams and the hounding of debt collectors? "Sighs by moonlight, long embraces, tears flowing over yielded hands . . . the balconies of great castles full of indolence . . . boudoirs with silken curtains and thick carpets, well-filled flower-stands . . . a bed on a raised dais . . . the flashing of precious stones and the shoulder-knots of liveries . . ."—do not all these ring with a strange modernity? Harry Levin suggests the answer when he points out that American readers recognize the kinship between Emma and Carol Kennicott of *Main Street*. "The vicarious lives that film stars lead for shop-girls, the fictive euphoria that slogans promise and advertisements promote, the imaginary flourishes that supplement daily existence for all of us, are equally Bovaristic."[24] Emma's mythopoeism seems uncomfortably familiar because Emma is the prototype of the perennial movie-goer. Instead of subscribing to the library, or buying novels by Balzac and George Sand, she now buys tickets to the latest CinemaScope. Could it be that the film-makers were as much transfixed by this theme as by Flaubert's sentient style? Did they see and, therefore, refuse Flaubert's

[23] Philip Spencer retails the episode in *Flaubert: A Biography* (New York, 1953).
[24] Levin, p. 3.

surgical portrait of their own patrons? Perhaps, under present conditions, Flaubert's Emma cannot be rendered cinematically (Georges Sadoul tells us that Jean Renoir's 1934 version was likewise a routine assignment).[25] For to do so would be to expose the face of the industry itself. Emma's dreams would become the dreams of Hollywood; her demise would correspond to our perpetual disappointment; and those last rites of Monsieur Bournisien would be intoned for us, the audience. Perhaps the film-makers failed so utterly because they realized, in some profound way, that Madame Bovary, to paraphrase her creator, was ourselves.

[25] Georges Sadoul, *French Film*, in the National Cinema Series (London, 1953), p. 67; see also the review of Renoir's film in William Troy, "Effigy of a Lady," *The Nation*, cxxxix (December 5, 1934) 657–658.

Epilogue

THE TREND CONTINUES. IN A PERIOD OF retrenchment and readjustment, Hollywood has reverted to a heavy reliance on literary and theatrical models. According to a report by Eric Johnston, president of the Motion Picture Association of America, only 51.8 per cent of the source material of 305 pictures reviewed by the Production Code office in 1955 represented original screenplays. The mysterious alchemy which transforms works of fiction into cinematic form is still being widely practiced without, perhaps, being sufficiently understood. Such reversion, however, is not a new phenomenon. Whenever the industry has been riddled with uncertainty about its proper role, it has shown a tendency to become dependent on other story forms.

Undoubtedly, the present trend toward adaptation is largely due to the appearance of wide-screen processes and stereoscopic films. It seems as if the screen, suddenly brimming with new dimensions, has learned to shout, with Cyrano, "Bring me giants!" The smaller canvasses of a W. R. Burnett or a Dashiell Hammett no longer suffice. Increasingly, the film-maker turns to novels whose created worlds encompass vast areas of space. The sweeping landscape is wanted, the grand design, as if the physical dimensions of the wide-screen require the imaginative dimensions of the large book. We await the release of Claude Autant-Lara's *Le Rouge et le Noir* and Christian Jacque's 1947 version of *La Chartreuse de Parme*. In America, we hear of plans for filming Faulkner's *The Sound and the Fury*, Wolfe's *Look Homeward, Angel*, Mann's *The Magic Mountain*. And we have already witnessed the release of filmed books which threaten to revise standards for normal running time. George Stevens' *Giant*, King Vidor's *War and Peace*, Mike Todd's *Around the World in Eighty Days*, Cecil B. DeMille's *The Ten Commandments* (based on that most venerable of all books) run just short of three hours or considerably more. Clearly, there is a bustling movement afoot to exploit the latest technical innovations by crowding the screen with spectacles-in-motion. The more grandiose the scheme, the larger the budget. No sooner does Dino de Laurentiis attend the *première* of his production, *War and Peace*, than he announces plans for filming *The Brothers Karamazov*. These are giants indeed. But whether they will give the alchemist the results he seeks is another matter entirely.

After the current vogue of adaptation and theatrical spectacle has run its course, the film will doubtless rediscover its central principles. For all the ballyhoo accompanying the new process, the essential methods of the cinema remain the same (note the instinctive awareness of combined space, vision and machinery in the various trade names—Todd-AO, CinemaScope, VistaVision, Cinerama).[1] The depth-illusion will take its place with sound and color as an additional but not primary line in film structure. What may be a more radical innovation, the surprising flexibility of the wide-screen, has gone largely unexplored (except for rare instances like *It's Always Fair Weather*, which makes use of three adjacent panels to follow the parallel stories of the ex-G.I.'s, a technique reminiscent of Abel Gance's neglected *Napoleon*).[2] What the possibility of breaking up the screen (reducing and enlarging the separate frames at will) may mean for montage (a new principle of simultaneity?) it is still too early to tell.

[1] See George Bluestone, "In Defense of 3-D," *Sewanee Review* (Autumn, 1956).

[2] Dudley Nichols' script for Cinerama, *Lewis and Clark* (as yet unproduced), employs concurrent and flexible frames.

What remains clear, however, is that the cinema continues to be at once the most mechanized and most spatially free of the arts. Machinery and imagination continue to interact, each conditioning the other. The film is still in no danger like Icarus of flying too near the sun, for the celluloid image, faithful to physical reality, will always draw it back to earth. Nor is the film, like leviathan, in danger of bogging down in mud. Since the plastic image is subject to endless variations, it will always defy restriction, will sooner or later break loose to fly on its own. Bound on the one hand by the realistic demands of the photographed object, and on the other by the formative principles of editing, the film gravitates endlessly between documentary realism and spatial fantasy. The fidelity of the one and the freedom of the other continue to provide the joint sustenance of motion pictures.

Similarly, the film, as a separate artistic entity, continues its war against thematic and technical limits. John Huston's *Moby Dick* and Otto Preminger's *The Man With the Golden Arm* have each been responsible for a significant innovation. Huston and his technicians have developed a new silvering process which tones down and softens technicolor images to make them resemble nineteenth-century steel engravings. And Otto Preminger, with the financial backing of United Artists, has insisted on releasing *The Man With the Golden Arm* without the industry's seal of approval, thus defying the Production Code's specific strictures against the dramatization of drug addiction. As we have amply seen in our specimen films, such struggles with medial and thematic restrictions are not new. When Theodore Dreiser tried to get the Supreme Court of New York to restrain Paramount from showing the 1931 version of *An American Tragedy* "on the ground that by not creating the inevitability of circumstance influencing Clyde, a not evil-hearted boy, they had reduced the psychology of my book so as to make it a cheap murder story,"[3]

[3] Theodore Dreiser, "The Real Sins of Hollywood," *Liberty*, IX (June 11, 1932), p. 6. In a later article, Fulton Oursler tried to defend the industry's position by quoting Supreme Court Justice Witschief of New York: "The defendant [Paramount] has submitted the opinions of an impressive list of critics, who find that the picture is a true representation of the letter and spirit of the book." Such support for the studios was less a comment on the film than on the analytical impoverishment of the critics.

he must have been voicing the frustration of every novelist before and since who has found the film image of his work beyond recognition. The court, upholding the studio, argued that "the great majority of the people composing the audience before which the picture will be presented, will be more interested that justice prevail over wrongdoing than that the inevitability of Clyde's end clearly appear." Thus the artistic and commercial license to alter literary texts received its legal sanction. Its aesthetic sanction had been granted long before. One has only to compare the opinion of the presiding judge in the Dreiser case with the decision of Judge John Woolsey for the United State District Court in the *Ulysses* case (December 6, 1933) to see that the novel has so far had more success in its struggle against censorial restrictions than the movies. And yet the film, struggling to meet new demands and new conditions, has continued its abrasive pressure on the Production Code. Perhaps a technically revitalized film, carrying with it a morally liberated content, will combine to shape the freer cinematic conventions of the future. Perhaps thematic and technical innovation can join to bring the cinema to the point where it will, at last, assert its independence from the traditional arts.

For it is still true, as these studies have tried to demonstrate, that cinematic and literary forms resist conversion. If the kind of analysis we have applied to the specimen films were applied to *War and Peace* or *Moby Dick*, it would reveal a similar range of resemblances and deviations; it would demonstrate that on the screen there is inevitably more King Vidor and John Huston than Tolstoy and Melville. Our conclusions are no less true for current productions than they are for William Wyler's *Wuthering Heights* or John Ford's *The Grapes of Wrath*. The film and the novel remain separate institutions, each achieving its best results by exploring unique and specific properties. At times, the differences tempt one to argue that film-makers ought to abandon adaptations entirely in favor of writing directly for the screen. More often than not, the very prestige and literary charm of the classics has an inhibiting effect, shriveling up the plastic imagination. Like Lot's wife, the film-maker is frequently immobilized in the very act of looking over his shoulder.

But considering the present abundance of literary adaptations, a policy of original work does not seem very likely for the immediate future. As long as the cinema remains as omnivorous as it is for story material, its dependence on literature will continue. The best one can hope for, then, is a minimal awareness of that metamorphic process which transforms pieces of fiction into new artistic entities. Once that process is understood, the alchemist's firing pit will surely yield less disappointing lead; it may even yield surprising deposits of gold.

Selected Bibliography

THE MOST COMPLETE BIBLIOGRAPHY ON
the film may be found in *The Film Index: A Bibliography*, edited
by Harold Leonard for the New York City Federal Writers Project, of which Volume I, *The Film As Art*, has been completed
(New York: H. W. Wilson Co., 1941). Items derived from personal interviews are acknowledged in the footnotes. Novels
upon which the specimen films are based do not appear, since any
standard edition may be consulted. Only books and magazine
articles directly referred to in the text are listed below.

Agee, James. "Comedy's Greatest Era," *Life*, xxvii (September 5, 1949),
70–88.
Algren, Nelson. "Hollywood Djinn," *The Nation* (July 25, 1953), pp. 68–70.
Ames, Van Meter. *Aesthetics of the Novel*. Chicago, 1928.
Anderson, Lindsay. *Making a Film: The Story of the "Secret People."* Lon-
don, 1952.
Angoff, Charles. "In the Great Tradition," *North American Review*, ccxlvii
(Summer, 1939), 387–389.
Arnheim, Rudolph. *Film*. Translated by L. M. Sieveking and Ian F. D. Mor-
row. London, 1933.
Asheim, Lester. "From Book to Film". Unpublished Ph.D. dissertation, Uni-
versity of Chicago, 1949.
Auerbach, Eric. *Mimesis: The Representation of Reality in Western Litera-
ture*. Translated by Willard R. Trask. Princeton, 1953.

Austen-Leigh, William and Richard Arthur. *Jane Austen: Her Life and Letters.* New York, 1913.

Bardèche, Maurice and Brasillach, Robert. *History of Motion Pictures.* Translated and edited by Iris Barry. New York, 1938.
Barnes, Walter. *The Photoplay as Literary Art.* (Educational and Recreational Guides.) Newark, 1936.
Balázs, Béla. *The Film: Character and Growth of a New Art.* Translated by Edith Bone. New York, 1953.
Bentley, Eric. "Monsieur Verdoux as 'Theater,'" *Kenyon Review* (Autumn, 1948), pp. 705-716.
Bentley, Phyllis Eleanor. *The Brontë Sisters.* A supplement to *British Book News,* for The British Council and National Book League. New York, 1950.
Birney, Earle. "The Grapes of Wrath," *Canadian Forum,* xix (June, 1939), 94-95.
Bluestone, George. "In Defense of 3-D," *Sewanee Review* (Autumn, 1956).
Bond, Kirk. "Film as Literature," *Bookman,* lxxxiv (July, 1933), 188-189.
Borneman, Ernest. "Rebellion in Hollywood," *Harper's Magazine,* cxciii (October, 1946), 337-343.
Boyle, Rev. E. Oliver. "Communication," *Commonweal,* xxiii (March 6, 1936), 525.
Bowen, Elizabeth. "Why I Go to the Cinema," *Footnotes to the Film,* ed. Charles Davy and Lovat Dickson. London, 1937.
Brontë, Emily. *The Complete Poems,* ed. Philip Henderson. London, 1951.
————. *Five Essays Written in French.* Translated by Lorine White Nagel. University of Texas Press, 1948.
Burton, Thomas. "Wine From These Grapes," *Saturday Review of Literature,* xxi (February 10, 1940), 16.

Caudwell, Christopher. *Illusion and Reality.* New York, 1947.
Cecil, Lord David. *Jane Austen.* (The Leslie Stephen Lecture.) Cambridge, 1936.
Chapman, Robert W. *Jane Austen: Facts and Problems.* Oxford, 1948.
Clair, René. *Reflections on the Cinema.* London, 1953.
Condon, Frank. "The Grapes of Raps," *Collier's* (January 27, 1940), p. 23; pp. 64-67.
Cooke, Alistair. "The Critic in Film History," *Footnotes to the Film,* ed. Charles Davy and Lovat Dickson. London, 1937.
Cowley, Malcolm. "American Tragedy," *The New Republic,* xcviii (May 3, 1939), 382-383.
Crane, R. S. "The Concept of Plot and the Plot of *Tom Jones,*" *Critics and Criticism* (Chicago, 1952), pp. 616-647.
Craven, Thomas. "The Great American Art," *Dial,* lxxxi (December, 1926), 481-492.

Daiches, David. "Jane Austen, Karl Marx, and the Aristocratic Dance," *The American Scholar*, XVII (Summer, 1948), 289–296.

————. *The Novel and the Modern World*. Chicago, 1939.

Daugherty, Frank. "John Ford Wants It Real," *Christian Science Monitor* (June 21, 1941), Magazine Section, p. 5.

Donat, Robert. "Film Acting," *Footnotes to the Film*, ed. Charles Davy and Lovat Dickson. London, 1937.

"The Drama, the Theater, and the Films: A Dialogue Between Bernard Shaw and Archibald Henderson," *Harper's Magazine*, CXLIX (September, 1924), 425–435.

Dreiser, Theodore. "The Real Sins of Hollywood," *Liberty*, IX (June 11, 1932), 6–11.

Duncan, Hugh Dalziel. *Language and Literature in Society*. Chicago, 1953.

Eisenstein, Sergei. *The Film Sense*. Translated and edited by Jay Leyda. New York, 1947.

————. *Film Form*. Translated and edited by Jay Leyda. New York, 1949.

Fadiman, Clifton. "Highway 66—A Tale of Five Cities," *The New Yorker*, XV (April 15, 1939), 81–82.

————. "The Ox-Bow Incident," *The New Yorker*, XVI (October 12, 1940), 84.

Farber, Manny. "Let Us Now Praise Movies," *The New Republic*, CVIII (May 17, 1943), 669–670.

Feldman, Joseph and Harry. *Dynamics of the Film*. New York, 1952.

Ferguson, Otis. "The Informer," *The New Republic*, LXXXIII (May 29, 1935), 76.

————. "Show for the People," *The New Republic*, CII (February 12, 1940), 212–213.

Forster, E. M. *Aspects of the Novel*. New York, 1927.

"The Fortune Survey," *Fortune*, XXXIX (March, 1949), 39–44.

Fox, Ralph. *The Novel and the People*. New York, 1945.

Gassner, John and Nichols, Dudley. *Best Film Plays, 1943–44*. New York, 1945.

————. *Best Film Plays, 1945*. New York, 1946.

————. *Twenty Best Film Plays*. New York, 1943.

Gissen, Max. "The Ox-Bow Incident," *The New Republic*, CIII (December, 1940), 764.

Goodman, Paul. *The Structure of Literature*. Chicago, 1954.

"The Grapes of Wrath," *Time*, XXXV (February 12, 1940), 70–72.

Greene, Graham. "Subjects and Stories," *Footnotes to the Film*, ed. Charles Davy and Lovat Dickson. London, 1937, pp. 57–70.

Handel, Leo A. *Hollywood Looks At Its Audience: A Report of Film Audience Research.* Urbana, Ill., 1950.

Hanson, Lawrence and E. M. *The Four Brontës.* Revised Edition. London, 1950.

Harrah, David. "Aesthetics of the Film: The Pudovkin-Arnheim-Eisenstein Theory," *Journal of Aesthetics and Art Criticism,* xiii (December, 1954).

Hartung, Philip T. "The Grapes of Wrath," *Commonweal,* xxxviii (June 4, 1943), 169–170.

————. "The Screen," *The New Republic,* xxxii (August 2, 1940), 311.

Hauser, Arnold. "The Film Age," *The Social History of Art.* Translated by Stanley Godman. New York, 1951, pp. 927–959.

Hecht, Ben. *A Child of the Century.* New York, 1954.

Hinkley, Laura L. *Charlotte and Emily.* New York, 1945.

Hitchcock, Alfred. "Direction," *Footnotes to the Film,* ed. Charles Davy and Lovat Dickson. London, 1937, pp. 3–15.

Hoellering, Franz. "The Grapes of Wrath," *The Nation,* cl (February 3, 1940), 137–138.

Huettig, May D. *Economic Control of the Motion Picture Industry.* Philadelphia, 1944.

Hurd, Reggie, Jr. "Academy Award Mistakes," *Films in Review,* vi (May, 1955), 209–215.

"The Informer," *The New Republic,* xlv (December 9, 1925), 93.

"The Informer," *New Statesman,* xxv (October 10, 1925), 727.

"The Informer," *Saturday Review of Literature,* ii (October 17, 1925), 227.

Inglis, Ruth. *Freedom of the Movies.* Chicago, 1947.

Jacobs, Lewis. *The Rise of the American Film.* New York, 1939.

James, Henry. *The Art of Fiction.* New York, 1948.

Jones, Dorothy B. "Quantitative Analysis of Motion Picture Content," *Public Opinion Quarterly,* vi (Fall, 1942), 411–428.

Kennedy, Margaret. *The Mechanized Muse.* London, 1942.

Kliger, Samuel. "Jane Austen's *Pride and Prejudice* in the Eighteenth Century Mode," *University of Toronto Quarterly,* xvi (July, 1947), 357–370.

Kracauer, Siegfried. "The Found Story and the Episode," *Film Culture,* ii, No. 1 (1956), 1–5.

————. *From Caligari to Hitler: A Psychological History of the German Film.* Princeton, 1947.

Kronenberger, Louis. "Hungry Caravan: The Grapes of Wrath," *The Nation,* cxlviii (April 15, 1939), 440–441.

Laffay, Albert. "Le Récit, le Monde et le Cinéma," *Les Temps Modernes,* No. 20 (May, 1947), pp. 1361–1375; No. 21 (June, 1947), pp. 1579–1600.

Langer, Susanne K. "A Note on the Film," *Feeling and Form*. New York, 1953, pp. 411–415.

Lascelles, Mary. *Jane Austen and Her Art*. Oxford, 1939.

Lawson, John Howard. *Theory and Technique of Playwrighting and Screenwriting*. New York, 1949.

Levin, Harry. "Literature as an Institution," *Criticism: The Foundations of Modern Literary Judgment*, ed. Mark Schorer, Josephine Miles, Gordon McKenzie. New York, 1948, pp. 546–553.

————. "Madame Bovary: The Cathedral and the Hospital," *Essays in Criticism*, II (January, 1952), p. 5ff.

————. "The Novel," *Dictionary of World Literature*, ed. Joseph T. Shipley. New York, 1943, pp. 405–407.

————. "What is Realism?" *Comparative Literature*, III (Summer, 1951), 193–199.

Lewis, C. S. "A Note on Jane Austen," *Essays in Criticism*, IV (October, 1954), 359–371.

Lindgren, Ernest. *The Art of the Film: An Introduction to Film*. London, 1948.

Lindsay, Vachel. *The Art of the Moving Picture*. New York, 1915.

Lubbock, Percy. *The Craft of Fiction*. New York, 1947.

MacGowan, Kenneth. "The Artistic Future of the Movies," *North American Review*, CCXIII (February, 1921), 260–265.

————. "Beyond the Screen," *The Seven Arts* (December, 1916), pp. 165–170.

Mann, Thomas. "On the Film," *Past Masters and Other Papers*, Translated by H. T. Lowe-Porter. New York, 1933, pp. 263–266.

Manvell, Roger. *The Cinema*, annuals for 1950, 1951, 1952, in the Penguin Books series.

————. *Film*. Revised Edition. London, 1950.

————. *The Film and the Public*. London, 1955.

Marsh, Fred. T. "The Ox-Bow Incident," *New York Times Book Review* (October 13, 1940), p. 6.

Mayer, J. P. *Sociology of the Film*. London, 1946.

"Men and Monsters: The Informer," *The Spectator*, CXXXV (October 3, 1925), 560.

Mendilow, A. A. *Time and the Novel*. London, 1952.

Merleau-Ponty, Maurice. "Le Cinéma et la Nouvelle Psychologie," *Les Temps Modernes*, No. 26 (November, 1947), pp. 930–943.

Meyerhoff, Hans. *Time in Literature*. Berkeley and Los Angeles, 1955.

Mizener, Arthur. "The Elizabethan Art of Our Movies," *Kenyon Review*, IV (Spring, 1942), 181–194.

Mok, Michael. "Slumming with Zanuck," *The Nation*, CL (February 3, 1940), 127–128.

Moore, Virginia. *The Life and Eager Death of Emily Brontë*. London, 1936.

"Movies: End of an Era?" *Fortune*, xxxix (April, 1949), 99–102, 135–150.

The Movies on Trial, ed. William J. Perlman. New York, 1936.

Muir, Edwin. *The Structure of the Novel*. New York, 1929.

Nicoll, Allardyce. "Literature and the Film," *English Journal*, xxvi (January, 1937), 1–9.

Noble, Peter. *The Negro in Films*. London, n.d.

O'Brien, Desmond. "Aspects of the Novelist," *Bookman*, lxxxiv (April, 1933), 7–8.

O'Connor, Frank. "Jane Austen and the Flight from Fancy," *Yale Review*, xlv (Autumn, 1955), 31–47.

Orme, Michael. "The Bookshelf and the Screen," *Illustrated London News*, clxxxvi (March 10, 1934), 368.

Ortman, Marguerite G. *Fiction and the Screen*. Boston, 1935.

Oursler, Fulton. "Is Hollywood More Sinned Against Than Sinning?" *Liberty*, ix (June 18, 1932), 22–25.

Panofsky, Erwin. "Style and Medium in the Moving Pictures," *Transition*, No. 26 (1937), pp. 121–133. Revised version appears in *Critique*, i (January–February, 1947).

Poulet, Georges. "The Circle and the Center: Reality and Madame Bovary," *The Western Review*, xix (Summer, 1955), 245–260.

————. "Flaubert," *Studies in Human Time*. Translated by Elliott Coleman. Baltimore, 1956, pp. 248–262.

Powdermaker, Hortense. *Hollywood: The Dream Factory*. Boston, 1950.

"Pride and Prejudice," *Time*, xxxvi (July 29, 1940), 45.

Pudovkin, V. I. *Film Technique*. Translated by Ivor Montagu. London, 1935.

Ragg, Laura M. "Jane Austen and the War of Her Time," *Contemporary Review*, clviii (November, 1940), 544–549.

Reisman, Leon. "From Caligari to Metro-Goldwyn-Mayer," *Kenyon Review* (Winter, 1948), pp. 157–161.

Repplier, Agnes. "The Unconscious Humor of the Movies," *Atlantic Monthly*, cxxxvi (November, 1925), 601–607.

Ross, Lillian. *Picture*. New York, 1952.

Rosten, Leo C. *Hollywood: The Movie Colony, The Movie Makers*. New York, 1941.

Sadoul, Georges. *French Film*. ("National Cinema Series.") London, 1953.

Salomon, Louis B. "Necktie Party," *The Nation*, cli (October 12, 1940), 344.

Sanger, Charles Percy. *The Structure of Wuthering Heights*. ("Hogarth Essays Series.") London, 1926.

Sartre, Jean Paul. *What Is Literature.* Translated by Bernard Frechtman. New York, 1949.

Schary, Dore. *Case History of a Movie,* as told to Charles Palmer. New York, 1950.

Schwegler, Rev. Edward S. "Communication," *Commonweal,* xxiii (April 3, 1936), 637–638.

Shaffer, Helen B. "Changing Fortunes of the Movie Business," *Editorial Research Reports,* ii (September 3, 1953).

Shaw, George Bernard. "The Cinema as a Moral Leveller," *New Statesman: Special Supplement on the Modern Theater,* iii (June 27, 1914), 1–2.

Spencer, Philip. *Flaubert: A Biography.* New York, 1953.

Stevens, George. "Steinbeck's Uncovered Wagon," *Saturday Review of Literature,* xxix (April 15, 1939), 3–4.

Terlin, Rose R. *You and I and the Movies.* (Y.W.C.A. pamphlets.) Woman's Press, 1936.

Thorp, Margaret Farrand. *America at the Movies.* New Haven, 1939.

Tourneur, Maurice. "Movies Create Art," *Harper's Weekly,* lxii (April 29, 1916), 459.

Trilling, Lionel. "Mansfield Park," *Partisan Review,* xxi (September–October, 1954), p. 490ff.

Troy, William. "Judas in Dublin," *The Nation,* cxl (May 22, 1935), 610, 612.

————."Effigy of a Lady," *The Nation,* cxxxix (December 5, 1934), 657–58.

Tyler, Parker. "Film Form and Ritual as Reality-Principle," *Kenyon Review* (Summer, 1948), pp. 528–538.

————. "The Film Sense and the Painting Sense," *Perspectives USA,* no. 11 (Spring, 1955), pp. 95–106.

Vardac, A. Nicholas. *Stage to Screen.* Cambridge, Mass., 1949.

Vaughan, James N. "The Grapes of Wrath," *Commonweal,* xxx (July 28, 1939), 341–342.

Villard, Léonie. *Jane Austen: Sa Vie et son Oeuvre.* Doctorat-ès-Lettres, l'Université de Paris, 1914.

Wald, Jerry. "Screen Adaptation," *Films in Review,* v (February, 1954), 62–67.

West, Anthony. "The Grapes of Wrath," *New Statesman and Nation,* xviii (September 16, 1939), 404–405.

Whittaker, Charles E. "Movies Destroy Art," *Harper's Weekly,* lxii (April 29, 1916), 458.

Wilson, Edmund. "John Steinbeck," *The Boys in the Back Room.* San Francisco, 1941, pp. 41–53.

Wolfenstein, Martha and Leites, Nathan. *Movies: A Psychological Study.* Glencoe, Ill., 1950.

Woolf, Virginia. " 'Jane Eyre' and 'Wuthering Heights,' " *The Common Reader,* First and Second Series. New York, 1948, p. 224ff.

————. "The Movies and Reality," *New Republic,* XLVII (August 4, 1926).

Wright, Andrew H. *Jane Austen's Novels.* London, 1953.

INDEX

Index